Ivan
the
Terrible

RUSLAN G. SKRYNNIKOV

Ivan the Terrible

Edited and Translated
by
Hugh F. Graham

Academic International Press

1981

THE RUSSIAN SERIES/Volume 32

Ruslan G. Skrynnikov, *Ivan the Terrible.*
Translation of *Ivan Groznyi* (Moscow, 1975).

English translation and special contents of this book
Copyright © 1981 by Academic International Press.

Library of Congress Catalog Card Number: 77-78432
ISBN: O-87569-039-4

Composition by Jayne Berndsen, Carol Casey,
Mary Virginia McDaris and Jean Grabowski
Title page by King & Queen Press

Printed in the United States of America

*A list of Academic International Press publications
is found at the end of this volume.*

ACADEMIC INTERNATIONAL PRESS
Box 1111 Gulf Breeze FL 32561

CONTENTS

Maps		vi, 52-53, 186
Illustrations		33, 59, 78, 90, 136, 158
Editor's Introduction		vii
Author's Introduction		xxiii
1	The Regency Council	1
2	The Administration of Elena Glinskaia	6
3	Ivan's Childhood	9
4	The Title of Tsar	14
5	The Moscow Uprising	18
6	First Reforms	22
7	Conquest of Kazan	32
8	Conspiracies	36
9	Last Reforms	42
10	The Livonian War	49
11	Adashev Falls	54
12	The Capture of Polotsk	56
13	Conflict with the Boyars	58
14	Kurbskii's Betrayal	72
15	The Oprichnina Decree	83
16	The Oprichnina Menace	87
17	The Land Assembly	94
18	Destruction of the Zemshchina Opposition	100
19	Terror	108
20	Onset of Ruin	117
21	The Sack of Novgorod	119
22	Victories and Defeats	131
23	The Moscow Affair	134
24	Novgorod Under the Oprichnina	139
25	The Last Oprichnina Government	142
26	The Rout of the Crimean Horde	151
27	The Abolition of the Oprichnina	155
28	The Purpose of the Oprichnina	157
29	A Tatar Khan on the Muscovite Throne	162
30	Ivan's Family Life	171
31	Triumph in Livonia	177
32	The Policy of Ivan's Court	180
33	The End of the War	183
34	Final Crisis	193
35	Ivan's Death	196
36	Conclusion	198
	Notes	200
	Author's Bibliography	212
	Index	213
	The Author	220

Russia in the Sixteenth Century

EDITOR'S INTRODUCTION

Professor Ruslan Grigorevich Skrynnikov, a leading authority on Russia in the sixteenth century, is the author of numerous monographs and three major studies, *The Beginning of the Oprichnina, The Oprichnina Terror,* and *Russia After the Oprichnina,* which deservedly were honored by Leningrad State University, the institution at which he serves. In these scholarly works Professor Skrynnikov minutely and meticulously has analyzed all available sources for the epoch and broken new ground, and he strongly believes that less technical books written by experts are most useful in attracting a wider audience to the study of history. This biography of Ivan the Terrible is a fruit of his conviction; it appeared in the Soviet Union under the auspices of the Scientific-Popular Press, a title that aptly describes the purpose of that organization. Professor Skrynnikov is following in the footsteps of a long and distinguished company; thus, it might be well briefly to consider views that other scholars have held about Ivan the Terrible before considering Professor Skrynnikov's own contribution. Ivan has stood the test of time to remain one of the most enigmatic and controversial rulers to occupy the Russian throne. He has stimulated the interest and exercised the imagination of generations of historians and men of letters in Russia and elsewhere.

The difficulties confronting the biographer of Ivan the Terrible are formidable. One stems from the character of the primary sources. Native ones are sparse, for the chronicles, upon which reconstruction of Russia's early history depends, largely fall silent during Ivan's reign, although Professor Skrynnikov has made effective use of official correspondence, decretals, charters, and other materials, as the notes to the text testify. The second problem lies in the sources' tendentiousness, which is as true of the writings of Prince A. M. Kurbskii as it is of accounts left by contemporary foreigners. All must undergo the rigorous scrutiny to which Professor Skrynnikov has submitted them.

The first full biography of Ivan the Terrible was composed by Paul Oderborn, a Protestant pastor living in Lithuania, using primary sources, which appeared in 1584, the year of Ivan's death. It is an early tract of Protestant morality, in which Oderborn employed Ivan's career in order to illustrate how God suffers the mighty to exult so that their fall may be the more grievous. The work is rich in detail and accurate in its discussion of the Livonian war, since Oderborn enjoyed access to state papers and high officials in Poland, but the author aimed at sensationalism and filled his narrative with unverifiable anecdote and scabrous gossip about the tsar and other figures at court, and so the biography must be treated with considerable caution and skepticism. However, Oderborn developed fundamental concepts that have remained influential in arriving at assessments of Ivan ever since. One of these was his "two-Ivan" theory: dividing the reign into approximately equal parts Oderborn detected a "good" period when Ivan, abetted by such upright coadjutors as Silvester and Adashev, reformed the government, which was followed by a "bad" period when Ivan created his personal fiefdom, the *oprichnina.* It is fascinating to see the native *Chronograph* of 1617 arrive at the same conclusion, separating the good and bad periods of the reign at the death of Ivan's wife Anastasiia in 1560, although it is hazardous to suggest that its author was familiar with Oderborn's narrative.

To obtain the hair-raising stories he told about Ivan's wicked behavior Oderborn, who seems not to have known of Kurbskii's writings, relied heavily on material he drew from accounts by other foreigners who were in Russia in Ivan's time. In the late eighteenth century a Viennese scholar, Gustaw Treuer, observed in an obscure publication that historians had failed to adopt a critical attitude towards such sources as Oderborn and overlooked the fact that foreigners uniformly had entertained strong feelings of hostility towards Ivan because they felt threatened by Russia's invasion of Livonia. Many subsequent commentators on the period, both Russian and foreign, have been prone to forget this sensible admonition.

The native Russian tradition in the historiography of Ivan's reign, which was slow to evolve, coincided with the growth of the discipline of history itself in that country during the eighteenth century, but after that Ivan captivated historians, who have striven to integrate his complex reign into the overall pattern of Russia's development. Estimates of his character and accomplishments have fluctuated wildly, not so much because later generations had access to new information (the meagre store of facts about Ivan was not substantially augmented until quite recently) but because many writers reacted to Ivan in a strongly personal way, a trait they frequently combined with their desire to use him as an excuse to deliver themselves of sentiments about the condition of Russia in their own time. In spite of this tendency, however, certain general trends of thought emerge, as may be seen from consideration of the views of representative figures.

V. N. Tatishchev (1686-1750) held the view that by curbing the power of factions Ivan left on balance a firmer and stronger monarchy than the one he had inherited, but M. M. Shcherbatov (1733-1790), though crediting the tsar with keen intellect, substantial achievement in foreign policy, and concern for juridical reform, censured him for refusing to share power with the boyars, a criticism he based on the contention that the rule of law is invariably preferable to individual caprice. On the other hand, I. N. Boltin (1735-1792) praised Ivan for the same reason that Shcherbatov condemned him: by strengthening the monarchy and putting down the members of the aristocracy when he destroyed the great landed estates that constituted the source of their power he rendered Russia an essential service.

The work most influential in shaping the view of Ivan that lasted for almost a century and of which traces still survive was *The History of the Russian State* by N. M. Karamzin (1766-1826), the product of the belletrist's later years while he served as Imperial Historiographer at the court of Alexander I. Staunchly maintaining that autocracy was responsible for Russia's power and success, Karamzin located its first clear and effective expression in the reign of Ivan III, because the grand prince recognized that he must base his rule on law and surrounded himself with wise advisors. Karamzin distinguished between the first phase of Ivan the Terrible's reign when he relied on Sylvester and Adashev and emulated the policies of his grandfather, and the second, after the death of Queen Anastasiia, when he rejected good advice and ignored the rule of law. Karamzin employed his formidable literary talents to compile a psychological portrait of a pathologically mad Ivan which has enjoyed great currency as a device to explain the cruelties perpetrated by the man he termed the "autocrat-torturer." Karamzin obtained his material for this dismal portion of his *History* almost entirely from foreign sources like Oderborn (whom he cited extensively), accepting them at face value without pondering their credibility, motivation, or bias. So great was the impression produced by Karamzin's powerful characterization that it is not too much to say his successors often were arguing either in favor of or in opposition to Karamzin's depiction of the tsar, not about Ivan himself.

Reaction soon began. Taking issue with Karamzin, N. S. Artsybashev (1773-1841) censured his uncritical use of foreign accounts and the writings of Prince Kurbskii, sources both avidly hostile to the tsar. Echoing Boltin he contended that the need to control the turbulent and fractious boyars was the reason compelling Ivan to take the actions he did. Others, too, praised Ivan for fostering enlightenment and culture and asserted that the moves he made to change Russia that had aroused Karamzin's horror were necessary, no matter how painful to the nobility and clergy who suffered as a result.

Nineteenth-century writers critical of autocracy as it functioned in their own time and anxious to expand Western influence in Russia might be expected to regard Ivan with hostility. This was true of the Decembrists, who, although granting Ivan certain merits, considered his struggle with the boyars the action of a tyrant, but it was not the attitude of Vissarion Belinskii (1811-1848) and Alexander Herzen (1812-1870). Belinskii saw Ivan as a man of masterful will (going so far as to call him a "fallen angel") who performed a service for the Russia of his time by checking the boyars, whose intransigence provoked the excesses he perpetrated against them. He even took a negative view of Silvester and Adashev as individuals who were determined to undermine the royal will. Herzen was more restrained; acknowledging that concerns of state may have justified Ivan's actions and helped to preserve Russia, in the process he felt the tsar had destroyed existing freedoms, and his tyrannical behavior illustrated the danger inherent in unbridled autocracy. N. A. Dobroliubov (1836-1861) and N. G. Chernyshevskii (1828-1889) put forward the hypothesis that in responding to popular demand (this is how they interpreted the pro-gentry aspect of the reforms) Ivan created a national state which superseded the dominion of the nobility, but his reign was tarnished by the spread of serfdom; the law code of 1551 placed no effective limit on exploitation of the poor by the powerful. It is no surprise that those holding such views regarded the sack of Novgorod as particularly heinous; Ivan destroyed a city that once had practised genuine democracy. Men of this persuasion were in essence saying that autocracy was necessary in the sixteenth century to overcome the past but such a mode of governance had outlived its usefulness in their own time.

The Slavophils, who participated in the ideological controversies of the nineteenth century, held their own views about Ivan's reign, which one of their leading exponents, K. S. Aksakov (1817-1860), effectively formulated. He too saw Ivan's time as the period when a decisive struggle took place to eliminate control of the government by a network of kinship relations among the nobility, but he refused to believe that the process produced major social upheavals because Slavophils denied that any conflict between the tsar and his people could have occurred in Old Muscovy. This is flying in the face of all available evidence, but Aksakov and his associates made a significant point when they criticized certain contemporaries for their exclusive concentration on the deeds of rulers and boyars while neglecting the peasants and other humble elements of society. Westernizers and Slavophils alike continued to be fascinated by Ivan's personality and kept trying to explain his behavior in psychological terms.

The historians to whom Aksakov referred were representatives of the statist or juridical school, fashionable in the nineteenth century, who contended that the state was an entity superimposed upon the population it embraced, and only those controlling its destiny were in a position to take action or formulate policy, a theory that inevitably demanded focusing attention on ruling elites. The members of this school, which included a number of distinguished adherents, under the influence of Hegelian thought made a valuable contribution by developing the concept that Russia was not static, but a dynamic organism in which each epoch was related to the one preceding and the one following it. K.D. Kavelin (1818-1885), seeing such a state emerge from the welter of kinship relations in the sixteenth century, believed that Ivan, who embodied this nascent state power, was only doing what was necessary to implement this change. Kavelin did not regard the oprichnina as an effort to destroy the boyars but as a device to forge a new class of serving-men from the lesser gentry, whose members would advance, as this new state required, on a basis of merit rather than pedigree, a task which, however, was not accomplished until the days of Peter the Great. Viewed thus, Ivan's conduct was not blameworthy nor a proper object of censure.

S.M. Soloviev (1820-1879) in his monumental *History of Russia from the Earliest Times* (volumes of which are now appearing in English from Academic International Press) was influenced by the statist school. He agreed with Kavelin that Russia became a centralized monarchy in the sixteenth century but he took a different view of the oprichnina, considering it the response the tsar had to make in order to overcome opposition to his new order manifested by the great boyars. In establishing it Ivan showed he was capable of dealing promptly and effectively with dissidence, a view that enabled Soloviev to condone many of the tsar's actions. Troubled, however, by the excesses of Ivan's reign, he investigated Ivan's psychological makeup, which he explained by assuming that the quarrels among the boyars Ivan witnessed as a child warped his intense and sensitive personality and made him unduly nervous and suspicious. Soloviev attributed the change in Ivan not to the death of his wife but to the failure of key boyars to support him during the succession crisis that arose when he became seriously ill in 1553.

Other writers offered other ingenious hypotheses: Ivan created the oprichnina in order to save Russia from the divisiveness of oligarchy, or that he was right to remove Silvester from office because the priest was striving to make Russia a theocracy. Still others merely embroidered upon Karamzin. Perhaps D.G. Ilovaiskii (1832-1920) best reflects this tendency: any merits Ivan's reign may have possessed were due to the influence of the "gentle and noble" Anastasiia or the "worthy and pious" Silvester and Adashev. N.G. Kostomarov (1817-1885), who, believing a ruler's spiritual qualities shaped the kingdom he governed, claimed Ivan was an incarnation of wickedness, an ignorant monster incapable of any positive, constructive action.

V.O. Kliuchevskii (1841-1911), who studied under Soloviev and succeeded him to the chair of Russian history at Moscow University, achieved a far higher degree of sophistication. In his *Course of Russian History* he emphasized internal developments and socio-economic issues rather than the purely political matters and foreign affairs his mentor had stressed, and he too saw Ivan's reign as the time when centralized monarchy superseded a government based on kinship relations. Kliuchevskii made a brilliant analysis of the psychological factors affecting Ivan's character and also drew attention to the traumatic experiences of childhood, but in this context he made a decisive break with Soloviev when he declared that the oprichnina was merely the product of the tsar's disordered imagination which had not contributed to the formation of a unified, centralized state because it failed to alter the system whereby Russia was governed. Ivan directed the oprichnina against individuals who had incurred his wrath, not against the system of which they were a part, and from this flows Kliuchevskii's ultimate conclusion that Russia would have developed in approximately the same way that it did if Ivan had never lived, save only that the process would have been more orderly, and less chaotic and destructive.

Undoubtedly reacting to Kliuchevskii's thesis S.F. Platonov (1860-1933) in his biography of the tsar (available as *Ivan the Terrible*, ed. and trans. by Joseph L. Wieczynski, with "In Search of Ivan the Terrible," by Richard Hellie, Academic International Press, 1974) endeavored to reassert the view that Ivan was following a consistent policy and had behaved sensibly and rationally throughout his reign. The tsar planned the oprichnina as the only possible (albeit radical) mechanism to shatter the power of the separatist-minded, fractious boyars by breaking up their estates. He always carefully plotted his course and strove conscientiously to build a strong centralized monarchy.

New currents of thought began circulating in Russian intellectual circles during the late nineteenth and early twentieth centuries, prominent among them Marxism with its emphasis upon socio-economic issues, and historians were not slow to respond. In treating the early period M. P. Pavlov-Silvanskii began to apply the term feudalism to Russian history, which later historians, including Professor Skrynnikov, utilize extensively. The term comprehends the kinship relations, and the way categories of vassals were articulated to one another in an agrarian society where appanage ownership existed; in short, the conditions obtaining in the sixteenth century which previous historians had been obliged to describe more elaborately. Pavlov-Silvanskii considered Ivan's reign the time when a monarchy supported by gentry serving-men superseded rule by the owners of autonomous appanages who formerly had held power.

The initial years of the Soviet era were not fruitful of studies in early Russian history, but one of the first Marxist historians, M. N. Pokrovskii (1863-1932), propounded a theory that in the sixteenth century the ratio between productive forces and productive relationships had become such that natural economy yielded to a money economy, which he termed "merchant capitalism." This economic change was reflected sociologically in a coalition of the rising urban middle class, or bourgeoisie, and landholders on service-tenure, which ousted the nobility from its position of privilege. In this schematic construction neither the actions of the tsar nor his advisors could have any appreciable impact on the course of events.

The single biography of Ivan that appeared in the early Soviet period was markedly different in tone and attitude from Pokrovskii. R. Iu. Vipper (1859-1954), whose previous work had been mainly concerned with classical antiquity, published his *Ivan the Terrible* in 1922, and it went through two subsequent editions in the 1940s. Less concerned with Ivan's place in Russian history than with the man, Vipper praised the tsar indiscriminately as a mighty, powerful ruler, who thoroughly understood the best interests and needs of the Russian people, which he deliberately and conscientiously undertook to fulfil, a task crowned with success both at home and abroad. Ivan's policies invariably were sound and well-conceived, his actions always rational, and even the harshest measures he took were amply justified because the boyars, who constantly opposed him, resorted to conspiracy and treason. Vipper considered that those who spoke ill of Ivan were actuated by jealousy, spite and malice. His adulatory portrait of the tsar is unacceptable, but his criticism of the foreign accounts on which Karamzin and others had relied so heavily may serve as a further reminder that much of the material vilifying Ivan comes from sources whose own credentials are far from impeccable.

In following decades Soviet historians assimilated new ways of criticizing and analyzing sources and developed interests in material culture—the daily life, work and economic activity of the lower classes in early Russian society. This led them to seek out and publish a great deal of new archival material, thereby facilitating the growth of a rich and varied monographic literature on many sixteenth-century topics. Instead of reacting instinctively and emotionally to Ivan's deeds historians tried to discover what the sources had to tell about the life of the Russian people, on the logical assumption that the more was known about it the more light would be shed on the policies those in power sought to implement. Several studies devoted to Ivan's reign that appeared after World War II illustrate these trends.

P. A. Sadikov wrote a series of monographs concerning Ivan and his epoch, which were collected and published in 1950. He combed the sources to find evidence demonstrating the changes that occurred in the modes of land tenure brought about by the oprichnina, the disruption that institution occasioned among the upper classes, and the effect Ivan's policies had upon the peasantry. His work provided much material to undermine the view that the oprichnina was a product of rational calculation, which had served as the cornerstone of Platonov's hypothesis.

Two biographies of Ivan, by S. V. Bakhrushin (1882-1950) and I. I. Smirnov (1909-1965) respectively, show the influence of these new approaches, although they cannot be said to have broken major new ground in their arguments, the gist of which is that Russia developed a centralized absolute monarchy out of feudal fragmentation in the sixteenth century. To facilitate the task Ivan made common cause with the lesser service gentry and the expanding ranks of merchant-traders, the new forces in the political arena most inclined to support him. Actions taken to benefit this new alignment were bound to provoke the old princely and boyar families, who resented attack on their entrenched privileges, above all on their hereditary estates, and led to genuine attempts to form conspiracies, which Ivan and his new supporters had to counter by establishing the oprichnina.

In 1956 a panel discussion under the auspices of the Institute of History of the Academy of Sciences of the USSR, stimulated by general interest in problems posed by the "cult of personality," was held in Moscow, at which Professor S. M. Dubrovskii raised provocative

questions concerning the historiography of Ivan's reign. Using Vipper's book as his paradigm, he asserted that the merits and achievements of a ruler who actually had done much damage to Russia had
been grossly exaggerated. Dubrovskii's comments elicited considerable discussion and coincided with the start of a new and exciting
phase of Soviet study of Ivan's era, in which Professor Skrynnikov
has played a prominent part.

At the end of his distinguished career Academician S. B. Veselovskii, who died in 1952, composed a series of essays on Ivan's reign
which were collected and published in 1963. Moving beyond the traditional view that Ivan and his associates restricted their attacks to
the great nobles he claimed the object of the tsar's wrath was nothing
less than the whole court elite, now composed of men whose power
derived as much from their monopoly of seats on the boyar council
as upon their possession of estates. As the conflict intensified the tsar
decided to establish the oprichnina, principally as a means to ensure
his personal safety. The institution cannot be considered the product
of a long period of careful planning, and it confiscated land from
many elements in society, not just the nobility, because it needed
revenue; to break up princely appanages was not its primary task.
Veselovskii conducted pioneering research on the Synodicals, the
lists of those who perished during his reign which Ivan ordered compiled at the end of his life, and stimulated the prosopographical approach that has proven its worth as a tool to elucidate the history of
the epoch.

Maintaining the trend towards greater flexibility of attitude and
more sophistication in treatment, A. A. Zimin, a scholar of outstanding capacity and wide interests, has made close analyses of the principal features of Ivan's reign, the reforms and the oprichnina. He believes
it simplistic and misleading to assume that all the nobility formed a
single homogeneous group opposed to the tsar, for frequently its individual members would pull in different directions and nobility and
gentry often found interests in common. This proposition holds true
even though urban gentry who had entered the fledgling bureaucracy
(the chancery apparatus) tended to support the desire of their rural
counterparts to acquire more land and greater control over the peasants who worked it, whereas nobles still possessing appanages wished
to keep the peasantry as a labor force enjoying at least limited mobil-
ity, for which their ampler resources would permit them successfully
to compete. The tsar thus was subjected to conflicting pressures simultaneously, first from the rising gentry, strong in the chancery appara-

tus, and from the nobility, whose members still retained their monopoly of the highest state offices. This tug-of-war ensured that the reforms carried out by Ivan, Silvester and Adashev would have to be
compromises. The operation of the same set of factors contributed
to the establishment of the oprichnina, but it eventually began to attack men the tsar disliked, feared, and rightly or wrongly (Zimin is
equivocal on this point) believed were conspiring against him. However, Zimin does not consider the oprichnina irrational, although his
argument might seem to be leading to such a conclusion. He avoids it
by taking refuge in the contention that centralized absolute monarchy could not be fully achieved in Russia until steps, as radical as
necessary, had been taken finally to overcome the three remaining
bastions of feudal fragmentation: the Staritsa appanage, the power
base of Prince Vladimir Andreevich, Ivan's sole legitimate rival for
the throne; Novgorod, where the ancient separatist tradition stubbornly persisted, and the church, which, despite its long record of cooperation with Muscovite rulers, was a state within a state. During
the oprichnina years Prince Vladimir was executed; Novgorod was
devastated, and the church was humiliated. Zimin claims these actions
were unavoidable in order to overcome clear and present dangers, although he deplores the cruelty with which they were carried out.

N.E. Nosov has likewise demonstrated that social relationships
were growing increasingly complex and, depending upon circumstances, components among the dominant groups might seek accomo-
dation or collide with one another. His careful scrutiny of monastery
and regional charters and similar documents has led him to the conclusion that in the sixteenth century new forces, such as groups of
merchant entrepreneurs in the far north, began appearing to compete
with the existing blocs because the reform of local administration
had given them greater authority and independence, but these changes
were not yet translatable into resources sufficient to enable such
groups to challenge the traditional elites. S.O. Shmidt also has contributed a number of important studies on similar themes, showing
that loyalties were fluid and shifting and elements within the nobility
were more supportive of the monarchy than had previously been assumed.

As has been seen, accounts composed by foreigners in Russia in
Ivan's time are essential primary sources for the period, but after
these foreigners were gone and Russia's bid to consolidate a position
on the coast of the Baltic sea met with failure, interest in early Russian history outside Russia virtually disappeared until modern times.

The revival of recent decades has led to the accumulation of a significant monographic literature on many aspects of the sixteenth century. Ivan's reign also has its place in general histories of Russia, among which the work of George Vernadsky occupies a commanding place. Such a section usually gives a short factual exposition based on secondary sources and the estimate of Ivan's character and accomplishments is generally negative. There are only a few biographies of Ivan, which for the most part are superficial and idiosyncratic, written by amateurs uninterested in or unable to take advantage of the serious scholarly literature. This is exemplified in the most recent production in this genre, published in 1975. Master biographer Robert Payne, assisted by Nikita Romanoff, brought out a large *Ivan the Terrible* that looks like a serious work of modern critical scholarship, but all the authors have actually done is to pen a highly emotional diatribe (with contemporary overtones) in which they attack Ivan more savagely than Karamzin or even Kostomarov would have cared to do. A refreshingly different atmosphere prevails in Professor Skrynnikov's book.

It is appropriate to comment on some features of Professor Skrynnikov's narrative. He has used the work of his predecessors in the field to provide the base from which to develop his own concepts; the author's bibliography at the end of this volume lists general scholarly works he has found valuable. The present *Ivan the Terrible* is a biography in the best traditional sense, but its straightforward format deceptively belies the amount of erudition that has gone into its composition. Utilizing the latest developments in recent Soviet historiography, it permits the reader to observe the interaction between those in power and those over whom they exercised it as the story proceeds from Ivan's minority to the day of his death. The tsar stands at the center and provides the mean against which the various forces at work within the realm can be measured.

Realizing they are almost as remote from Soviet readers as they are from others, Professor Skrynnikov carefully defines the technical terms appearing in the book which were employed in the administrative and military apparatus and used to denote the various components of the social structure in sixteenth-century Russia, including the complex, highly-charged, and ultimately untranslatable words oprichnina and zemshchina. He shows the pervasive importance of birth as a passport to high office, as demonstrated during the various boyar regimes that followed one another during Ivan's minority. Although these groups governed in their own interest Professor Skrynnikov draws attention to the fact that certain reforms, particularly of local administration, began at that time and others were carried out by the factions existing during the regency of Ivan's mother, Elena Glinskaia.

Professor Skrynnikov is skeptical of the psychological school that finds the clue to Ivan's future course of action in the experiences of his childhood. He notes that the only information available concerning these experiences is what Ivan himself said about them long after they supposedly occurred; he exaggerated some and attached less significance to others than later commentators, who often have magnified them out of proportion.

Professor Skrynnikov accepts the generally-held view that Ivan's reign was the time when centralized autocracy evolved from feudal fragmentation, and he carefully analyzes the factors contributing to it. He shows that the forces striving to achieve or retard this development were roughly equal in strength, though by no means homogeneous, a circumstance that heightened tension, led to frequent rise and fall of noble cabals, and aroused the fury of the commons in 1547, over which the ruler could exercise little or no control. The nobility zealously guarded the archaic institutions of maintenance and precedence (both of which Professor Skrynnikov defines) in the hope of maintaining their ancient privileges, although precedence sometimes helped the ruler, allowing him both to adjudicate and manipulate the mutual rivalries and jealousies among the various factions.

The forms of land tenure existing in Russia in the sixteenth century are Professor Skrynnikov's next concern. He discusses the ways in which the government tried to advance the lesser gentry and equalize the military obligations (with which landholding was indissolubly linked) of nobility and gentry alike. This motivation was a prime reason for the reforms that took place during the first decade and a half of Ivan's administration. Reformers like Adashev (himself of gentry origin) wanted to benefit the gentry at the expense of and as a counterpoise to the nobility, but strength was so evenly divided that neither side could decisively prevail. Eventually the tsar became disenchanted with reform in the growing conviction that it would not enhance his power as he had hoped initially.

Professor Skrynnikov is interested in military strategy and tactics, and the book contains several lively descriptions of battle, including the succinct account of the successful Russian campaign to conquer Kazan, clashes in Livonia, and the extended account of the Battle of

Molody in 1572 that saved Russia from the Crimean Tatars. There are numerous references to the long and debilitating Livonian war, which Professor Skrynnikov believes Ivan was justified in undertaking in order to allow Russia access to the Baltic sea and assure direct communication with western Europe. His view leads him to criticize Adashev, a determined advocate of war against the Crimea, for using his influence to arrange a truce in Livonia soon after the war began in 1558, that allowed Russia's opponents to come together and cost her the initiative, which she was never able to regain.

When the tsar fell ill in 1553 the boyars split between those supporting Dmitrii, Ivan's infant son and heir, and those refusing to do so. In the light of the crisis Professor Skrynnikov examines the available evidence to determine whether serious internal opposition to Ivan subsequently formed and comes to the conclusion that it did so. Certain members of the nobility hoped to replace Ivan on the throne with his cousin, Prince Vladimir Andreevich, in the belief the latter would prove more amenable to their interests and were prepared to accept help from the king of Poland, who was happy to proffer it, to achieve their purpose. It is in this frame of reference that Professor Skrynnikov extensively analyzes the circumstances surrounding Prince Kurbskii's defection to Lithuania in 1563. As the notes to the text indicate, the authenticity of the exchange of epistles between Kurbskii and the tsar has recently been challenged, but Professor Skrynnikov, who has prominently defended the traditional attribution, feels entitled to use the correspondence as a primary source while offering as much corroborative evidence from other sources as possible. He is aware of Kurbskii's faults and weaknesses and considers that his treachery was more comprehensive than has previously been assumed. Kurbskii's defection was an essential step along the road to the establishment of the oprichnina; if so powerful a noble, a man whom Ivan had trusted and regarded as a personal friend, would betray him, what might be expected from others less favorably disposed? The tsar grew convinced he must seek protection for his person because he now believed he was in real danger from those close to him.

Professor Skrynnikov advances a significant new theory to explain why the oprichnina was established early in 1565, based on his research in the cadastral books of the Kazan region. They reveal that Ivan compelled a large number of prominent families to forsake their appanages and move there. Fearing such an unprecedented action might provoke an armed uprising Ivan prepared to meet it, and encouraged by his new mentor, Aleksei Basmanov, a man who favored the use of force to solve intractable problems, set about recruiting a personal bodyguard from among those he believed he could trust, regardless of their social origin. This was the nucleus of the oprichnina. An alternative existed: granting further concessions to the gentry at the expense of the aristocracy, but this Ivan refused to entertain because he was sure such a policy would additionally compromise his autocratic power, to the preservation of which, as Professor Skrynnikov again points out, he was ready to sacrifice all other considerations.

If centralization of the government to replace feudal fragmentation is regarded as essential to the development of the Russian state, by creating the oprichnina Ivan made a regressive move, for although larger and stronger than the estate of any nobleman, the oprichnina was basically an appanage. This was no aberration, and appanage concepts remained rooted in Ivan's thinking, as may be seen from the fact that after removing Simeon Bekbulatovich from office Ivan named him grand prince of Tver, and the principality thereby reverted to appanage status. This serves as but one example of the anomalies and distortion the oprichnina introduced into Russian society; it is to questions like these that Professor Skrynnikov turns in the second portion of his book.

His work on the Synodicals marks an advance on Veselovskii's research. They have helped him obtain further insight into the workings of the oprichnina. Originally devised as an immediate response to the fear that the nobles exiled to Kazan might retaliate, once in existence it failed to remain consistent, changed directions, and soon started attacking the chancery apparatus and gentry serving-men, the elements in Russian society Professor Skrynnikov thinks were most disposed to support the tsar. In its third phase the oprichnina became a terror machine which those manipulating it were no longer able to control, and finally it turned upon itself and devoured its own leaders, until the tsar at last was persuaded to abolish it after the Battle of Molody showed that its continuation might place the existence of the nation in jeopardy.

The sack of Novgorod receives considerable attention. Professor Skrynnikov characterizes it as the most repulsive episode in the violent history of the oprichnina. Scholars long have debated the reasons why the tsar should have undertaken a massive punitive raid against the city early in 1570. Professor Skrynnikov documents his ingenious theory that it was caused by a successful provocation staged by the

Lithuanian secret service, which took advantage of the fact that some leading Muscovites assigned to Novgorod did engage in conspiratorial activity; apparently the separatist tradition died hard and affected those exposed to it. The damage the oprichnina caused in Novgorod was substantial enough, but Professor Skrynnikov criticizes other historians for the sensational ways in which they have presented the episode and believes the number of the slain has been exaggerated.

In the wake of the oprichnina various incidents made Ivan continue to feel that treason still stalked the land, and among the moves he made to combat it were the creation of what came to be known as his own special court, which functioned as a kind of mini-oprichnina, and the temporary elevation of Simeon Bekbulatovich to the office of grand prince in 1575-1576, an action which many scholars have dismissed as mere caprice. Ivan's private life is judiciously passed in review; political calculations determined his choice of wives, although it is intriguing to speculate whether perhaps Ivan's alliance with the widow Vasilisa Melenteva may have been a genuine love match! Ivan had struggled desperately to perpetuate his dynasty; there is grim irony in the fact that the tragic denouement of his quarrels with his older son, which Professor Skrynnikov considers politically, not personally motivated, brought the sway of the house of Rurik over Muscovy to an end.

Ivan's confiscations and banishments undermined the power of the old aristocracy and facilitated the rise of the next layers in society, the non-titled nobility and the gentry, many representatives of which found their niche in the chancery apparatus. The boyar council was temporarily weaker and less effective than it had been before. However, new men like Boris Godunov who came to prominence through the oprichnina soon began behaving like their aristocratic predecessors; Roman Alferev brought a precedence suit against Prince Mosalskii and won it, and the issue of promoting men on the basis of merit never arose.

Professor Skrynnikov clearly does not subscribe to the view that the oprichnina followed a consistent, cohesive policy throughout its existence. He expresses distaste for the arbitrary violence that accompanied it and for individuals prominent in it, especially during its final phase when it was in the hands of the brutal Maliuta Skuratov and the vain Vasilii Griaznoi. It was Russia's further misfortune that a string of natural disasters in the late 1560s happened to coincide with the worst period of oprichnina excess. This produced disastrous results which mightily taxed the country's recuperative powers. The final debacle of the Livonain war a decade later created additional difficulties.

One of Professor Skrynnikov's fundamental conclusions, which flows from his narrative, is that Ivan and the oprichnina perverted Russia's development in the second half of the sixteenth century but failed to alter the structure of the government, no matter how much they may have changed its personnel, and here too the changes were more often apparent than real; names of members of the Belskii and Mstislavskii families are heard as frequently as ever. Ivan had no wish to heed Simeon Gordyi's apostrophe, when his fourteenth-century ancestor told his brothers to "honor, respect, and consult with your boyars," but he could not do without them. It is again ironic that the Romanov dynasty that came to power after the Time of Troubles following Ivan's death, was more dependent upon the nobility than its predecessors. Professor Skrynnikov parts company with Professor Zimin, who has followed Platonov, to draw closer to the intuitive ideas of Kliuchevskii, but he has based his conceptions on a mass of data that was not available in Kliuchevskii's time and has introduced a subtle refinement by contending that the oprichnina degenerated from a device that initially possessed a rational, if narrow, purpose to become a haven for opportunists and careerists of every sort and finally an irrational instrument of terror that directed its blows indiscriminately against members of every level of Russian society.

Since serious interest in Ivan and his reign developed more than two centuries ago historians have been too prone to seek a single cause to which they can attribute all the events of the period. Most frequently they have discerned this single cause in the tsar's personality, which means that Ivan was in full control of all that happened and made it happen. Professor Skrynnikov has demonstrated that the solution is much more complex. The alignment of forces in Russia, which was perhaps less centralized in Ivan's time than is usually supposed, often changed position and personnel, but it always remained in an approximate balance; hence, neither the tsar nor any other individual or group could win permanent unchallenged authority and enforce stable consistent policies. Ivan's power was not unlimited and he was as much at the mercy of circumstance as his subjects. Tragically, he longed for what he could never obtain, and his efforts to become an untrammeled autocrat provoked hostile responses from those who stood to lose if he succeeded, provoked savage conflict, and strained the fabric of the state to its utmost. Russia was to reap the whirlwind in the Time of Troubles. Professor Skrynnikov has come close to grasping the elusive essence of Ivan's epoch and those active in it. All students of early Russian history stand in his debt for his thoughtful, stimulating and sophisticated biography of Ivan the Terrible. It will not be superseded for a long time.

AUTHOR'S INTRODUCTION

New developments changed the face of Europe in the sixteenth century. Feudalism still prevailed on the continent, but bourgeois relationships were forming imperceptibly in the advanced countries of the West. A worldwide trade network and a nascent colonial system, which enriched the bourgeoisie, had resulted from remarkable geographical discoveries. The initial era of bourgeois revolution, now dawning, won its first victory when the Low Countries succeeded in freeing themselves from Spanish dominion. The German Reformation, directed against feudal reaction, produced an ideological transformation. All Europe was in the throes of change. Italy and Germany could not overcome feudal fragmentation, but France and England had become centralized absolute monarchies, and the unified Russian principality had developed into a mighty power in eastern Europe.

In the sixteenth century eastern Europe made substantial economic gains, including burgeoning trade, artisan manufacture, and the growth of towns, but feudal reaction still reigned despite such solid progress. The German nobility brutally suppressed peasant revolts and enserfed the peasantry. This process next spread to the Polish-Lithuanian state and then made its way to Russia in the latter part of the century. Unfavorable historical conditions, to which the cruel Tatar invasion substantially contributed, had retarded somewhat the growth of the Russian state. The pernicious consequences of a foreign yoke were long felt, until the Russian people at last shook off their torpor and national consciousness quickened. Men appeared who were highly skilled in literature,, publicistics, chronicle-writing, book production, art and architecture. Remote Muscovy felt the European Reformation and its culture experienced, albeit slightly, the impact of the Italian Renaissance.

Russia's political development in the sixteenth century was fraught with contradictions. Unification of the Russian land had failed to eliminate many survivals of the feudal fragmentation which continued to beset Russian society, although the exigencies of political centralization rendered it vital to change such an outmoded structure and made reform imperative. However, Russia's growing military power enabled it to achieve major foreign-policy goals. Muscovy's relations with the Tatars and its western neighbors were placed on a new basis. Russian armies struggled to reunite the west-Russian lands that had fallen to Lithuania after the Tatar sack, but the country still possessed no outlet to the sea, which would facilitate the establishment of close economic ties with the developed countries of the West. The need to acquire such an outlet became of primary concern.

This was the age when the centralized Russian state emerged and grew strong, and also the time that forged the personality of Ivan the Terrible, who in turn influenced the period. Few other figures in Russian history have occasioned such intense disagreement in subsequent epochs. Some have considered him an outstanding military leader, diplomat, and man of letters, an incarnation of political sagacity, while others have regarded him as a savage, almost insane tyrant. What is true? Which view is correct? Only facts, which must be studied as carefully and patiently as possible, can provide answers to such questions.

Chapter One

THE REGENCY COUNCIL

Ivan the Terrible's grandfather, Ivan III, was married twice, first to a princess of Tver, and then to the Byzantine princess Sophia (Zoe) Paleologue. Members of the senior line, Ivan III's eldest son, Ivan, and after the latter's death, his son Dmitrii, were destined to inherit the throne. The grand prince crowned his grandson Dmitrii, but later imprisoned him and bestowed the throne upon Vasilii III, the son of his second marriage. Vasilii, like his father, was also married twice. On the first occasion a circular letter was dispatched throughout the country summoning daughters of the gentry to attend a bride-show, where Vasilii chose Solomoniia Saburova from 1500 aspirants. Their marriage was childless, and twenty years later Vasilii immured his wife in a nunnery. The Orthodox church and some influential boyars disapproved of divorce in the family of the Muscovite grand prince. Chronicles composed later insisted that Solomoniia had accepted tonsure voluntarily, but in fact the grand princess did everything in her power to prevent the divorce. Rumors circulating in Moscow insinuated that Solomoniia had borne a son, Yurii Vasilevich, the lawful heir to the throne, in the nunnery, but this was mere idle talk, which the nun Solomoniia was seeking to use in order to prevent Vasilii from marrying again.

The grand prince's second wife was Princess Elena Glinskaia, a girl from Lithuania, whose family did not belong to the high nobility, although her ancestors could trace their descent from Khan Mamai.[1] A union with her was not calculated to exalt the dynasty, but Elena, who understood foreign customs and bore no resemblance to the boyar ladies of Moscow, knew how to make herself agreeable. Vasilii was so smitten with his young wife that in order to please her he did not hesitate to violate traditional taboos by shaving off his beard.

The Muscovite aristocracy disapproved of the grand prince's choice and the monks of Beloozero called the marriage adulterous, but a greater misfortune was that this marriage too was initially barren. It was five years after the royal couple were married when Elena bore a son, who was named Ivan. Boyars hostile to the ruler hinted that Ivan's father was a favorite of the grand princess. Legend holds that a frightful storm burst over the entire realm as the child was born. Thunder crashed in a cloudless sky and shook the earth to its foundation. On learning of Ivan's birth the wife of the khan of Kazan said to Muscovite envoys: "A tsar is born among you: two teeth has he. He will devour us (Tatars) with one and you with the other."[2] Other portents and prodigies about Ivan's birth were reported, but all of them were composed after the event. The birth of a son occasioned the normal concerns and joys in the grand prince's household. Whenever Vasilii had to leave Moscow without his family he would send impatient letters to his wife in which he instructed her to inform him about Ivan's health and what the child was eating. Day after day Elena would tell her husband that the baby had "squawked," or how a "large strong place" had broken out on his neck.[3] Ivan was barely three years old when his father fell ill and soon died.

The relationship between the grand prince and his nobles was clearly revealed at the time of Vasilii III's illness and death. The grand prince's will has not survived, and thus his final dispositions cannot be precisely known, but the Voskresenskii chronicle of 1542 states that Vasilii blessed his son Ivan with the realm, entrusted him with the sceptre of mighty Russia, and instructed his wife to maintain the state in their son's interest until he attained his majority.[4] In Ivan's lifetime, during the 1550s, the chronicles began claiming that Grand Prince Vasilii had consigned the sceptre to his wife, not his son, because he considered her wise and courageous, with a heart filled with "mighty tsaric intelligence."[5] Ivan loved his mother and surrounded her with a special halo. The royal chronicles thus naturally depicted Elena as Vasilii's lawful successor. The chronicle tradition, altering with the passage of time, transformed her into a champion and defender of centralized monarchy, a ruler firmly opposed to the intrigues of reactionary boyars. Unofficial sources represent Elena's accession in a different way from the official chronicles. A well-informed Pskov chronicler wrote that Vasilii "consigned the grand duchy to his elder son, Prince Ivan, designated him grand prince during his own lifetime, and ordered a small group of his boyars to watch over him until he reached the age of fifteen."[6] This source, if credible, implies that the grand prince transferred power to a boyar regency and Elena usurped authority which lawfully belonged to the guardians.

The issue is whether the official or unofficial account is the more credible. The earliest chronicles, composed by someone who actually witnessed Vasilii's last days, supply the answer. The grand prince was taken mortally ill while hunting near Volokolamsk in autumn. When his physician told him his condition was hopeless, Vasilii demanded his will be brought from Moscow. Couriers gave him the document, concealing it from the grand princess. After the sick man was conveyed to the capital a ceaseless round of conferences began in the palace to discuss the disposition of the realm. Counsellors and boyars attended the meetings, but the grand prince never invited his wife. He tried to defer explanation with her to the last minute, but when the crisis set in and the sick man's hours were numbered his councillors entreated him to send for the grand princess and give her his blessing. At last Elena was ushered into the sickroom. Sobbing bitterly, the young wife asked her husband what was to become of her: "Sovereign grand prince! To whom do you commend me and to whom, sire, do you entrust our children?" Vasilii replied briefly but explicitly: "I have blessed our son Ivan as sovereign grand prince. You are designated in our will as former grand princesses have been designated in the wills of our fathers and grandfathers, in accordance with your deserts." Elena understood her husband perfectly well. Long-established custom among the descendants of Kalita[7] provided that widows of Muscovite sovereigns should receive a widow's appanage as their portion. Elena wept. "Pitiable was it then to see her crying and sobbing," is how the witness sadly concludes his narrative.[8]

This Muscovite version supports the Pskov account. The grand prince had given power to the boyars, not the grand princess. Vasilii III was over fifty and Elena was twenty-five years his junior. Their correspondence shows clearly that the husband never consulted his wife about affairs. Vasilii did not tell the grand princess of his plans before he died because he did not trust her youth and had little confidence in her judgment or experience of life. Another factor was of even more importance. Time-honored custom denied women participation in affairs of state; thus, had he entrusted the government to his wife the grand prince would have violated ancient Muscovite tradition.

Scholars have interpreted chronicle testimony concerning the transfer of power to the boyars in various ways. The distinguished historians A. E. Presniakov and I. I. Smirnov have expressed the view that Vasilii III created a regency council from among the boyars who attended him on his deathbed, which was to function during his son's minority. Disagreeing with them, A. A. Zimin concluded that the grand prince entrusted the state to the entire boyar council and named two princes, Mikhail Glinskii and Dmitrii Belskii, to serve as guardians

during Ivan's minority. A closer look at the sources is needed. Examination of Muscovite rulers' wills convincingly demonstrates that the
grand princes invariably assigned responsibility for carrying out their
final instructions to three or four executors chosen from the boyars
who were their closest advisors. This is essentially what the dying
Vasilii did. To attest his will he summoned three boyars, Mikhail
Yurev, and Princes Vasilii Shuiskii and Mikhail Vorontsov, and his
younger brother Andrei, whom he esteemed and fully trusted. In discussion with the future executors the grand prince reminded them
that he intended to grant his wife's relative, Prince Mikhail Glinskii,
full regency powers. The boyars agreed, but tried to place their own
relatives on the council. Vasilii Shuiskii advanced his brother, Ivan
Shuiskii, as a candidate, while Mikhail Yurev put forward the name
of his cousin, Mikhail Tuchkov. In this way the regency council was
constituted.

The Pskov chronicle states that the tsar consigned the administration to a "small number" of boyars. Their number can be precisely
determined: Vasilii III entrusted affairs to seven executors. This information helps solve the frequent, puzzling references to groups of
"seven boyars" in Muscovy. The appearance of a group of seven during the Time of Troubles[9] need no longer be regarded as happen-
stance. The registers of the Military Records office indicate that groups
of seven boyars frequently managed Moscow during the reigns of Ivan
and his son Fedor. Vasilii's seven boyars evidently served as the
model.

During his lifetime Vasilii was criticized for deciding issues with
two or three close associates in private, without consulting the boyar
council. Creation of the special regency council showed that the grand
prince intended to perpetuate his administrative system. In time the
seven-boyar regency council came to display characteristics of the
boyar oligarchy, but when it first came into existence it was regarded
as a device to reinforce the authority of the central government.
Vasilii placed his most trusted advisors on the regency council; his
favor had led to their rise, but their humble origins effectively excluded them from aspiring to high positions. Vasilii relied on them to protect the throne from attacks by the powerful boyar aristocracy and
check the influence of the boyar council. The chosen advisors were
to rule the country and watch over the grand prince's family for
twelve years, when the heir would attain his majority.

The regents crowned Ivan (then three years old) soon after the
grand prince died. They moved swiftly in order to prevent a rising by

Prince Yurii,[10] who had been planning for twenty-five years to succeed the childless Vasilii. Even after Ivan was born Yurii refused to abandon his ambitious plans, and the regents feared he might try to remove his nephew from the throne. To prevent disturbances they seized Yurii and threw him into prison, where he was held for three years until he died a pitiful death from starvation.

The boyar council resented the transfer of power to the regents and relations between Vasilii's executors and the council's leaders grew strained. Polish agents furnished a vivid picture of the situation in Moscow in the wake of Vasilii's death: "There boyars are at each other's throats. The fact that everything is in the hands of men the grand prince designated is the source of contention. The chief boyars, Princes Belskii and Ovchina, hold positions senior to the regents but can make no decisions."

Prince Ivan Ovchina-Telepnev-Obolenskii, whom the Poles considered one of the council leaders, emerged as the regents' most formidable opponent. He succeeded in attracting Grand Princess Elena's attention, and the young widow had no sooner buried her husband than she made Ovchina her favorite. It was subsequently rumored he was the real father of Ivan, but this was merely spiteful gossip about the royal family. Ovchina early had acquired military distinction. During the major campaigns of the early 1530s he commanded the army's advance guard, and his successful service as commander provides the strongest testimony to his military prowess. Shortly before his death Vasilii III, out of regard for the prince's service, had made him a boyar and also, according to certain reports, Master of Horse, who was the senior boyar in council. The grand princess chose to appear before the people at Vasilii's obsequies attended by three of the regents (Shuiskii, Glinskii, and Vorontsov) and Ovchina.

The slightest acquaintance with Ovchina's service record convincingly demonstrates that he achieved success on the battlefield, not in the grand princess' bedroom. He was descended from a noble family close to the court. His sister Cheliadnina, of boyar rank, was Ivan's nurse. Before he died Vasilii had entrusted his son to her hands and told her never to leave him. Ovchina's family also was connected with the regent Mikhail Glinskii, but their kinship failed to prevent conflict. Political rivalry caused the family quarrel. The boyar council, endeavoring to end the regents' domination, supported Ovchina, while the regents, rent by factionalism, stood behind Glinskii. However, the favorite rendered Glinskii an invaluable service. As senior boyar in council he boldly challenged the grand prince's executors and managed to abrogate the regents' control of the grand princess. They ruled the country for less than a year, and their authority began to crumble the day the palace guard arrested Glinskii.

Chapter Two

THE ADMINISTRATION OF ELENA GLINSKAIA

Before he died Vasilii III asked Glinskii to be responsible for the royal family's safety. "Pour forth your blood and let your body be hacked to pieces for my son Ivan and for my wife,"[1] was the grand prince's final injunction. The grand princess, who was Glinskii's niece, prevented her uncle from fulfilling the charge. The Austrian ambassador, Herberstein,[2] said that Glinskii fell because he undertook to interfere in Elena's private life and sternly insisted she break with her favorite. Herberstein was an old friend of Glinskii and wished to present the latter's conduct in the most becoming light. He failed in his attempt. All Europe was aware of Glinskii's escapades and it seems unlikely that a decline in his niece's morals could have upset such an inveterate opportunist.

The clash between Ovchina and Glinskii, which genuinely alarmed Elena, confronted her with a difficult decision. She could dismiss her favorite and throw herself on the regents' mercy, or sacrifice her uncle, keep her favorite, and thus be extricated from the unenviable condition of a princess living on a widow's mite. Ivan's mother chose the second course, thereby proving that indomitable will was a characteristic of all members of the family. Elena became regent although Vasilii III had clearly expressed his opposition to such a move. Ovchina helped her to engineer a genuine *coup,* after which she immediately removed Glinskii and Vorontsov, and later Prince Andrei Staritskii, from the regency council. Later chronicles declared that Glinskii and Vorontsov were disgraced because they wished to rule the Russian state through the grand princess or, in other words, to rule it in her name. The chroniclers distorted the truth to curry favor with Tsar Ivan IV, who considered his mother his father's lawful successor. In reality Glinskii and Vorontsov had been ruling in accordance with Vasilii's wishes, for he had designated them protectors of his family.

However, once the boyar council had prevailed over the regents, what had been legal became illegal, and the boyars' protectorate over the grand princess was now assumed to be high treason.

Rumors circulated that Glinskii had poisoned Vasilii and planned to hand the royal family over to the Poles, but they are difficult to verify. The actual reason for Prince Mikhail's fall was that he was an outsider among the Muscovite boyars. The authorities starved him to death in prison but conveniently forgot to punish Vorontsov, who was sent to Novgorod after receiving the honorific titles of chief commander and lieutenant of that city. Such behavior fully demonstrates the mendacity of official statements charging that Glinskii and Vorontsov had hatched a conspiracy. Yurev, the most influential figure among the regents, was arrested before Glinskii was, but his punishment was even lighter than Vorontsov's. Released after a brief incarceration, he remained in Moscow, and was permitted to take his seat in the boyar council even after his cousin[3] had fled to Lithuania.

After the regency's collapse Andrei Staritskii, Vasilii III's younger brother, who possessed a large principality and disposed of an impressive military force, withdrew to the town of Staritsa, the capital of his appanage, but this was not enough to allay the concerns of Elena's supporters about him. He was required to sign a formal undertaking to serve Elena faithfully, and was expelled from the regency council on which Vasilii III had placed him. In retirement Andrei lived in constant fear of falling under official displeasure, while Elena suspected the former regent of intriguing against her. Ovchina advised her to summon Andrei to Moscow and arrest him. The latter discerned the ruse and declined the invitation by pretending to be ill, but anxious to convince Elena of his loyalty, he transferred almost all of his military forces to her service. Elena and her favorite lost no time in taking advantage of his naive action, and Muscovite units moved secretly towards Staritsa. Warned at night of their advance, Andrei hastily left Staritsa for Torzhok. From there he could have fled to Lithuania, but instead turned aside to Novgorod. Andrei hoped the Novgorod gentry would help him defeat Ovchina and bring his power to an end. He wrote to Novgorod: "The grand prince is a child; the boyars control the realm, and I shall be happy to reward you."[4] Although he received support from some members of the gentry Andrei was afraid to do battle with Ovchina; instead, trusting in the oath he had sworn, he proceeded to Moscow to beg Elena's pardon. Apprehended as soon as he set foot in the capital, he was sentenced to prison for life, forced to wear a heavy kind of iron mask, known as the "iron hat," and starved to death in six months. Gallows were erected along the main highway between Moscow and Novgorod on which gentry who had supported Prince Andrei were hanged.

Prince Mikhail Glinskii and Andrei, the grand prince's brother, the strong figures in the regency council, were the ones Ovchina punished most severely. Vasilii III's other executors, the Shuiskii princes, Yurev and Tuchkov, remained on the boyar council until Elena died, and apparently this group, composed of Vasilii's old advisors, was precisely the men who promulgated the significant reforms carried out during these years. The first changes the boyars made affected local government, assigning elected members of the gentry (known as district elders or circuit judges) responsibility for apprehending criminals. They also stimulated building and beautification in Moscow and accomplished a major reform of the monetary system. As trade increased more money was constantly needed, but the stock of precious metals in Russia was extremely small. Inability to obtain currency led to massive counterfeiting of silver coins and many counterfeiters appeared in the towns. Those found guilty of this practice were severely punished; their hands were cut off and lead was poured down their throats, but no measures proved of avail. Elena's regency finally adopted a radical means to solve the currency crisis: the government withdrew old units of various denominations from circulation and struck a new standard coinage. The silver Novgorod *denga* became the basic unit. It was known as a kopeika [lance], stamped with a representation of a knight holding a lance, whereas the old Moscow *denga* showed a knight carrying a sword. The heavy Novgorod *kopeika* superseded the slight Moscow "sword-bearer."

Elena's administration lasted only five years. In Old Russia women rarely stepped outside the world of domestic concerns to engage in politics, and very few of these prisoners of the woman's quarter have found a place in history. Elena Glinskaia was one of the few. She succeeded in usurping the power Vasilii III had conferred upon the regency council, and the ensuing reforms could never have taken place without her approval. However, the facts are inadequate to answer the question whether she was actually the wise ruler the royal chronicles portrayed her to be. The boyars, who hated her for flouting tradition, slyly deprecated her as an evil seer.

During the final year of her life Elena was often ill and went on frequent pilgrimages to monasteries. She most likely died a natural death. Herberstein reported the grand princess had been poisoned, but, growing dissatisfied with unfounded rumor omitted further spec-

ulation in the second edition of his *Commentary* that Elena had died
a violent death. Tsar Ivan never thought she had been poisoned, although he was angry with the boyars because of the scant respect they
had shown his mother. The boyars greeted Elena's death with rejoicing. Former members of the regency council were unsparing in their
abuse of a woman who had no right to rule. Ivan later declared that
one of them, Boyar Mikhail Tuchkov, uttered many bitter words
when she died and likened her to a viper spewing forth venom.

Chapter Three

IVAN'S CHILDHOOD

On Elena's death power reverted to the regency council, which lost
no time settling accounts with Prince Ovchina, since its members were
united in their detestation of the favorite. But their harmony was to
prove of short duration. When Andrei Staritskii fell, Prince Vasilii
Vasilevich Shuiskii assumed leadership of the council. When more
than fifty he married Anastasiia, a member of the royal house who
was a cousin of the young grand prince. Becoming part of the royal
family, he decided to enjoy a life that reflected his new status and
moved from his old residence to quarters at the court of the Staritskii
family.

Although Ivan never grew tired of asserting that Princes Vasilii and
Ivan Shuiskii arbitrarily had attached themselves to his person and
"acted like tsars,"[1] this was not actually the case, for Grand Prince
Vasilii had chosen them to be his young son's guardians. One of Russia's most aristocratic families, the Shuiskii princes had no desire to
share power with men whom Vasilii III's patronage had brought to
prominence. The hostility between princes of the blood, as foreigners
called the Shuiskii clan, and Vasilii's old counsellors, such as the boyars Yurev and Tuchkov, and the secretaries of the boyar council, provoked an open clash. Six months after Elena's death the Shuiskii
group arrested and executed Fedor Mishurin, a royal secretary, and
soon completely eliminated the regency council, the task Elena had
begun. One of the regents, Boyar M. V. Tuchkov, was exiled, and his
nephew, V. M. Yurev, died less than a year after these events took

place. Tuchkov's closest ally in council, Boyar I. D. Belskii, was arrested and imprisoned. The deposition of Metropolitan Daniel, an associate of Vasilii III, completed the Shuiskii triumph.

The Shuiskii victory, though complete, was of short duration. Prince Vasilii survived Mishurin by only a few weeks and died at the height of the disturbance his family had caused. Lacking both Vasilii's authority and experience his younger brother, Ivan, finally quarreled with the rest of the boyars and ceased to attend their meetings. Taking advantage of the situation, opponents of the Shuiskii faction secured pardon for Ivan Belskii and brought him back to Moscow, while Ivan Shuiskii was sent with army detachments to Vladimir. Ivan refused to accept defeat. Fomenting a rising, he returned to the capital with a substantial gentry force that deposed Metropolitan Ioasaf and exiled Prince Belskii to Beloozero, where he was secretly murdered. When Prince Ivan, the last of Vasilii's executors, died, Prince Andrei Shuiskii emerged as the head of the faction, but he received no support from the other boyars and was slain late in 1543. This brought the Shuiskii administration to an end, when the grand prince was barely thirteen years old.

Ivan lost his father when he was three and was orphaned at seven and a half. Four-year-old Yurii was incapable of sharing boyish pleasures with his brother because he was born deaf and dumb. The mature Ivan often recalled his childhood with bitterness. His ink turned to gall as he described the insults the boyars had forced him to endure. Historians have felt the fascination of the tsar's powerful evocation. V. O. Kliuchevskii constructed a remarkable psychological portrait of the young Ivan, based on his letters. Kliuchevskii wrote that the orphan's mind was early imbued with feelings of isolation and rejection, growing up amid scenes of disorder caused by the boyars' highhanded and violent actions, which transformed shyness into nervous timidity. Ivan once experienced convulsive shock when the Shuiskii boyars burst into his bedroom at dawn, awoke and terrified him. As time passed Ivan grew suspicious and developed a profound distrust of mankind.

How credible is the image of Ivan this talented artist has created? In order to answer this question one must remember that Ivan was the object of his mother's love until he was seven, while his basic nature was forming. The regents never involved Ivan in their disputes save when the Shuiskii partisans arrested their opponents, including Metropolitan Ioasaf, in his presence. A chronicler hostile to the Shuiskii princes observes that the disturbances in Moscow frightened the ruler. Ivan supplemented the chronicle narrative with statements that render the outline of the uprising much clearer. Seeking to arrest the metropolitan, the boyars noisily invaded the sovereign's bedchamber in the palace. They awakened him at the unseasonable time of three hours before dawn and made him chant in front of the cross. The boy apparently had no real suspicion an uprising was taking place before his eyes, for the tsar's letter to Kurbskii makes no allusion to the terror he was supposed to have felt and refers incidentally and indifferently to the metropolitan's deposition: "and they drove out Metropolitan Ioasaf with great dishonor."[2] He obviously had forgotten about an event which supposedly had left him terrified for the rest of his life. It is reasonable to assume that the immediate impressions of childhood, at least until Ivan was twelve, had not given him serious grounds for charging the boyars with behavior disrespectful towards him.

Ivan's later complaints produce an odd effect. They convey an impression that he was borrowing other people's words rather than directly recalling his own childhood experiences. He scolded the boyars at length for craftily plotting to appropriate his family's possessions, or personal fisc. Members of the Shuiskii family were the most covetous. Ivan darkly observed that Ivan Shuiskii had only one fur coat, which everyone knew was in tatters. How could he make a display of gold and silver vessels; what resources did he have to craft them? It would have been better for Shuiskii to exchange his fur coat and make the vessels with the extra money.[3] The grand prince's court undoubtedly contained people who gossiped about Shuiskii's coat and utensils, but a ten-year-old orphan who was a ward of the Shuiskii princes would be unlikely to comprehend their meaning. Ivan would naturally have to be much older before he would worry about conserving family property, and it was many years later when those seeking his favor told him that his fisc had been rifled.

All his life Ivan harbored animosity towards his guardians. He made no effort to conceal his irritation in his letters. He wrote: "I recall once when we were playing childish games Prince Ivan Shuiskii sat on a bench, his elbow on my late father's bed and his feet on a chair, not looking at us." The barrage of words at last permitted a lively recollection of childhood to shine through, but Ivan interpreted it perversely. Conjuring up the memory of a feeble old man at death's door, Ivan went on to upbraid his guardian because he sat in the presence of his ruler showing no signs of respect and behaving neither like a parent, nor a master, nor a servant before his lord. "Who could endure such insolence?" was the question with which Ivan concluded his account of the Shuiskii administration. When the tsar's erstwhile friend Kurbskii read his letter he could not refrain from an ironical riposte. He mocked the clumsy attempt to compromise the former guardians and tried to make Ivan understand how impolite it was to write about "beds and bed-warmers" (he meant Shuiskii's coats) and insert what were no more than "other innumerable and inexhaustible old wive's tales."[4]

Ivan complained bitterly that he had been insulted and coerced as a child. He lamented: "I was never free to do anything; I could never do what I wanted or what a boy should." However, proud and cunning boyars could not be blamed for this. The spirit of the *Domostroi*[5] had reigned in the ceremonial chambers of the grand princes for centuries; established custom invariably dictated the norms of court life. Ivan was crowned at the age of three; it became his duty henceforward to sit through protracted ceremonies and obediently discharge exhausting rituals that held no meaning for him and constantly deprived him of a child's pleasures. This was how it had been during his mother's lifetime and this is how it remained under the regents. According to Kurbskii, the boyars made no attempt to initiate Ivan into their affairs, but they kept a sharp eye on his friends and soon removed from the palace anyone who showed signs of becoming a confidant. After the last regents died the system of training the royal children inevitably altered. Patriarchal severity was succeeded by a permissiveness which did Ivan more harm than the boyars' presumed strictness. As Kurbskii noted, his tutors "praised him (Ivan) for being an unruly boy."

Physically Ivan developed rapidly and at thirteen was already a sturdy youth. The ambassadorial bureau officially announced to other countries that the grand prince was becoming a man, had already matured fully (!), and with God's grace was planning to marry. The crown secretaries had described the tall young man's outward appearance with some accuracy, but they were mistaken in ascribing to him serious thoughts of marriage. In youth Ivan bore little resemblance to a child who had been thwarted by a strict regimen. Once free of the tutelage and authority of the senior boyars he gave himself up to pursuits and games which had formerly been banned. His entourage was struck by Ivan's violent, savage temperament. At twelve he would ascend tall towers and hurl cats and dogs, which he called dumb brutes, down from the height. At fourteen he turned his attention to humans. These vicious activities delighted the young sovereign, who behaved like a regular criminal. With a gang composed of sons of highly prominent boyars his own age he roamed the streets and squares of Moscow, lept and ran about everywhere in an unseemly manner, trampled people with his horse, and beat and robbed ordinary citizens.

When his guardians died and the grand prince reached maturity the boyars began to involve him more often in their disputes. Ivan vividly remembered the time he saw a fight break out in the boyar council. Andrei Shuiskii and his partisans attacked the boyar Vorontsov, struck him on the cheek with their fists, pushed him, tore his clothing, and hauled him from the chamber in order to kill him. Some six months after this palace incident one of Ivan's associates urged him to execute Andrei Shuiskii. Huntsmen seized the boyar near his residence by the Kuriatnyi gate and his naked corpse lay near the gate for two hours. The chronicler noted: "From this moment the boyars began to fear and obey the sovereign."[6] Many years were to pass before Ivan managed to make the boyars obey him; in the meantime he himself became the tool of his palace entourage. Kurbskii wrote: "They began to instruct him and one would use him in order to wreak vengeance upon another."[7]

The Master of Horse, Ivan Ivanovich Cheliadnin, died at approximately the same time as the last regent. He had been the grand prince's close mentor and tutor, and with him the traditional mode of life in the royal household came conclusively to an end. Much later Ivan was prone to tax his boyars with the charge they had looked after their rulers poorly. He complained: "My brother Yurii and I were fed like foreigners or peons. We had no food or clothing. Many times our meals were not delivered on time. It is impossible to tell how terribly I suffered in my youth." So went Ivan's pathetic cries, and no doubt these complaints echoed actual recollections of his childhood. It is by no means clear to what time he was referring, although almost certainly he was lamenting the period after he had freed himself from tutelage and become his own master. Ivan's subservient attendants, who sought to acquire the young prince's favor, made no real attempts to instruct him. They lacked authority to admonish him for the disorderly life he lived or compel him to eat at the proper time.

Chapter Four

THE TITLE OF TSAR

Vasilii III, as has been seen, had requested the boyars to watch over his son until the latter reached the age of fifteen, when he would have to rule independently. The sixteenth century considered fifteen the age of maturity, the time when gentry children first entered military service and sons of the nobility began their careers as courtiers. Vasilii had hoped the regents he had named would instruct his heir in affairs of state, but they had departed before they could accomplish the charge. At fifteen Ivan was poorly prepared to rule a large and powerful state, and surrounded by chance acquaintances. He marked attainment of his majority by meting out sentences of displeasure and ordering executions. As soon as he had celebrated his birthday the grand prince ordered Afanasii Buturlin to have his tongue cut out as punishment for impolite words he had uttered, and a month later pronounced sentence of displeasure on five great boyars.

The boyar council urged the young grand prince to take command of a force proceeding against the Tatars. Ivan regarded the campaign as an excuse to indulge in pursuits that took his fancy. In camp he joined in spring ploughing, planted seeds, walked on stilts, decked himself out in a shroud, and compelled boyars to participate in the royal amusements. A few days later he had three boyars beheaded who were planting seeds with him. No one knew exactly why prominent commanders were put to death, but it was most likely because they had criticized the grand prince.

An event of great political significance signaled the beginning of Ivan's independent reign: the head of the Russian state adopted the title of tsar. Medieval man conceived of the international political system as a strict hierarchy. In accordance with Byzantine teaching Constantinople, the center of the universe, had assumed the mantle of the Roman Empire. Russia became acquainted with Byzantine doctrine in Kievan times and Moscow had not forgotten it. In the fourteenth century Muscovite grand princes occasionally were called the cupbearers of the Byzantine tsar [emperor], but at the time the rank was devoid of political significance. The devastating Tatar sack and the triumph of the Golden Horde had brought Russia into an unfamiliar political configuration, the empire of the mighty Mongol khans who ruled half the world. Russian princes, who now had to receive permission to administer their ancestral realms from the khans of the Golden Horde, called their Tatar overlords tsars. The grand princes of Moscow had long been called "grand princes of all Russia," but not until Ivan III managed finally to overthrow the Tatar yoke did they become fully sovereign autocrats instead of vassal princes. The collapse of the Golden Horde and the destruction of the Byzantine Empire in 1453 ended Russia's factual subjection to the Tatars and invalidated the views Russians traditionally had entertained concerning the superior authority possessed by the Greek emperors. When a strong, unified Russia succeeded the weak and fragmented state tributary to the Tatars, the situation in eastern Europe altered radically and new concepts reflected Russian political awareness of the changes that had taken place, the most striking of which was the theory of Moscow the Third Rome. According to this concept Muscovite princes were now the direct successors of the rulers of New Rome, or the Byzantine Empire. Ivan III had called himself tsar of all Russia, but he refrained from adopting the title officially. Assuming that adjacent states would refuse to recognize it, he confined its use to relations with the Livonian Order and a few German princes.

The boyars were in no hurry to inform other countries that Ivan III's sixteen-year-old grandson had been crowned as tsar. Two years later Polish envoys in Moscow at last discovered that Ivan had been proclaimed tsar in the fashion of his ancestor Monomakh,[1] and had adopted the appropriate title. As soon as the envoys learned of this highly significant development they demanded documentary proof. The boyars cunningly refused, fearing that if the Poles obtained a written answer they might contrive objections which would be difficult to overcome. Couriers dispatched to Poland attempted to explain the meaning of what had taken place in Moscow in such a way as to avoid arousing hostility at the Polish court. They said that since their sovereign now ruled the Russian land independently the metropolitan had crowned him as tsar with the crown of Monomakh. The Muscovites considered the coronation, which occurred in the fourteenth year of Ivan's rule as prince, to mark the start of his independent reign.

The coronation took place on January 16, 1547. After a solemn service in the Cathedral of the Dormition in the Kremlin Metropolitan Makarii placed the Cap of Monomakh, symbolic of tsaric power, on the grand prince's head. In their testaments the earliest princes

of Muscovy invariably had bequeathed a Golden Cap, the crown sig-
nifying their control of Muscovy, to their successors. Their wills never
mentioned their own grand-princely crown, for the all-powerful Horde
had reserved the right to dispose of it. When Russia shook off the
harsh Tatar yoke the rulers of the strong new principality continued
to wear this traditional Golden Cap, but now they called it the Cap
of Monomakh. Herberstein, the inquisitive Austrian, saw Vasilii III
wearing it, sewn with jewels and ingeniously adorned with gold sheet-
ing that quivered whenever the prince moved. The Cap was an obvious imitation of Tatar headgear, but after the Horde collapsed the
Eastern style went out of fashion. A legend was devised to explain
the Cap's origin. When Monomakh was victorious in a campaign
against Constantinople his grandfather, the Emperor Constantine
(who actually had died long before) took a purple cap from his own
head and gave it to his grandson in exchange for peace. The imperial
regalia descended from Monomakh to the sovereigns of Muscovy.

As official chronicles portrayed the event, the sixteen-year-old boy
himself decided to be crowned with the Cap of Monomakh and assume the title of tsar. When the metropolitan and the boyars ascer-
tained their sovereign's intent they burst into tears of joy and the
whole matter was settled. In reality the initiative came not from Ivan
but from those who ruled in his name. Before the coronation the
grand prince's maternal grandmother Anna and his uncle, Mikhail
Vasilevich Glinskii, wielded the greatest influence at court.

Vasilii III's marriage to Elena Glinskaia had raised her family to
first rank among the boyars of Moscow, but the fall of the regent,
Mikhail Lvovich, and Elena's death relegated the family to a subordinate position for some time. The status of its members altered when
their nephew, Ivan, attained his majority. Mikhail Vasilevich, the eldest Glinskii brother, immediately announced his candidacy to be
Master of Horse, anticipating he would occupy a position in the state
with power comparable to that which Ovchina had exercised in that
office during Elena's administration. The most powerful figures in
the realm constantly vied for the position of Master of Horse. It had
passed from Ovchina to the grand prince's tutor, I.I. Cheliadnin, and
next to I.P. Cheliadnin-Fedorov. Mikhail cleverly contrived to secure
passage of a death sentence upon Cheliadnin, who was stripped naked
and consigned for execution on Ivan's orders. The price of his pardon was total humiliation. A few months later the grand prince ordered the execution of two young cousins his own age, Princes Ivan
Dorogobuzhskii and Fedor Ovchinin. One was impaled on a stake

and the other was beheaded on the ice of a frozen river. This grue-some affair was not the result of a youthful quarrel; the chronicles indicate that Mikhail Glinskii and his mother, Princess Anna, caused the death of the noble courtiers. The Glinskii faction thus managed to settle accounts with the old Master of Horse, I.P. Cheliadnin. They stripped him of all his titles and he lost his sole heir, his stepson, Prince Dorogobuzhskii.

The coronation substantially benefited members of the tsar's family. Anna, the tsar's grandmother, and her children acquired vast ap-panage territories and at the coronation Prince Mikhail was named Master of Horse and his brother Yurii was made a boyar. It is im-possible to accept the view that Ivan's coronation and the executions which preceded it brought the boyar regime to an end. These moves were really no more than a reshuffling of the groups at the top of the power pyramid, which ushered in a brief period during which the Glinskii faction predominated.

The tsar and most of his subjects believed the change in his title constituted a first proof that Ivan was functioning as a genuinely in-dependent monarch. Recalling the time, the tsar subsequently wrote that he personally had decided to establish a tsardom, and "with God's grace its beginnings were auspicious."[2] The title of tsar sud-denly made Ivan's subjects see him as the successor of the Roman emperors and God's annointed on earth. However, Ivan was not long to enjoy the power he had so easily acquired. Life quickly taught him a sanguinary lesson. Reared as he had been in the rarified atmosphere of the court, Ivan had little understanding of his people. When he amused himself trampling crowds in the marketplace with his horses he saw terrified individuals, and he saw only happy faces on great holidays, but his submissive folk possessed another mien, which the tsar was fated soon to behold.

Chapter Five

THE MOSCOW UPRISING

The population of Russia barely exceeded eight or ten million people in the middle of the sixteenth century. Most lived in tiny hamlets scattered over the limitless eastern European plain, where a process was imperceptibly at work preparing for the future greatness of the realm. Peasants were on the move, settling the empty borderland known as the Wild Field. The first half of the century was relatively kind to the rural population. Crop failures were frequent, but they did not occur everywhere simultaneously and were not fraught with disastrous consequences. Feudal lords burdened peasants with every conceivable impost, but even so failed to tie them to the land or deny them the right of departure on St. George's Day.[1]

Town-dwellers comprised no more than two percent of the inhabitants in agrarian Russia. Towns were centers of artisan production and trade. In a natural economy commodity exchange usually was limited to local markets. The country had not yet recovered from the legacy of economic dislocation inherited from the period of feudal fragmentation. Nevertheless, towns were prospering and their populations were increasing. The growth of Moscow was particularly rapid, and foreigners compared the Russian capital with leading cities in western Europe. According to contemporary calculations (which were highly inexact), Moscow contained some 100,000 people. Next came Novgorod, which had a population of 25,000 or 30,000 people; after the collapse of the feudal republic[2] Great Novgorod had lost its former prominence as a center of industry and trade. The rest of the towns in Russia lagged far behind.

Town life was marked by deep social contrasts. Wealthy merchants were constantly at odds with the impoverished lower classes. Exactions levied on the towns were one of the main sources of revenue for the crown treasury, and the government required the citizenry to pay pecuniary tribute and make heavy contributions in kind. In wartime towns were compelled to outfit contingents of soldiers equipped with firearms. A perpetual source of friction between rich merchants and the commons was the issue of who was to perform military service. One such dispute involved Novgorod during one of the earliest campaigns against Kazan. Novgorod fusiliers sent to the tsar's camp at Kolomna tried to obtain redress from the young sovereign, and attempted to hand him a petition while he was walking outside the camp. The grand prince ordered the petitioners to disperse immediately, and his attendants undertook to clear the road. The men of Novgorod responded by hurling pieces of turf at them and discharging their weapons. More than ten men died and many were wounded in the encounter. His courtiers failed to rout the fusiliers and the grand prince had to return to his headquarters by a circuitous route. Ivan remembered the disturbance at Kolomna well; many years later he inserted an account about the refractory men of Novgorod into some old chronicles he was scrutinizing. Six months after the disturbance Ivan appeared personally in Novgorod, accompanied by four thousand soldiers. A local scribe states he did nothing for three days but after that his entire army behaved in an arrogant manner. The people of Novgorod were aroused, however, more by Moscow's exactions than by the army's arrogance. They were forced to pay three thousand gold pieces to demonstrate their esteem for the grand prince.

Ivan proceeded from Novgorod to Pskov, whose inhabitants were impatiently awaiting his arrival in order to demand redress against the boyars who governed the city, but he merely harassed employees of the posting service and paid no attention to the complaints he heard. The townspeople, although they suffered substantial loss and experienced much difficulty, refused to abandon hope. After Ivan's departure they sent a numerous delegation to petition him. The suppliants found the tsar at leisure in a village on one of the royal estates. Venting his rage, Ivan ordered them arrested and harshly dealt with: he plunged them in boiling wine, burnt their hair with candles, singed their beards, had them stripped naked, and stretched on the ground. If an accident had not intervened it is hard to say how the affair might have ended. The tsar was informed the great Kremlin bell had suddenly fallen and he rushed to Moscow to marvel at the portent. The men of Pskov returned empty-handed and their tales provided their fellow-citizens with fresh fodder to fuel their discontent. Disturbances were momentarily anticipated and the local commander fled the city in fear. A rising soon broke out in the Pskov region; dissidents seized the strong border fortress of Opochka and imprisoned the crown secretary in charge of it. The events in Opochka so greatly alarmed the authorities in Moscow that they rushed substantial forces to Pskov. Although two thousand men from Novgorod occupied the unruly fortress and the rising in Pskov was crushed, the unrest spread to Novgorod and Moscow. The archbishop of Novgorod dolefully wrote several letters stating that robbers on the roads made it impossible to enter or leave the city, but Moscow was preoccupied with its own problems. A revolt had broken out in the capital.

The rise of the Glinskii faction had complicated the general situation. Like previous boyar administrations, the new favorites plundered the treasury and extorted large sums of money from the citizenry. Long out of power, the Glinskii group was trying to make up for lost time, and soon earned universal detestation. The chronicler relates that the nobility behaved with great lawlessness in Moscow and everywhere else in the country: its members committed acts of violence, gave unjust judgments in return for bribes, and exacted heavy tribute from the populace. Glinskii's servitors in Moscow acted like conquerors, and the common people expected nothing but violence and rapine from them.

Fierce fires broke out in Moscow during the hot summer months of 1547, hastening the denouement. Many lost their possessions and their lives, and those who suffered held the Glinskii faction responsible for their misfortunes. A revolt began in Moscow on June 26, 1547 when armed men burst into the Kremlin demanding the surrender of Glinskii and his supporters. The boyars tried to sooth the people, but to no avail. The grand prince, who had been attending service in the Cathedral of the Dormition, was forced to drain the cup of humiliation to the dregs. The angry townspeople tore his uncle, Yurii Glinskii, from the cathedral and stoned him to death in the square. People plundered the homes of Glinskii's partisans and killed a host of their armed retainers, as well as many royal courtiers. The tsar and his entire court were obliged to withdraw to the village of Vorobevo, a suburb of Moscow, which proved an unsafe refuge. On the third day of the rising the Moscow executioner convoked a huge crowd in the square. People who had suffered in the conflagration loudly shouted that the city had been burned by warlocks, and the person chiefly responsible was Anna, the tsar's grandmother, who was a witch. She conjured people's hearts from their bodies, sprinkled them with water, and flew over the city like a magpie, scattering the water over it. The enraged mob set out in a body for Vorobevo to settle accounts with the hated rulers. The crowd terrified the tsar. Ivan later said his life was in danger and "traitors had urged the mob to kill us."[3] The boyars managed with difficulty to calm the people and convince them that Glinskii and his supporters were not in Vorobevo. The armed bands returned to Moscow without incident. Those who participated in the Moscow revolt came from various levels in society. The lowest ranks of the commons formed the backbone of the movement, but they lacked any clear political program and their attack on the Glinskii faction was reminiscent of the "primitive surges" (in S. O. Shmidt's phrase) characteristic of the middle ages. People of substance who originally took part in the rising eventually were able to secure substantial concessions from the government.

When the turbulence abated the authorities finally managed to regain control of the capital, but these events had shown Ivan how totally he had failed to comprehend the gulf dividing what he imagined he could do from what it was actually possible for him to do. He had believed his autocratic rule emanated from God, but the first acts of his independent administration had brought him into confrontation with his people, who had raised unruly hands against the royal family. Although this was not the first time Ivan had risked the lives of others with impunity, it was the first time he had been compelled to think seriously about the safety of himself and those close to him.

These events in the capital constituted a watershed in Ivan's development. He was obliged to expel the Glinskii family from the boyar council, since its members were compromised and had been adjudged guilty of the earlier boyar executions. Prince Mikhail dared not return to Moscow and tried to flee to Lithuania from his estate near Rzhev, but was apprehended enroute. The boyars insisted he be stripped of his title of Master of Horse, and executions ceased as if by magic. The collapse of the Glinskii administration brought to a final close that phase in the political development of Russia known as the boyar regime. The great Moscow revolt showed the boyars how highly insecure was their rule. The social antagonisms it revealed blunted the power of the possessing classes, temporarily checked the feuding in which the boyars indulged, and had much to do with shaping the course of the ensuing reforms.

Chapter Six

FIRST REFORMS

Russia's political structure was invigorated in the mid-sixteenth century, but although the unification of the country had endowed the Muscovite sovereigns with remarkable powers, they were not unlimited. The monarch had to share power with the strong aristocracy, which actively upheld the divisive traditional principle of fragmentation even after the discrete feudal duchies had been united in a single principality. "The tsar proposes and the boyars dispose" was the formula used in adopting laws and deciding questions of peace and war. The nobility's central mechanism was the boyar council, which also controlled all local administration. The boyars had been granted the largest towns and districts in the country as maintenance (kormlenie). The term *maintenance* denoted the right of local administrative officials to collect taxes for their personal use, so that they literally maintained themselves at public expense. The system of maintenance was one of the most archaic institutions of the sixteenth century.

In attempting to guard its privileges the boyar aristocracy took advantage of the custom according to which a man's service rank was not determined by his capacity and experience but by his pedigree or level of nobility, and the positions occupied by members of his family, such as his father, grandfather and other relatives. This system, known as *precedence* (mestnichestvo), divided the nobility into rival clans and guaranteed a tiny clique of the greatest noble families exclusive rights to top offices. By the middle of the sixteenth century the institution of precedence was also largely outmoded. Although the nobility zealously championed its ancient privileges the disputes in which the boyar factions engaged and the abuses they perpetrated during Ivan's minority had called the old order into question and made it essential for the administrative system to be reconstructed along centralized lines.

After the country was unified the feudatories' hieratical structure experienced numerous vicissitudes. Sometimes a large boyar clan would break up into individual families. The ancient title of boyar was reserved exclusively for great landowners, who constituted the upper level of the feudal class. Possessing huge estates which they

ruled in a patriarchal manner, they could sell, alienate or mortgage
their property. The lower and more populous level of this rank was
filled with petty landowners (called junior or lesser boyars) and servitors at the grand prince's court, who once had been slaves, or court
menials, which eventually came to be known collectively as the gentry. These serving people. or gentry, usually held land on service-
tenure, and could keep it only as long as they rendered the grand
prince service. The service-tenure estate developed into the main type
of feudal landholding in the sixteenth century. Service-tenure enabled
the grand prince to bind the serving ranks closely to himself, and the
monarchy acquired firm, massive support from these landholders, the
men on service-tenure. The army was first to feel the impact of the
changes taking place in the feudal ranks. A single force composed of
gentry superseded the numerous bands belonging to princes, and
thousands of gentry served in its ranks. This meant the importance
of the gentry increased so greatly that any clique of boyar rulers
would have to reckon with its demands. However, the direct influence
exercised by the gentry upon the rulers did not correspond with its
numbers and weight. The gentry had no permanent representatives in
the boyar council, and the rules of precedence effectively barred its
members from higher office. The gentry refused to accept this state
of affairs and demanded establishment of an administrative apparatus
corresponding to the new set of historical conditions.

The Moscow revolt of 1547 revealed the instability of the boyar
regimes and created a splendid opportunity for the gentry to enter
the political arena. Soon after the revolt gentry publicists began to
be heard from and gentry representatives were permitted to participate in convocations of the estates, or those assemblies which subsequently became known as land assemblies, again as Shmidt has observed. Gentry apologists drew up plans aimed at fundamental
reconstruction of Russia's governmental apparatus and the flood of
reform ideas at last attracted the attention of the young tsar.

Metropolitan Makarii, who by virtue of his office had become the
tsar's mentor, is thought to have had considerable influence in shaping Ivan's general attitude. A well-educated man, though a mediocre
writer, Makarii possessed qualities that enabled him to survive all the
boyar regimes and retain Ivan's favor for twenty years. A seasoned
ecclesiastical diplomat, he subtly adapted his pastoral mission to the
interests of secular authority, and became an apostle of autocracy.
He crowned Ivan tsar, and shed fresh luster on the concept that Russian autocrats were chosen by God, which had grown sadly tarnished

during the boyar regimes. He taught Ivan this belief, which became the fundament of the tsar's philosophy of life. The head of the church militant made a substantial contribution to the theory of autocracy, heretofore the domain of writers, to which Ivan was subsequently to give practical implementation.

After Ivan was crowned the Orthodox tsar of his realm Makarii carried out a reform of the church. An ecclesiastical council he convened canonized a number of local holy men, who were proclaimed new miracle-workers. The Russian church discovered more saints than it had possessed during the previous five centuries of its existence. The reform was designed to enhance the importance of the native church and show that the sun of piety, which had grown dim in ancient Rome and Constantinople, shone with new force in Moscow, the Third Rome. Makarii's activity exerted an influence on Ivan, but the metropolitan was not alone.

At the outset of his independent administration Ivan had formed close ties with a small group of men in the higher chancery bureaucracy responsible for operating the government apparatus. These bureaucrats were among the best-educated members of contemporary society. One of them, who had risen from humble origins, was the celebrated crown secretary, Ivan Viskovatyi, whose rare talents had brought him from obscurity to the highest rung of the official ladder. Viskovatyi had considerable influence with Ivan, but the tsar's particular favorite was Aleksei Adashev.

A petty landowner from Kostroma, Aleksei Adashev was neither a great noble nor a wealthy man, but the tsar somewhat exaggerated when he said that in expectation of loyal service he had plucked Adashev from the gutter to the court and made him the equal of potentates. Adashev exemplified all the qualities of a devoted servitor, but this alone was insufficient to achieve a successful career at court. Like Viskovatyi, he owed his success to his effective service in the chanceries, the new organs of the centralized administration. The tsar's future favorite began his service career in the petitions bureau, which examined pleas addressed to the tsar and was an object of his special concern. Adashev transferred to the treasury bureau, where his service was so outstanding that he soon achieved the rank of crown treasurer, which afforded him access to the boyar council. Informed contemporaries believed that Adashev eventually came to rule Russia from his chancery office near the Cathedral of the Annunciation.

The senior chancery bureaucracy, which political centralization had brought into existence, naturally became the conduit for ideas about restructuring the government apparatus. Adashev and his circle put these ideas into practice and the reforms they sponsored constituted a major event in Russia's development. New people entered the Kremlin, and Ivan's acquaintance with them ushered in a new epoch in the tsar's life. Opportunities for social engineering never before suspected now lay open to him; real maturity was close at hand, and Ivan's concealed dislike for the great boyars, receiving fresh stimulus, took a new direction.

The reformers first made their presence felt at what is known as the reconciliation assembly convoked in 1549 and attended by military commanders, lesser boyars, the boyar council and church leaders. Appearing before its members the eighteen-year-old tsar publicly declared changes must occur. He began his speech with threats directed against boyars who subsisted on maintenance, oppressed the lesser boyars and peasants, and grossly affronted serving-men everywhere. Scoring their abuses, Ivan held the nobles responsible for the impoverishment of the gentry.

Criticism of boyar wrongdoing, approved from on high and becoming, as it were, official doctrine, aroused many to reflect on the condition of society. For a brief period, never to be repeated, publicistics flourished in Russia. Advanced thinkers discussed urgent problems of reform, and Ivan Semenovich Peresvetov was one of the most striking of them. Born in Lithuania to a family of petty gentry, he had travelled over almost the whole of southeastern Europe before coming to Russia. Surviving members of the regency council still possessed some influence in Moscow, and one of them, Mikhail Yurev, was attracted to Peresvetov when he learned of his scheme to reequip the Muscovite cavalry with shields of the Macedonian type. Although the time was clearly not yet ripe to formulate broader plans for reform, Yurev nevertheless became Peresvetov's patron and helped him achieve material independence. After Yurev's death Peresvetov grew impoverished, and his decline coincided with the onset of the boyar regimes, which he came to view as the incarnation of all the evils in society, ruining ordinary soldiers and threatening the state with destruction.

Having lived in poverty for many years Peresvetov at once grasped the splendid opportunity afforded him by the reform movement of the late 1540s. Taking advantage of the situation he dreamed and tendered his famous petitions to the tsar, and the simple soldier turned out to be one of the most talented writers ever to produce a basic theory of autocracy. Since it was unsafe to criticize Muscovite institutions overtly, Peresvetov took refuge in allegory. Sketching an idealized form of unlimited monarchy supported by the gentry he used as a paradigm the menacing Ottoman Empire, which had arisen from the ruins of the Byzantine Empire. As he put it, the Orthodox Greek empire of Constantine had been destroyed by its nobility, composed of lazy rich men, whereas the realm of Sultan Mohammed owed its success to its soldiers, who brought the ruler power and glory. The sweep of Peresvetov's views dumbfounded contemporaries; in ways he was ahead of his time. He wrote that men's deeds must be judged by their righteousness, for God loves justice, not faith. Calling for the liberation of the enslaved soldiers he wrote, "evil is perpetrated in any country that has been enslaved . . . and the entire realm is impoverished."

Interestingly enough Peresvetov had nothing to say about land grants for serving-men, although this issue was the most burning one of the time and greatly agitated the feudal gentry. Peresvetov proposed that serving-men should be guaranteed an adequate salary, for which townsmen could furnish the necessary financial resources if fixed prices were established at town markets. He advised the tsar that generosity to his warriors would be a sign of wisdom and levelled threats at the treacherous nobles. Peresvetov was the first to state unequivocally that change in Russia's administrative or service structure was out of the question unless the political domination of the nobility was restricted and the gentry allowed to participate in affairs of state. Peresvetov protested boldly and passionately against boyar excesses. Such impudent assaults on the mightiest officials of the land inevitably would have brought this insignificant member of the gentry to prison or the scaffold had not the reformers, his new protectors, stood behind him.

The reform party, headed by Adashev, became the heart of the administration. In the historical literature it is called the chosen council, a term which is not entirely accurate. The young tsar became its spokesman. After addressing the reconciliation assembly he appeared before what is known as the Stoglav assembly,[1] where he posed a series of questions that contained a far-reaching program of reform. In his speech the ruler raised economic issues, as, for example, internal customs duties, and social ones, such as restricting precedence, a general land census, reexamination of land tenure, and the fate of maintenance. His questions showed how seriously the tsar took the reform movement. The discussions generated by the plans for reform and the first attempts to carry them out gave Ivan the practical experience he sorely needed, honed his naturally inquisitive mind, and initiated him into state affairs.

In 1549 the reconciliation assembly authorized a measure to bring the law code up to date. The chanceries set to work at once and within a year had produced a new code for the council to ratify. The treasury department seems to have taken the lead in the legislative work, over which the treasurers presided. It was no coincidence that Adashev became a treasurer while the new code was in preparation and left the treasury bureau when the work on it was virtually completed. The compilers of the code left intact the laws defining relationships between lord and peasant, and the rule of St. George's Day survived with a few small changes, so that peasants were still free to leave their landlords during a two-week period in late autumn. The lawgivers concentrated on the system of central and regional administration. The new code stimulated the formation of chanceries, increased the responsibilities of the chancery bureaucracy, and somewhat curtailed the authority of local governors subsisting on maintenance. New entries in the code provided for direct participation by elected local officials, elders and men of substance, in cases heard by the governor's court.

While they were engaged in juridical reform Adashev and his group undertook to regulate the system of precedence. Its anachronistic rules manifested themselves with singular force in the army. Assigning the highest command posts on the basis of patent and noble birth at times led to catastrophic results on the battlefield, but the boyar council and the nobility refused to accept changes in the system of precedence advocated by gentry spokesmen and thus the modifications made concerning it were indecisive and compromising. They prohibited commanders from quarreling over precedence on active service and made certain changes in the command structure. Under the new regulations the government might assign more courageous and experienced, though less high-born, officers to the commander-in-chief, invariably the most pedigreed boyar. They were protected from suits brought by all the other officers. The reform of precedence and the struggle to broaden the privileges of the middle gentry coincided with the career interests of Adashev's family, whose members soon obtained commands of their own. Adashev considered these initial reforms to be his most significant. Shortly before his retirement he deliberately recalled his achievements by including an account of them out of sequence in the final volumes of a chronicle he was editing. He wrote: "The sovereign calculates pedigree when appointing commanders. A man of noble birth is entitled to keep his military rank." Adashev's views differed greatly from Peresvetov's radical demand to abolish precedence. His reform introduced minor changes but preserved the system.

In addition to regulating administrative and military service, the government resolved to select one thousand principal servitors from the nobility and gentry and assign them lands near Moscow. Located close to the capital, these men could be summoned at any time to perform important tasks. The proposed reform was intended to involve the cream of the provincial gentry in the administration. Historians are divided concerning the fate of this reform. I. I. Smirnov considers the formation of the one thousand a substantial achievement of the chosen council, but A. A. Zimin doubts the project was ever implemented.

To strengthen the armed forces Adashev's administration organized a permanent unit of fusiliers and established a detachment of three thousand men to serve as the tsar's bodyguard. The fusiliers gave a good account of themselves during campaigns in the years following. The basic fighting force of the sixteenth century still remained the feudal levy, consisting largely of petty gentry, and the government often discussed redistributing the land in the gentry's interests. Ivan addressed this issue in at least five of the twelve questions he put before the Stoglav council. In support of land redistribution Ivan drew attention to the fact that during the boyar regimes many boyars and gentry had acquired land without rendering service while others had grown impoverished. Men whose fathers had possessed an estate of more than 100 acres now had three times as much to hand on to their children while others went hungry. The tsar asked the metropolitan to examine patrimonial and service-tenure holdings and maintenance of the boyars and gentry, consider whether they had earned what they had, and determine how to compensate those in need.

Plans to divide the land were very popular with the gentry, but their realization posed the practical problem of where the land petty serving-men needed would come from. The gentry was perfectly satisfied to improve its condition at the expense of the church, the extent of whose landed property aroused envy. In the central districts of the country monasteries had succeeded in sequestrating approximately one third of the land, which was inhabited by peasants. Foreigners noted that Russia contained more monks and monasteries than any other country. Russian monks were by no means ascetics, who shunned secular life. They were active in trade and money-lending and by these means had acquired great wealth. Since they had money they bought up patrimonial estates whose owners had been ruined, and the authorities were alarmed as they saw monasteries increasing their holdings by acquiring the land of serving-men. At last some tentative efforts were made to secularize church property. The move was supported by the Transvolga elders, whom the tsar had summoned to Moscow. The elders long had lived in tiny enclaves scattered among the thick forests surrounding the Kirillov monastery. The founder of the Transvolga anchorites was Nil of Sorsk. He and his successors taught their followers to live in remote regions without possessions, hold no property, and earn their living by the sweat of their brow. The non-possessors allowed considerable latitude in interpreting scripture and rejected the methods of the inquisition. They also criticized Makarii's reform and refused to believe in the new miracle-workers. Elder Artemii, their leader, insistently recommended limitation of church lands and proposed to deprive monasteries of their villages. The government openly raised the question of the future of monasterial landowning at the Stoglav council. "Is it proper for monasteries to acquire land?" was one of the issues the tsar brought before that body.

This attack on ecclesiastical landowning was opposed vigorously by the church's militant wing, the Josephites, followers of Joseph of Volokolamsk, who had been the chief opponent of Nil of Sorsk and the non-possessors. The majority of the Josephites supported Makarii and thwarted the government's program of secularization, so that it was only partly able to achieve its goals. A rescript issued in May, 1551 ordered confiscation of all arable land the boyar council had assigned to bishops and monasteries since the death of Vasilii III. The statute categorically forbade the church to acquire new lands without informing the government. Determined to check loss of land by serving-men, the authorities introduced several restrictions affecting the patrimonial estates of princes. They were prohibited from selling or bequeathing them to the church without specific approval, and lands already transferred to monasteries without approval were confiscated and returned to the service-tenure fund. This new land legislation permitted the government slightly to augment the amount of land available for serving-men at the expense of the church and even princely patrimonies, but the basic wealth the church held in land remained untouched. It managed to preserve its lands, but it was forced to give up certain substantial tax benefits, known as immunities. Since the days of feudal fragmentation the nobility and princes of the church had paid no taxes on lands they owned. The authorities were determined to reform this system by curtailing immunities. The tsar's law code enacted that no future immunity charters should be granted and existing charters should be collected from anyone possessing them. As N. E. Nosov has demonstrated, privileged landowners, both clerical and secular, felt the impact of the new legislation.

The government announced another reform in the tax structure when it introduced a new unit of measurement determined by the class to which a landholder belonged. State peasants were taxed on the basis of 500 acres of arable land, church feudatories on the basis of 600, and serving landowners and gentry on the basis of 800. Secular feudatories thus obtained perceptible tax advantages in comparison with clerical and especially the peasantry. The measures taken to eliminate immunities undermined the system of feudal privilege and helped transform the status of the gentry. The reform of taxation units also contributed to satisfying gentry demands.

Adashev's initial reforms were very important. They strengthened centralized authority and did much to satisfy gentry interests, but on balance they were only compromises, for the conservative boyars were not anxious to make way for serving people. The conflicting views held by nobility and gentry had to be reconciled if the reform program was to continue. The one other person, besides Adashev, who sought solutions to this problem was the court priest Silvester. It was he who taught Ivan the real lessons of life.

Silvester was born in Novgorod to the family of a poor priest and adopted a spiritual calling. Moving to Moscow he took service in the Cathedral of the Annunciation in the Kremlin. The Annunciation priest, "worthless Silvester, a humble beggar, sinner, abandoned and depraved slave" (as he referred to himself), appeared modest among the greedy, covetous and drunken princes of the church. His appointment at the court presaged a remarkable career. With his influence he might well have obtained a profitable post as bishop or abbot, but he lacked the skills necessary to secure preferment. After the Moscow conflagration Silvester had a chance to become an archpriest or even the tsar's official confessor, but he chose not to take advantage of his opportunities. He began his career as a simple priest in the Cathedral of the Annunciation and rose no higher during the rest of his life.

Silvester was presumably an educated cleric. He possessed a good library by the standards of the time and Ivan gave him books from the royal repository. It is even possible that Silvester knew Greek. Ivan was considerably indebted to the priest for his own educational attainments, but after he broke with him the tsar deprecated his former mentor's mental capacities and bestowed upon him the derisory epithet of Dunce-Priest, which reflected rather on the tsar's spitefulness than on Silvester's ignorance.

Silvester compiled, or at any rate edited, the well-known *Domostroi.* He formally dedicated this compilation of precepts to his son Anfim, but there is reason to believe he intended the work for the young tsar's consumption. Ivan stood in great need of instruction as an orphan who recently had embarked upon family life. The first pages of the *Domostroi* inculcated belief in God and then Silvester took up the more immediate theme of "how children are to honor their confessor and obey him in all things." Ivan's duties toward his confessor were minutely defined. He was told often to summon his confessor to his chambers, go to him, give him as many gifts as he could afford, frequently to consult him about how to lead a useful life, or how a husband should instruct and love his wife, to repent, defer to his confessor in all things, and obey if his confessor should express reservations about any individual.[2] Recalling his relationship with Silvester, many years later the tsar wrote that he had followed Biblical injunction and unreservedly submitted to his worthy tutor. Taking advantage of his charge's submissiveness, Silvester used the *Domostroi* in an attempt to regulate every aspect of his life. He taught Ivan the right way to attend church, go on pilgrimage, and manage his personal affairs. The tsar eventually came to resent the restrictions Silvester imposed upon him whether away from home, at leisure, attending church, and on all other occasions.[3] Silvester was obviously a hard, demanding taskmaster, who reviled his pupil when he chafed under his mentor's tutelage. In Silvester's day, the tsar lamented, even in trivial and insignificant matters "I was granted no freedom. How to put on shoes, how to sleep—all was done at the instance of my mentors, while I was like a child."[4] Whether true or not, this period of Ivan's life left its mark upon him.

At the age of seventeen Ivan gave Silvester his first responsible assignment: to make a list of Kremlin cathedrals the great fire had damaged. Silvester submitted a report, and summoning icon-painters from Novgorod, told them to set about their task. They adorned the walls of the Golden Chamber with uplifting scenes depicting the young tsar as righteous judge, or brave warrior, or generous ruler distributing gold pieces among the poor. Using art as a medium, Silvester played upon his charge's emotions, and his efforts were soon crowned with success. Silvester possessed an unbounded faith. His religion was one of exaltation. He heard heavenly voices and beheld visions. Court circles were considerably annoyed by the prophet who had newly appeared among them. Even Kurbskii, who had praised the tsar's mentor, thought his miraculous visions were ridiculous. He claimed that Silvester abused Ivan's credulity, telling him the visions he saw were emanations from God. "I do not know," Kurbskii observed, "whether these miracles were genuine or whether Silvester contrived them in order to make the tsar have fearful dreams, abate his violence, and correct his savage temper."[5]

Silvester's tales produced a devastating effect on Ivan and the fanatical priest succeeded in arousing the tsar's religious feelings. Religion enticed him and he soon excelled in devotion. He zealously discharged all forms of church ritual, and at times of extreme nervous tension experienced hallucinations. The night before the decisive assault on Kazan the tsar, now twenty-three, prayed for hours and distinctly heard the bells of the Simonov monastery ringing in Moscow.

Silvester originally confined himself to useful instruction on life and morals, but the complex political situation that developed after the war with Kazan gave him an opportunity to become Ivan's political advisor as well. When Silvester entered the government the entity known as the chosen council reached its apogee.

Chapter Seven

CONQUEST OF KAZAN

While engaged in domestic reform Adashev and his group also devised an elaborate foreign policy, which paid special attention to the eastern question. Upon the collapse of the Golden Horde the Tatars seemed hopelessly fragmented, but after the Turks subdued the khanate of the Crimea there was real danger the Tatar tribes would be unified under the auspices of the Ottoman empire. Moscow had temporarily succeeded in bringing the khanate of Kazan under its influence, but later the Crimean royal house of Girei asserted its authority there. The Kazan feudatories raided Russia incessantly. Their flying squads devastated border regions and thrust as far as Vladimir, Kostroma and even remote Vologda. Ivan later wrote: "The Crimea and Kazan emptied half our land."[1] The Tatars enslaved the Russian prisoners they took, forced them to work in their orchards and fields, and sold Russian captives in the slave marts of Astrakhan, the Crimea, and Central Asia.

The khanate of Kazan was notoriously unstable, and pagan tribes of the Volga region, such as the Chuvash, Mordva, Mari, Udmurty and Bashkirs, which the Tatar feudatories had subjugated, were anxious to throw off the Tatar yoke. Constant quarrels among the Kazan princes kept the khanate in a state of turmoil. In 1545-1546 a con-

The Siege of Kazan. Sixteenth-century miniature. State Historical Museum, Moscow.

test between the Crimean and Muscovite factions first led to the ouster of the Crimea's puppet, Khan Safa-Girei, and then of Moscow's servant, Shah-Ali. At this point Moscow began planning the total subjection of the khanate.

The church administration portrayed the struggle with Kazan as a holy war against the godless sons of Hagar and the idea of taking

Kazan enjoyed substantial support among the gentry, who had long coveted its rich terrain. Reflecting the serving-men's attitude, Peresvetov wrote: "We are greatly surprised that our strong and puissant tsar has so long tolerated this realm close to his bosom, and permits it to cause him sorrow. Even if such a realm were agreeable and friendly it would be impossible to endure such friendship."[2]

The Russian army twice campaigned against Kazan in 1548-1550 but failed in its objective. On the first occasion the ice melted prematurely; it was impossible to cross the Volga and the army became bogged down near Nizhnii Novgorod. Ivan wept when he returned. The second time the tsar's commanders besieged Kazan for eleven days. Before the start of the third campaign the Russians constructed a fortress called Sviiazhsk on the opposite bank of the Volga, facing Kazan. Alarmed by his military preparations the people of Kazan made an appeal to the tsar and allowed Shah-Ali, Ivan's vassal, to enter the city, but he failed to establish himself on the throne. In 1552 war again swept the Kazan region, and the final, decisive assault on the city began when the army commanded by A. B. Gorbatyi reached Sviiazhsk. The Crimean Tatars attempted to divert the Russians by attacking Tula, but Muscovite troops expelled them from the southern district and advanced to the east. Late in August the Russians invested Kazan: they bombarded its wooden walls, and built a three-tiered siege tower eighteen feet high to breach the main Royal Gate. The cannon it carried poured murderous fire into the city. Sappers bored tunnels deep beneath the fortress walls, and an explosion destroyed the wells supplying the city's water. The Russians stormed the fortress on October 2, fought hand-to-hand in its narrow crooked streets, and the Tatar capital fell.

The commander, Prince Aleksandr Gorbatyi, was the man most responsible for the capture of Kazan. Kurbskii, who participated in the campaign, called him the heart and soul of the tsar's army. During the first days of the siege a large Tatar army operating outside the fortress ceaselessly attacked the Russian camp. Gorbatyi decoyed it into an ambush and destroyed it. A few months after the campaign with the tsar's approval Silvester wrote to Gorbatyi: "Kazan has been captured at the tsar's command and by your courage and bravery, as well as by your firm efforts and leadership."[3]

The young tsar had to be content with an honorable, but actually secondary role in the campaign, although even those unfavorably disposed to him had to admit that Ivan, an ardent supporter of the war, often attacked the enemy without regard for his person. He failed to distinguish himself during the conflict. Early in the siege he helped deploy troops and circled the Tatar fortress incessantly, but he later took up a position some distance away with his detachment. A decision of the boyar council empowered the royal regiment to enter the fray on October 2, the day Kazan was finally stormed. As the attack began Ivan was praying in the field church. The commanders twice sent to remind him it was time to advance, but the tsar refused to stop praying, and Russian flags were flying from the fortress walls by the time his regiment arrived. Ivan's tardiness gave rise to hostile rumors among the troops. Kurbskii reported that when the fighting in the city streets became critical the commanders ordered the royal banner unfurled at the main city gate, and the tsar willy-nilly checked his horse and halted beside it.

The boyar council strongly advised Ivan to remain in the conquered territory during the winter to follow up the victory and bring matters to a conclusion, but the tsar hastily returned to Moscow. Fighting in the eastern borderlands did not cease with the capture of Kazan, and four years were to pass before Russia had the region firmly under control. Russian forces next took Astrakhan. The overthrow of the two khanates brought Tatar domination of the Volga region, which had endured for three centuries, to an end, and a huge territory extending from the northern Caucasus to Siberia came under Russian influence. The Bashkirs voluntarily announced their association with Russia, and the rulers of the Great Nogai Horde,[4] the Siberian khanates,[5] and the princes of Piatigorsk and Kabardia[6] in the north Caucasus declared themselves vassals of the tsar.

These gains in the east were profoundly significant for Russia's historical destiny. Acquisition of the entire trading route along the Volga provided access to rich eastern markets and fostered the growth of Russia's internal trade. Russian peasants began intensively to colonize the fertile lands along the middle Volga. The people of the region were freed from the yoke of the Tatar feudatories, but tsarist oppressors soon arrived to take their place.

Chapter Eight

CONSPIRACIES

The war with Kazan, which lasted seven years, diverted the attention of Adashev and his circle from domestic reform. A dynastic crisis that occurred when Ivan fell seriously ill substantially affected future developments.

The tsar hastily quitted his army and went back to Moscow because his wife was expecting a child. The conqueror's return was a genuine triumph. The tsar rode into the capital in full military regalia, attended by a brilliant entourage. A host of people awaited Ivan in the fields outside the city walls and escorted him to the Kremlin gate. "Young and old," says the chronicler, "shouted at the top of their lungs, and their cries of welcome drowned out everything else." Winter had barely begun when Ivan hastened to Troitsa to have the monks christen his son Dmitrii, but early in spring he was suddenly seized with severe fever. His temperature soared; he no longer recognized those around him, and his death was expected daily. On the evening of March 11, 1553 the boyars closest to him took an oath to the infant Dmitrii as heir to the throne, and March 12 was designated for the boyar council and leading personages in Moscow to follow suit.

One source, the celebrated interpolations in the official chronicle, provides information concerning the events of March 12 but its veracity is suspect. Virtually all historians agree that Ivan was himself responsible for the insertions. The chronicle states that on March 12 the boyars openly refused to take an oath of fealty to a child, whereupon the council chamber became a scene of noisy disorder as the boyars who refused to serve an infant made many speeches. When the shouting and wrangling was at its height the tsar twice spoke sharply to the boyars despite his serious illness. The sovereign's words had a magical effect: "All the boyars were frightened by the sovereign's angry remarks and proceeded to kiss the cross in the antechamber."[1]

Careful scrutiny shows the chronicle entry to be contradictory and evasive. The tsar was so ill that the boyars were obliged to take the oath in the antechamber. He was obviously too ill to make speeches. Furthermore, the chronicler could not identify a single malcontent refusing to support the heir. Before the ceremony Boyar Prince Ivan Shuiskii had stated they should kiss the cross in the tsar's presence, but his observation by no means implied he refused in principle to take the oath. As the senior man present he was annoyed because V.I. Vorotynskii, a minor boyar, had been asked to preside at the ceremony. Boyar I.I. Turuntai-Pronskii made unflattering remarks about Vorotynskii, but he too was perfectly willing to kiss the cross. Fedor Adashev, the tsar's confidant, also agreed to support the heir, but this did not mean Daniel Zakharin and his brothers: "Before you attained your majority we beheld many evils from the boyars," he observed on the occasion.[2] Adashev was expressing openly the concern many felt that a boyar regime might be restored. Critical analysis of the chronicle entry concerning the disturbance in council reveals that on the whole the boyars manifested no disloyalty in their discussions; no one was openly disobedient, and the tsar had no cause to speak harshly. It is thus safe to assume that the words he uttered were fabricated and inserted in the chronicle many years later.

Chronicle reports that the Staritskii branch of the royal family was making secret preparations to seize power in the event of Ivan's death deserve greater credence. During the tsar's illness Prince Vladimir and his mother summoned their troops to Moscow and showed them favor. Ivan's supporters demanded an explanation, whereupon the Staritskii faction grew angry and vented its spleen upon them. As a result Prince Vladimir categorically refused to swear fealty to his infant relative and threatened to disgrace Vorotynskii. Staritskii's protest proved abortive. The right time for it was past, since all members of the boyar council had taken the oath. The tsar's intimates indicated they would not let Vladimir leave the palace and so forced him to take the oath against his will. His mother, Evfrosiniia, was more stubborn. Ivan's supporters had to go three times to her residence before she agreed to attest it with her royal seal. Prince Vladimir lacked the qualities which could have won him support for the throne. An unintelligent, feeble young man who had spent his early years in prison, he lacked a will of his own. Evfrosiniia was the chief intriguer. She possessed an uncompromising nature and hated the tsar; she could not forgive him or his mother for destroying her husband nor for the humiliations she had subsequently endured.

Many boyars sympathized with the Staritskii faction, and with good reason. If the throne passed to the infant Dmitrii a regency council headed by the queen's relatives, the Zakharin boyars, would rule in his name, and the princely aristocrats regarded the Zakharin family as baseborn parvenus, whose desire to usurp power had aroused immense discontent in the council. This condemnation embraced the tsar's entire family, not just the Zakharin branch. Boyar Prince Semen Rostovskii, a Staritskii partisan, summed up the boyars' reaction to the possibility of a Zakharin regency at a covert meeting with a Lithuanian envoy that occurred shortly after the tsar was taken ill. He said: "The sovereign spares none of us; he scorns the great families, brings in new people, and uses them to harass us. He has already dishonored us. He has married the daughter of a boyar and made her his slave. How can we serve the sister of one of us?"[3] Having experienced Elena Glinskaia's rule the nobles were making it abundantly clear they would not allow Queen Anastasiia Romanovna and her family to come to power.

Arrested and interrogated, Prince Rostovskii admitted that in March, 1553 Princess Evfrosiniia had invited him to enter Prince Vladimir's service and many boyars joined him at secret meetings with the Staritskii partisans. Just before he took the oath Boyar Prince D.I. Nemoi secretly urged council members to serve the uncle rather than the nephew "Why should we serve the young instead of the old?" he inquired. "Do you not see that the Zakharin family will lord it over us?" Other boyars, among them Prince P.M. Shcheniatev, were also quietly saying: "If the Zakharin family is to lord it over us and we are to serve a young master, better we should serve an older, Prince Vladimir Andreevich." If the chronicle interpolations deserve credence, even people close to the tsar sympathized with the Staritskii cause. Prince Kurliatev kissed the cross in favor of the heir but told the Staritskii faction he was prepared to serve them. Silvester, the tsar's mentor, condemned the Zakharin family's decision to deny the Staritskii people access to the tsar. He supposedly said: "Why will you not let Prince Vladimir see the sovereign? Our sovereign's cousin is better disposed to him than you boyars." The author of the chronicle interpolations concludes: "From this time on, enmity existed between the Zakharin family and Silvester and his associates."[4]

Successful resolution of the dynastic crisis depended on the church's attitude. Its leaders showed no disposition to support the pretensions of the Staritskii faction, but the chronicle interpolations strangely make no mention of Makarii nor allude to his presence at the oath-taking ceremony, although it could not have taken place in his absence. This is conducive to the view that the supple ecclesiastic preferred to stay out of the limelight while the internecine struggle wore on and to adopt a position of neutrality between the Zakharin and Staritskii groups.

The heir and the regents had been objects of a conspiracy, but its members had failed to realize their aims. Their plan to stage a palace revolt proved abortive because the tsar recovered and the succession issue thus was rendered moot. On his recovery Ivan and his family made a pilgrimage to the Kirillov monastery, where he held a long conversation with Elder Vassian Toporkov, once an advisor to Vasilii III. Vassian was regarded as a champion of strong monarchical power, and the tsar, who had learned something of the recent conspiracy, discussed with him the sedition that had been uncovered. He incidentally asked the elder a question: "How can I rule well and make the mightiest and strongest of my subjects obey me?" Toporkov replied by urgently advising the tsar to curb the power of the boyars. The elder's warnings were not limited to the nobility, as was demonstrated when non-possessors and heretics were persecuted savagely directly after Ivan's return from Kirillov.

The tsar, a man of inquiring mind, was interested in foreigners. He eagerly invited a German, Hans Schlitte, to come and discuss achievements in science and art in Germany with him. The reports of the experienced foreigner so intrigued Ivan that he decided to send Schlitte to Germany to seek skillful physicians, artisans, and even learned theologians and invite them to Moscow. One of Ivan's cherished desires was to introduce printing. He was advised to ask Denmark to send a printer. In 1552 King Christian III, responding to the appeal, sent Master Hans Meissenheim, typographical equipment, and a Bible in Luther's German translation. The Orthodox clergy was extremely suspicious of the Danish printer. Cursory examination of the books he brought indicated they were heretical, and the church employed all its resources to prevent the introduction of printing into Russia, considering it to be a ruse of the Danish heretics.

The investigation of the Danish Lutherans soon brought to light facts church leaders found disagreeable. Heresy had sprouted in Holy Russia. Silvester was the first to sound the alarm. He told the tsar: "Heresy is abroad in Moscow. People have doubts and utter improper words about the Divinity." Ivan summoned Matvei Bashkin, a member of the gentry suspected of heresy, and bade him read and interpret the Gospel. On hearing Matvei's heretical views the tsar had him confined to a shed in the courtyard and demanded an investigation, which discovered that the Staritskii court was a nest of heresy. Its principal members belonged to the gentry Borisov family, second cousins of Princess Evfrosiniia, who held high positions at her court. Bashkin and the Borisov family propagated unprecedented views:

they claimed icons were accursed idols, rejected the official church, blasphemed Christ Himself, and considered the Bible a collection of fairy tales. Bashkin also condemned slavery and called for an end to bondage. An ecclesiastical council anathematized the heretics. Matvei Bashkin was tortured and imprisoned in the Joseph of Volokolamsk monastery; his brother Fedor was condemned to be burnt at the stake, and Ivan Borisov was banished to the remote island of Valaam.

At Bashkin's trial the crown secretary, Ivan Viskovatyi, charged that Silvester and Artemii, leader of the non-possessors, were in communication with the heretics. The Josephites seized upon these charges, and Artemii was excommunicated and permanently confined to Solovki. The Orthodox Viskovatyi also claimed that the murals in the Cathedral of the Annunciation done under Silvester's supervision were heretical. In his lengthy campaign to discredit Silvester Viskovatyi tried to arouse the people against these new icons. Silvester retaliated by complaining to the tsar that those who worked in the chanceries had become shameless. Church leaders refused to support Viskovatyi, for if doubts were cast on the icons the metropolitan and even the tsar might become involved because they had approved the murals in the Kremlin cathedral. More significantly, Silvester permitted the Josephites to conduct reprisals against his recent allies, the non-possessors.

As soon as the heretics had been condemned new details concerning the conspiracy of Staritskii's partisans came to light. Fearing discovery, some prepared to flee abroad. Rostovskii had imparted major council decisions to the Lithuanian envoy and urged him not to make peace with Moscow because the realm was impoverished and "the tsar cannot hold Kazan; he has already abandoned it."[5] Asking the envoy to provide him refuge in Lithuania, Rostovskii sent his son Nikita to the king to obtain a letter enabling him to go abroad, but a border guard seized Nikita at the Lithuanian frontier and the treason became known. When brought to trial Rostovskii made damaging admissions about the Staritskii conspiracy. The Staritskii cause was judged in jeopardy; their court was full of heretics, and Prince Vladimir and his mother were guilty of anti-government intrigue. Moscow expected trials and executions, but the clergy and the boyar council intervened to stop the investigation, although a boyar court sentenced Rostovskii to death for his grave crimes against the state. He and his associates were brought to the block, but at the last moment he was granted clemency, scourged, and imprisoned in Beloozero.

Prince Rostovskii owed his life to Silvester. The tsar's mentor took advantage of the right to intercede for condemned men to put an end to talk about a boyar conspiracy on behalf of Vladimir Andreevich. The Staritskii faction greatly appreciated the court preacher's services, and Silvester became a frequent advisor to Princess Evfrosiniia, who grew very fond of him. The Annunciation priest also acquired other influential patrons—the distinguished commander, Prince A. B. Gorbatyi, and Prince Dimitrii Kurliatev-Obolenskii. The tsar eventually reproached his teacher for abusing trust by insinuating Kurliatev into his privy-council, which possessed enormous power and was the court of final appeal in deciding questions of great moment. Silvester used Kurliatev to influence the actions of a body to which he lacked formal access. Many representatives of the upper titled nobility received conciliar rank during the time Silvester and Kurliatev were at the height of their power, and the treasury gave these new boyars thousands of acres of land and a host of villages.

The writer who corrected the official chronicle after Silvester's retirement has left a vivid portrait of the favorite, a man who could decide every issue with a word. No one dared initiate action without his approval because, like tsar and bishop as one, he controlled everything in both the ecclesiastical and secular spheres. The chronicler offered a simple explanation of Silvester's power when he said that everyone obeyed the priest and dared not oppose him because of the favor he enjoyed with the tsar. It is true that the humble court priest had extraordinary influence in shaping the personality of the young tsar, but he did not owe his prominence to this circumstance alone.

Silvester reached the apex of his career after the dynastic crisis, which divided the privy council and led to the struggle between the Staritskii and Zakharin factions. This allowed him to serve as mediator between the contending camps. His own political views are unknown and politics probably held little interest for him. He knew how to maintain good relations with the tsar's young friends, who dreamed of major reforms, and his noble patrons, who entertained reservations about them. Silvester made Adashev one of his friends as soon as he understood the latter's role in the government. Ivan later conplained: "Priest Silvester plotted cunningly, became friends with Aleksei, and, holding us incapable of judgment, began counselling with him apart from us." It is hard to say who derived greater benefit from this association. Silvester was indifferent to rank and position, unlike the attitude of Adashev and his family to material rewards. In spite of their humble origin Adashev took pains to make his father a

boyar and himself became an associate boyar. He and his fellow reformers got both titles and thousands of acres of land. During his
chancery service Adashev became a large landowner and an influential
member of the boyar council.

Chapter Nine

LAST REFORMS

Once complete victory over Kazan had been achieved and Adashev
had consolidated his position at court, he returned to domestic issues.
The second wave of reforms restructured the central government de-
partments and produced a unified chancery system. Essential administrative functions came under the control of individual chanceries: foreign affairs were consolidated in the ambassadorial bureau,
military affairs in the military records bureau, and land problems in
the service-tenure bureau. The ancient local institutions known as pal-
aces were not abolished, but lost their previous significance. The chancery system was not completely homogeneous, but it met Russia's
needs for political centralization. The boyar council supervised the
chanceries and periodically attached associate boyars and boyars to
them. They became the council's eyes and ears throughout the country, and the whole system was controlled by the chancery bureaucracy.

The establishment of a chancery system required the government
to reorganize the archaic method of local administration known as
maintenance. The abolition of maintenance and transformation of
the system of military service during the second wave of reform are
usually considered the chosen council's greatest accomplishments.
That body's reputation largely stands or falls on the basis of an ap-
praisal of the effectiveness of these actions.

Soviet historians have discussed extensively the reforms of the
1550s. Virtually all of them hold the opinion that the reforms benefited the gentry, but they disagree as to how concessions were implemented. I.I. Smirnov emphasized that the reforms took on a markedly anti-boyar character as soon as the chosen council came to power,
while A.A. Zimin believed the early reforms were compromises and

the council made no decisive moves to restrict the aristocracy's privileges or systematically to introduce changes favoring the gentry until after the capture of Kazan. Comparison between the two stages of the reforms of the 1550s rests on the sources that tell of Adashev's final reforms. The original text of the principal decrees has not been preserved; only literary revisions survive. Shortly before his retirement Adashev inserted an account in the official chronicle designed to glorify his reforming activity. His narrative is self-serving and needs careful examination.

Adashev's main decree of 1555-1556 was concerned with maintenance and military service. He was unsparing in his criticism of the archaic system of local administration whereby provincial authorities, governors and hereditary landowners were maintained at the people's expense. The chronicle relates that when the tsar learned about the abuses perpetrated by such persons he assigned elected officials who could participate in the judicial process to towns and districts and substituted a special tax on those subsisting on maintenance that went to the treasury in place of the imposts they had been collecting. The statute on maintenance contained one glaring omission. It failed to specify the towns and districts in which local administration was to be reformed. Sharp critics of maintenance had assumed such an outmoded system must be abolished entirely, but the chronicle indicates that his scrutiny led the tsar to establish "the proper measure of maintenance for boyars, nobles, and all soldiers the birth and ancestry of each entitle him to receive."[1]

The government moved to abolish maintenance in the early 1550s, and it was eliminated in large areas, such as Riazan, Kostroma, and so forth, in the central part of the country. But after the capture of Kazan the boyars, in their search for wealth, appropriated the most profitable areas for maintenance there and the ruler assigned a good deal of land to maintain gentry noblemen. Moreover, the first successes in the Livonian war in 1558 occasioned substantial distribution of fresh maintenance lands. The decree of 1555-1556 thus failed to abolish the maintenance system in its entirety. Rivalry between the boyars and gentry noblemen, who could use deputies in the areas they were maintained, delayed abolition of the custom for many years. Local administration was completely changed in a comparatively short time only in the north, where there were few peasants living on state lands and scarcely any feudal landowners. Administration of justice and collection of taxes, tasks which those subsisting on maintenance had performed previously, now passed into the hands

of trusted men popularly elected. Local self-government provided traders, artisans and rich peasants with greater advantages than the gentry. In the opinion of N.E. Nosov this administrative reform may be
considered to have completed the general reorganization of the state
apparatus to accommodate the new relationship among the social
groups. Administrative reform in the central region, which had begun
as early as 1539, favored the gentry from the outset. The government
transferred supervision of local affairs to district and town officials
chosen by the provincial gentry. Instead of governors subsisting on
maintenance, these officials now presided over major criminal cases,
and the robbery chancery in Moscow assumed immediate jurisdiction
over their activities.

The chronicle account of the reform of military service is as contradictory as the one about maintenance. Adashev always had considered the issues of military service and gentry land grants to be
vitally important. For the first time the famous royal questions to
the Stoglav assembly had declared it was essential to equalize gentry
allotments by compensating those who had suffered loss and lacked
sufficient land: "A decree should be passed to requite him who has
suffered through no fault of his own, and he who has an abundance
should compensate him who is unfortunate." Land tenure was the
principal question preoccupying and agitating the entire mass of the
gentry. The theme of gentry impoverishment received its most comprehensive treatment in the writings of Ermolai Erazm, a distinguished
publicist of the 1550s. His treatise on surveying embodied a project
that would have led to thorough reorganization of the system of land
tenure for service gentry. Wishing to save the impoverished petty
gentry and lighten the burdens of the peasantry, Erazm advocated
having the gentry perform service strictly proportionate to the extent
of its members' holdings. The government should conduct a general
land survey to achieve this goal.

Erazm's social concerns and genuine sympathy for the oppressed
peasants were foreign to Adashev and his group, who were only interested in carrying out military and administrative reforms to benefit
the gentry, but his bold concepts may have influenced Adashev's
views. Traces of them can be found in the chronicle narrative of the
service reform of 1556, which reported that the statute was designed
to foster equalization of gentry landholding: "This the sovereign has
determined. Nobles and warriors owning much land but performing
little service hold their patrimonies against the sovereign's wishes. The
sovereign has taken steps to equalize holdings, has surveyed them,

has given each his due, and has distributed the surplus among those who lack."[2] This is a literary revision of the original text of the law. One searches in vain for answers to such questions as what was the size of an estate used as the norm to decide how holdings should be equalized, or how the amount of land held by nobles rendering inadequate service was determined excessive. Succeeding passages in the chronicle lead to the conclusion that the reform was actually no more than the ordinary army review, when regular soldiers and those beginning service took possession of the lands they were assigned and those who had failed to render service were deprived of their holdings. Naturally landholders who lost what was deemed surplus were not only nobles: widows, minor children, and impoverished members of the petty gentry unable to serve were affected also. Adashev's most radical project was a plan to survey the land in order to equalize holdings, but its application apparently fell short of a decisive redivision of the land between nobles and ordinary warriors. The real significance of the reform lay elsewhere. The government now regarded proprietors of hereditary and service-tenure estates as equal, and landowners and landholders alike were required to perform service and appear for campaign with horses, men and weapons. A proprietor had to furnish one soldier fully equipped for battle for every 400 acres of arable land. Adashev's military reforms succeeded in regulating conditions of gentry service, and increased the army's fighting capabilities just in time for the decisive battles of the Livonian war.

The reforms of the 1550s generally satisfied gentry interests and contributed to the development of the state by furthering centralization of the administrative apparatus and making it better accord with the new historical circumstances that emerged as feudal fragmentation was abolished, but they were half-hearted and showed marked signs of compromise. Gentry apologists demanded that precedence be abolished completely, a step which was not taken for 100 years, and plans radically to redistribute the land in the interests of the gentry likewise were largely unrealized. Decisively affecting the outcome of the reforms was the circumstance that Adashev and his group were apparently unwilling to give sustained energetic support to gentry radicals and felt they could not make the gentry full partners in their reform activity.

In the 1550s gentry bureaucrats consolidated their position in the chancery apparatus and individual representatives worked their way up into the boyar council. Members of the gentry constantly appeared at meetings of the estates, which gradually were becoming general convocations, known as land assemblies. As the political role of the gentry expanded Russia acquired certain characteristics of a representative monarchy, but no matter how many successes the gentry won, political control of the country remained vested in the boyar nobility. Russian autocracy was tempered by the boyar council and the boyar aristocracy down to the seventeenth century, as Lenin noted; the ruling boyars were unwilling to accommodate the gentry and jealously scrutinized any equivocal moves the monarchy made in its direction.

No account of the reforms of the 1550s would be complete without reference to the personality of Adashev, who initiated them. He was endowed with the exact qualities needed for a career in the chancery bureaucracy. His incorruptibility won him great popularity. As judge in and later head of the petitions bureau he sternly rebuked all who interfered with the chancery's operation regardless of rank and including boyars. The ruler's displeasure, prison and exile awaited the guilty. Adashev's contemporaries later recalled his administration as a time of prosperity, when Russia "knew great tranquility, happiness and righteousness."[3] Men were also struck by the illustrious favorite's extraordinary piety. Kurbskii was serious when he wrote that Adashev was like an angel. The tsar's favorite manifested his angelic characteristics in ostentatious piety and sanctimonious habits reminiscent of the priest Silvester. The leading minister of the realm, it would seem, was determined to outdo monks in mortifying the flesh. He prayed incessantly and fasted for long periods, eating nothing but a wafer a day. His house was filled with itinerant pilgrims and holy fools.[4] If Kurbskii is to be believed, Adashev kept a sanctuary in his home where he maintained sick people, secretly fed them, and washed off their filth, often with his own hands. The ideas of progressive gentry ideologists appear to have had some influence on Adashev's views, but he and his circle could meet but few of the gentry's demands. Unable to overcome the conservatism of the ruling boyars, Adashev had to be content with partial reforms and often abandoned attempts to carry them out. Kurbskii, the boyar apologist, strongly approved of Adashev's willingness to compromise, which he considered to be in the common interest.

The influence Adashev enjoyed ultimately depended upon the personal trust the tsar placed in him. What was Ivan's own role in the reforms, which were accomplished while he was still in tutelage? On attaining his majority the tsar was not equipped to rule a large state and was for some time subordinated to chosen mentors. In youth he had not received a systematic education, but as an adult he impressed his associates with the range of his attainment, and at the age of thirty-four he began to write and became perhaps the most fertile author of his generation. His writings are testimony to his intelligence and wide reading. However, none of the tsar's works has survived in the original and no one has yet been able to discover a line written in his hand or even a document affixed with his signature; thus, suspicion inevitably has arisen as to whether Ivan was actually literate. Muscovite tradition must be taken into consideration when deciding this question. A tradition, which first developed because the earliest Muscoviet princes were illiterate, categorically forbade sovereigns to sign documents, even their wills. This was still the rule in the sixteenth century, but other influences had been gradually undermining the hallowed fundaments of antiquity. Ivan's grandmother, the Byzantine princess Sofia, educated in Italy, was renowned for her learning and knowledge of the arts. When she came to Moscow she was accompanied by a large retinue of physicians, architects, and craftsmen. Sofia naturally took an interest in her son's education. When necessary Vasilii III wrote notes to his wife Elena in his own hand; hence, he was clearly not illiterate, but regard for ancestral custom inhibited further composition on his part. As a young man Boris Godunov signed decrees, but he ceased to do so once he assumed the throne. The First False Dmitrii wrote frequently in his own hand, but he paid a high price for flouting Muscovy's ancient standards.

The absence of writings in Ivan's own hand should not be taken as proof he was illiterate. The attempt of the American historian, Edward L. Keenan, to demonstrate that all Ivan's work is a forgery cannot be taken seriously.[5] Contemporaries had no doubts about the first tsar's learning and literary capabilities. They called him an orator, a wizard of words, and asserted he "was a master of learning and a highly skilled speaker."[6] Prince Kurbskii, once the tsar's friend and later his bitter enemy, who used Biblical quotations in his contest with Ivan, was so sure of his correspondent's learning that he sometimes gave no more than the first lines of a citation. In such instances he wrote: "The rest of the verse I do not cite, for you know the Scripture by heart." Ivan was well acquainted with historical works, which he often quoted in speeches to foreign diplomats and to the council. The Venetian ambassador was astounded at Ivan's close knowledge of Roman history. Lithuanian theologians shown the tsar's library saw rare books by ancient Greek and Byzantine authors.

In the early 1550s Ivan espoused the bold reform programs that advanced social thought had promulgated, but he interpreted their purpose and results in his own way. Early in life he had assimilated the concept that tsaric power was of divine origin, and had combed sermons and Biblical texts in order to discover the awesome images of men of ancient times in whom, as in a mirror, he tried to discern himself and his unique tsaric presence and find reflection of his own glory and might, as V.O. Kliuchevskii has put it. However, the idyllic picture Ivan had conceived of the origin and unlimited extent of royal power failed to correspond with reality, which guaranteed the mighty boyar aristocracy political predominance. Ivan felt that sharing power with the nobility was irritating and unjust.

The tsar's interest in reform was aroused originally because those advocating it promised to eliminate all traces of the boyar regime, and sharp criticism of boyar abuses initially spurred on the entire program of change. Ivan eagerly listened to proposals to end boyar arbitrariness, which came to him from all sides. Peresvetov told the tsar that in order to have justice in the state those heretics who used pedigree instead of service or wisdom to draw close to the throne must be consigned to a cruel death. The aged Josephite monk Vassian Toporkov echoed Peresvetov's view. Kurbskii thought his advice paved the way for the tsar's subsequent persecution of the boyars. He made a gloomy pun on Toporkov's name: "Toporok means 'little axe,' but it has become a great big axe to cut down noble and glorious men throughout the whole of mighty Russia." The advice Ivan received to buttress his rule with terror fell on fertile soil, but the tsar was not in a position to follow it as long as he was unable to transcend the traditional political order. This was the ultimate reason why his zeal for reform slackened.

Gentry publicists and activists one and all had painted an alluring picture of strong autocracy and mighty tsaric power, and advocated abolition of the survivals of the boyar regime, but they failed to make good on their promises. After ten years of reform Ivan came to the conclusion that his power was no longer autocratic because of the restrictions his advisors and the boyars placed upon it. Ivan complained that Silvester and Adashev "were the real rulers; you did as you pleased, and took the sovereignty away from me. I was ostensibly the sovereign, but actually controlled nothing."

In determining his political goals Ivan was guided by the simple formula that whatever strengthened his autocratic power was good, and the results produced by the chosen council failed to meet this criterion. Silvester and Adashev, asserted the autocrat, "gradually began leading all the boyars into contumacy, took away the beauty of our power from you (boyars), led you into opposition, made you virtually our equal in honor, and made young lesser boyars your equals in honor. Thus little by little was this evil accomplished."[7] In venting his irritation Ivan unfairly blamed his advisors for the boyars contumacy. He forgot that his favorites had not created the boyar aristocracy. The tsar's annoyance over elevating petty gentry is even more remarkable. They had, apparently, damaged the "beauty of the autocracy" as much as the boyars' arrogance. In these few words the tsar renounced the program of reforms to benefit the gentry which Adashev and he had worked for many years to accomplish. The tsar broke completely with his advisors in evaluating the goals of the reforms and the direction they should take. Differences over domestic issues were compounded by disagreement about foreign policy. A split was inevitable.

Chapter Ten

THE LIVONIAN WAR

After capturing Kazan Russia turned her attention to the Baltic area. Moscow had tested its strength in a brief war with Sweden in 1554-1557, and fired by this initial success drew up plans to conquer Livonia and become established on the Baltic sea. Livonia was characterized by internal instability and rent with national and social divisiveness. The princes of the church and the German knights, whose ranks constantly were swelled by new arrivals from Germany, dominated the native population of Letts and Estonians, who had been reduced to the status of serfs. The Livonian confederation lacked political centralization and its components, the Order,[1] the bishoprics, and the towns, were continually at loggerheads. The Reformation had increased the fragmentation. The Order and the bishoprics remained within the Catholic church, though their authority had diminished, but the gentry and the townsmen had become Protestants.

The Livonian war converted the eastern Baltic region into an area of conflict among the states seeking to control the Baltic sea, which were Lithuania and Poland, Sweden, Denmark, and Russia. Russia had good reasons for starting the war. The wealthy Livonian towns long had monitored trade between Russia and the West. The Order and the German merchants were hampering development of Russian commerce at a time when economic growth rendered it essential for Russia to establish close economic ties with the advanced countries of western Europe.

After English merchants arrived on the White sea in 1553 Russia established regular trading relations with England. Prior to the outbreak of the Livonian war the Muscovite government had allowed the English to build a harbor on the White sea and granted them the right of free trade throughout the country, but the harsh climate severely restricted trade on the White sea. The Baltic was far more suitable for this purpose. Just before the Livonian war Russia had acquired much of the shoreline along the Gulf of Finland and the whole length of the Neva river, down which the old trading route from the Varangians to the Greeks[2] had run. Russia also controlled the right bank of the Narova river, at whose mouth ships from many European countries put in. As soon as the war with Sweden was over the government decided to build a port there. In July, 1557 a crown secretary, Ivan Vyrodkov, an excellent engineer, constructed a town on the Narova, the first Russian port on the Baltic, where ships from abroad could anchor. The tsar's rescript forbade merchants from Novgorod and Pskov to trade in the Livonian towns of Narva and Reval and ordered them to trade with foreigners only on Russian soil, but the attempt to bring maritime commerce to the mouth of the Narova was abortive. The harbor was ready, but foreign merchants continued to use the German port of Narva.

Two factions had formed in the Muscovite government. Adashev insisted on continuing a vigorous eastern policy and launched expeditions against the Crimea, while his opponents, with gentry support, favored war with Livonia. The first Russian invasion of Livonia apparently took place against Adashev's wishes. Military activity intensified when the boyar Aleksei Basmanov, a strenuous advocate of the Livonian war, arrived in Ivangorod. Without waiting for the outcome of diplomatic negotiations in Moscow, he attacked Narva, and when fire broke out in the town ordered his men to storm the fortress. Although the force at Basmanov's disposal was small the Livonians could not sustain the sudden and vigorous attack. The impregnable fortress the Knights had built on what used to be the old border with Novgorod fell; the tsar's commanders occupied Dorpat (formerly Yurev), and pillaged southern Livonia. The success enjoyed by Russian arms might have been greater had not a dispute in high government circles broken out, which caused great confusion and made it impossible to carry out a uniform foreign policy. Instead of continuing the invasion of Livonia that had begun so auspiciously the Muscovite government, at Adashev's insistence, made a truce with the Order from May to November, 1559, while it prepared for a new expedition against the Tatars.

The military operations against the Crimea, which consumed substantial resources and sacrificed large numbers of men, failed to achieve the results Adashev had promised, and a splendid chance to conquer Livonia was decisively lost. Master Kettler signed a treaty which brought the Order under the protection of Lithuania and Poland, sharply altered the course of the war, and was a serious defeat for Russian diplomacy. The conflict in Livonia quickly was transformed into a major contest with Lithuania and Poland just when Russia was involved in a war with the Crimean khanate. The Livonian knights took advantage of the truce to muster their forces. A month before the truce was due to expire detachments appeared near Dorpat and defeated scattered Russian contingents. Ivan learned of the setbacks in Livonia while on a pilgrimage to Mozhaisk, and ordered Prince Mstislavskii, the commander-in-chief, to proceed at once to Livonia, but the bad roads of autumn caused delay and the troops became bogged down in mud along the main highway from Moscow to Novgorod. While the army was marching to the northern border word came that the Tatars had invaded the southern district. The military difficulties caused the ruling authorities to panic. Adashev and Silvester asked the tsar to return to Moscow as soon as possible, and Ivan had to set out with his wife although she was seriously ill. After an exhausting journey the royal family reached the capital, where the tsar learned there had been no reason for haste, since the garrison in Dorpat had beaten back the Livonian attack and the Tatars had vanished into the steppe. This led to a sharp exchange between the tsar and his mentors. As the influence of Adashev and Silvester waned the general line in foreign policy shifted. Moscow accepted peace overtures from the Crimea and hurled large forces into Livonia. The tsar dispatched Prince Kurbskii, one of his closest friends, there and Adashev followed with the field army.

The tsar's commanders decisively routed a crack army of knights below Ermes, took the fortress of Fellin, which was the residence of the Master, and captured almost all the Order's artillery. Livonia's military forces were shattered. It seemed possible to bring the Livo-

An Early Seventeenth Century English Map of Russia

NOVA ZEMLA

ANSKOY SEA

Tingoesi PART

BAIDA OT

Obdora

SIBIRIA

Iugoria

TART A

Condora

Permia

Ridiche Narva

Wiatka

Archangel

Ceremisi Lugova

CAZAN

The Emperours Court

Ceremisi Nagorni

MORDWA

A Hott House

A Mill of Russia

PEREKOPENS CAN

RI A

TURMEN

ASTRACAN

ETIGORA

CIR

MARE CASPIUM

ARMENIA

GILAN

nian war to a successful conclusion, but Adashev and his associates, fearing an attack by Lithuanian troops assembled near Riga, failed to take advantage of the favorable opportunity. After an unsuccessful siege of the fortress of Paida (or Weissenstein) the advance of the Russian armies came to a halt.

Chapter Eleven

ADASHEV FALLS

All through the campaign of 1560 Ivan displayed great impatience and dispatched one courier after another to his commanders. He thought all Germany could be conquered in a summer if the boyars ceased to be deliberately slow and sluggish. Adashev was effectively in control of the army operating in Livonia and thus the tsar held him responsible for the delay. He was ordered to take charge of the fortress of Fellin, which removed him from overall direction of military activity. Ivan next transferred him to Dorpat, where he was subordinated to the local commander and experienced bitter humiliation when Khilkov, the local commander, refused to admit Adashev to the fortress to serve as his assistant. Conciliar rank and the connections he had in Moscow apparently emboldened Adashev to put up a struggle and protest the Dorpat commander's arbitrary action, but he was shattered by the disgrace. He abased himself before Khilkov, who spurned him again, and once more submitted a petition to him. The government announced that Adashev's lands in Kostroma and Pereiaslavl had been confiscated. Silvester, who remained in Moscow after Adashev had left for Livonia, did everything in his power to prevent the latter's dismissal, but without success. He then informed the tsar that he wished to retire to a monastery; Ivan made no attempt to restrain his mentor and sent him to the Kirillov monastery with his blessing.

Adashev's case came before a court composed of council members and higher clergy. The metropolitan and some of the boyars urged the tsar to allow Adashev, now formally in disgrace, to be present at the trial, but the Zakharin faction insisted on a trial *in absentia*. They alarmed Ivan by saying that the former favorites enjoyed greater authority and popularity than the autocrat ("all your soldiers and your people love them more than they do you"), so that the people and the army would be inclined to support Adashev.[1] Furthermore, Silvester and Adashev had had no use for Ivan's wife, Anastasiia Zakharina, and had tried to limit her involvement in state affairs. She died early in August, 1560, and malicious rumors at once began circulating to the effect that enemies had bewitched her. Suspicion fell on the former favorites and an assembly convoked in Moscow condemned them as known criminals. Silvester was banished permanently to Solovki and Adashev remained under arrest in Dorpat. Soon after the assembly met he came down with a high fever and died a month or two later. Ivan promptly sent one of his intimate courtiers to investigate the circumstances of Adashev's death, for it was suspected he had committed suicide.

Having thus disposed of his counsellors Ivan sought to efface all traces of them. What had been regarded as proper behavior in Silvester's time now was considered ridiculous. Lavish revels and entertainments succeeded gloomy fasts. The tsar invited boyars who secretly detested him to court and made them drink heavily. The following became the custom at a party in the palace. Ivan drank the first cup filled with intoxicating liquor, and similar potions were distributed to the other revellers until all grew hopelessly drunk. A guest who tried to resist and avoided draining his cup was reproached as an enemy of the tsar, a man who had not yet shaken off the temper and habits of Silvester's and Adashev's era. The palace drinking bouts affronted the pious. Acknowledging his impropriety, the tsar nevertheless claimed that high state interests required these changes at court. Ivan often asserted that games and entertainments were making him popular with the people and gentry: "I accommodate their weakness (*sic*) so they may know I am the sovereign, not you (boyar) traitors!"[2]

Ivan took advantage of any available means to bolster his prestige, and the clergy rendered him valuable assistance. Fifteen years after his coronation representatives of the patriarch of Constantinople brought Ivan the decree of an ecumenical council confirming his right to the title of tsar. The head of the universal Orthodox church had consecrated the power of the Orthodox Muscovite tsar. The triumphant services held to celebrate this event were designed to buttress Ivan's authority.

Chapter Twelve

THE CAPTURE OF POLOTSK

Contemplating war with Lithuania the government sent an embassy to make peace with the Crimea, a move which marked Moscow's final rejection of Adashev's eastern policy. The determined efforts to make peace with the Crimea were caused by Russian reverses in Livonia. Following Lithuania's lead, the major Baltic powers, Denmark and Sweden, which had joined in dismembering Livonia, became involved in the war. In April, 1560 Duke Magnus, the Danish king's brother, became ruler of the island of Oesel, and a month later Sweden acquired control of Reval[1] and northern Estonia.

Determined to prevent formation of a broad anti-Russian coalition in the Baltic area, the Muscovite government made an alliance with Denmark and concluded a 20-year truce with Sweden in order to concentrate its forces against Lithuania. The Russian command decided to strike at Polotsk, a key border fortress guarding the routes to the Lithuanian capital of Vilna. Virtually all of Russia's armed forces took part in the assault on Polotsk: 18,105 gentry, attended by 20,000 or 30,000 armed slaves, 7219 fusiliers and cossacks, and more than 6,000 Tatar auxiliaries, to make a grand total of 31,546, which, with the armed slaves came to some 50,000 or 60,000 men. This large Russian force left Velikie Luki in January, 1563. The narrow road to Polotsk could not accommodate the great mass of soldiers and their transport. The army was constantly bogged down in the thick forests and swamps, and finally units lost all semblance of order; infantry, cavalry and wagons became entangled with one another and movement came to a standstill. Order was restored with great difficulty. The tsar personally rode along the road with his close associates to separate those who had become stuck, ably assisted by the efficient transport commander, Afanasii Viazemskii, who now first came to the tsar's attention.

Early in February the Russian army reached Polotsk and began a siege. Training artillery on the fortress the commanders battered down its walls and forced the Lithuanians to retreat to the upper fort. In an unexpected night sortie they tried to capture the Russian batteries, but the boyar Sheremetev and the advance guard drove them back. During the battle a bullet creased his ear, but Prince Kashin took his place. Next day the commander, Prince Repnin, set up artillery in the burnt fortress and bombarded the upper fort for two days. Fires broke out all over the town and at dawn on February 15 the Polotsk garrison surrendered. The capture of Polotsk was Russia's greatest triumph in the Livonian war, but it was followed by a decline, characterized by failures in the field and fruitless negotiations. Moscow refused to accept Sweden's capture of the fortress of Paida on the frontier with Russian Livonia. Annoyed by Swedish pretensions, the tsar wrote King Erik XIV an unseemly letter: ". . . he wrote the king . . . many abusive mocking words, reproaching his folly."[2] The tsar's angry letter might have seriously complicated Swedish-Russian relations, but the Swedish king was in such a difficult position that he swallowed the insults uncomplainingly. Somewhat later Ivan grew dissatisfied with the behavior of the Danes and wrote an offensive letter to their king which the Danish ambassador refused to deliver when asked to do so. Ivan's letters to the kings of Sweden and Denmark are milestones in the history of Muscovite diplomacy. They show that after the fall of Polotsk the influence of Ivan, now aged thirty-three, on matters of diplomacy had markedly increased, but in charting Russia's foreign policy he was swayed more by impatience and arrogance than by sober reflection.

After making a field truce with Lithuania near Polotsk Ivan summoned the king's envoys to Moscow and unequivocally demanded they evacuate Livonia as far as the river Daugava. When the envoys refused and went home the tsar immediately moved forces into Lithuania. Moscow intended to have the army advancing from Polotsk link up in enemy territory with another one from Smolensk in order to assault Minsk. The Lithuanians seem to have known the Russian plans. They concentrated their forces on the army from Polotsk and routed it at the Battle of Ula before the two Russian armies could unite. The army from Smolensk was forced to beat a hasty retreat from Lithuania, and the disaster at Ula worsened Russia's military posture. The Crimean khan refused an alliance with Moscow.

Chapter Thirteen

CONFLICT WITH THE BOYARS

Vasilii III had made decisions with the aid of two or three trusted intimate advisors. After dismissing Silvester and Adashev Ivan attempted to revive his father's practice. When he married again[1] he attached several important codicils to his will: in the event of his death a regency council should be formed to guard Ivan, his seven-year-old son and heir, and following Vasilii's precedent Ivan named seven executors. Armed with full powers as regents the boyars swore an oath of fealty to the heir and inscribed their signatures on a document that is extant. Although Ivan manifestly was following his father's procedures closely, his regency council was far less influential than its predecessor. Vasilii III had made a powerful man possessed of substantial resources, his younger brother, Prince Andrei Staritskii, head of the council, but Ivan assigned this office to a colorless individual, his relative, Prince Mstislavskii. In addition to his brother and counsellors, Ivan's father had included the strongest leaders in the boyar council, the Shuiskii boyars, among the regents, whereas Ivan's executors, besides Mstislavskii, were Boyars Daniel Romanovich and Vasilii Mikhailovich Yurev-Zakharin, Ivan Petrovich Yakovlev-Zakharin, and Fedor Ivanovich Umnoi-Kolychev, as well as Princes Andrei Teliatevskii and Petr Gorenskii, who were not of boyar rank. Three of the five boyars on the regency council belonged to the Zakharin family and the fourth was related to it. Relatives of the late queen Anastasiia thus effectively controlled the council, but they were neither influential nor popular among the nobility. Their assistants were two of the tsar's young friends, Teliatevskii and Gorenskii, new men who were little known.

In contrast to his father Ivan established a regency council devoid of authority. Old appanage princely houses, like Staritskii and Belskii, boyars who had been members of his privy council, such as Prince Dmitrii Kurliatev, Ivan Sheremetev, Mikhail Morozov, Prince Aleksandr Gorbatyi, the conqueror of Kazan, and other leaders of the boyar council, who had stood at the summit of affairs when the chosen council existed, were excluded from the new administration. The nobility easily forgave Ivan the dismissal of his humbly-born

Ivan the Terrible. Fresco from the Sviiashk Monastery. Second half of the six-teenth century.

favorites Silvester and Adashev, but it had no mind to overlook his attacks on the boyar council's prerogatives. Ivan's attempts to rule independently with the help of a few relatives and without the advice of the great boyars aroused general discontent. Proud of its royal blood the aristocracy always had despised Anastasiia Zakharina's family and now began to consider its members usurpers.

The Zakharin family succeeded in gaining control of the entire administration. On the occasion of his second marriage the tsar made a disposition in favor of his sons and placed members of the Zakharin family in charge of their councils and courts. The minor heir now formally was declared the ruler whenever Ivan was away, but it was the Zakharin family that exercised the actual power. Its members fully understood the importance of the new chancery apparatus and sought to control it. Their representative, Nikita Funikov, had been disgraced in Adashev's time, but he was brought back from exile and put in charge of the treasury, the main financial chancery. Funikov's associate, the crown secretary Ivan Viskovatyi, became Keeper of the Seal, and important chancery documents had to be stamped in his office. The new chancellor (as foreigners called him) began his activity by replacing the small old seal the grand princes had used with a large one adorned with the symbols of the autocracy, "a two-headed eagle framing a mounted man and a two-headed eagle framing a unicorn on the obverse."[2]

For all practical purposes the tsar had removed the aristocratic council leaders from direction of affairs and was attempting to rule alone, and this perceptibly increased the influence of the higher chancery bureaucracy. Kurbskii, the boyar ideologist, who had witnessed the collapse of the chosen council, strongly protested this infringement of noble privilege and the transfer of administrative duties to chancery bureaucrats. He declared: "The grand prince places all his trust in Russian scribes and to provoke his nobles chooses them not from the gentry nor from the well-born, but among sons of priests or common people."[3] Timokha Teterin, scion of an old secretarial family, was equally severe in his condemnation of the new officials. He wrote to one of the disgraced that the tsar no longer trusted his boyars: "His new confidants are secretaries who give him half of what they get while keeping the other half for themselves. Your fathers would never have had the fathers of such secretaries as their slaves, but now such men have land and trade in your heads."[4]

All involved in the conflict were well aware that the power of the noble princes and boyars depended upon land, and Ivan, embarking on his struggle with the boyars, never lost an opportunity to inform everyone he intended to restrict princely landowning, as his father and grandfather had done. In the heated controversy with Kurbskii the tsar claimed the chosen council had destroyed the traditional customs of land tenure but Silvester had failed to deprive the boyars of their huge patrimonial estates and "had lavishly and improperly distributed such patrimonies, thereby nullifying our grandfather's statute and winning many people to his side."[5]

The tsar had directed his chancery heads to devise a law concerning princely patrimonies, which came into effect when the council approved it on January 15, 1562. The new law categorically forbade princes to sell or alienate their ancestral estates. The treasury claimed exclusive jurisdiction over escheated property, which formerly had gone to monasteries. The tsar's consent was required for nephews or brothers to inherit the patrimony of a deceased prince. Widows and daughters also might not inherit large patrimonies, but were compensated at a fixed rate. The government announced its intention to review the status of all land princes had added to their patrimonies from the death of Vasilii III to implementation of the 1556 service statute. The treasury was empowered to confiscate, with or without compensation, patrimonies princes had transferred to others. Although the act clearly identified the appanage groups to which the new land law applied, as, for example, the Vorotynskii family, the nobility in the Suzdal region, including the Shuiskii princes of Suzdal proper, and the princes of Yaroslavl, Rostov, and Starodub, its restrictions did not apply to great families like Staritskii, Glinskii, Belskii, and Mstislavskii. This is conducive to an assumption that those in charge of land policy in the early 1560s had not yet decided to use it as a means to break up hereditary estates.

The princely aristocracy bitterly opposed the new land law. Kurbskii, its champion, charged that Ivan had destroyed the Suzdal nobility by seizing its wealth and immovable property.[6] The intensity of his anger shows how deeply the feudal nobility resented measures attacking patrimonial landowning. The rise of the Zakharin family and the new land law directly challenged the powerful titled aristocracy. The boyars loudly complained that the council's traditional privileges had been abridged. First to protest were the tsar's relatives, proprietors of appanage duchies who possessed considerable forces of their own and enjoyed comparative freedom of action.

The collapse of the chosen council led members of Prince Glinskii's family to think they might return to power, but their calculations proved incorrect. The tsar placed none of them on the regency council. During Vasilii III's lifetime Prince Mikhail Glinskii, as has been seen, had grown dissatisfied with Muscovite ways, had tried to flee to Lithuania, but ended up in prison. His son, Prince Vasilii Glinskii, also attempted to do what his father had done, but his punishment was lighter. After a brief incarceration and in disgrace he promised to break off the secret relations he had maintained with the Polish king, and swore not to defect to Lithuania or the Staritskii appanage, nor communicate to anyone decisions reached in council or the gist of any speeches he might hear at court.

A short time later Prince Dmitrii Vishnevetskii, one of Ivan's uncles, formed a more serious conspiracy among the appanage magnates. This great Lithuanian lord had been given Belev as an appanage when he came over to Moscow. A vigorous proponent of Adashev's foreign policy, he took part in every campaign against the Crimea and ended up as the virtual ruler of Cherkasy. Expelled from his holding by the tsar, the prince entered into secret negotiations with the king and fled to Lithuania at the moment Muscovite forces were preparing to cross the Lithuanian frontier.

Ivan Belskii, another appanage prince of Lithuanian origin, was arrested in Moscow a few months before Vishnevetskii fled. Regarded as the titular head of the boyar council, he disagreed with the tsar on principle, and thus was automatically placed under restraint when Ivan demanded the council ratify the highly unpopular law concerning princely patrimonies. Unable to approve of Ivan's policy, Belskii tried to flee to Lithuania and when apprehended, rescripts from the king guaranteeing him refuge and a detailed map showing the road to the Lithuanian frontier were found on his person. Prince Rostovskii had been condemned to death (a sentence later commuted to exile) for a comparable crime, but Belskii managed to escape such punishment when clergy and council members interceded on his behalf. The government released him when influential boyars and a hundred gentry went surety for him. The new land laws did not immediately affect the interests of the Glinskii and Belskii families but the three heirs to the Vorotynskii appanage, who were not related to the dynasty, were in a different position. When the estate was distributed Prince Vladimir, the eldest heir, received the best third of it, which escheated to his widow at his death, but his two younger brothers, Mikhail and Aleksandr, also laid claim to it. The statute of 1562 had ruined their prospects; they were told they must cede this best third of the appanage to the treasury. They refused to do so and Prince

Mikhail, according to the official chronicle, criticized the tsar. Lithuanian sources imply that Ivan suspected the Vorotynskii brothers intended to go over to the king with all their lands, which were situated on the border with Lithuania. Prince Mikhail was brought to trial and convicted on testimony by his retainers of trying to bewitch the tsar and inciting certain old women to cast spells upon him. The boyar council and higher clergy tried to intervene on behalf of the Vorotynskii brothers, but managed only to obtain clemency for Aleksandr, the younger. Mikhail Vorotynskii was imprisoned in Beloozero and the treasury confiscated the ancestral property of the disgraced family.

Besides appanage proprietors, powerful boyars who had exercised great authority during the chosen council's administration also were subject to harassment. The government disgraced Boyar Prince Dmitrii Kurliatev, a member of the intimate council and Silvester's principal patron. The official chronicle is deliberately vague concerning Kurliatev's treason and does not choose to explain it, but the catalog of the sixteenth-century royal archive also mentions the incident. After Silvester's trial Kurliatev was sent as commander to Smolensk and wrote the tsar a letter after his arrival. It was deposited in the archive with the following notation: "Here is a letter from Prince Dmitrii Kurliatev, which he sent to the sovereign. Prince Dmitrii wrote that he had not gone by that road. Here is a roster of the commanders of Smolensk."[7] At first sight Commander Kurliatev's attempt at exculpation seems insignificant, but the tsar believed it contained hidden meaning and forwarded it to the archive, where the most important state papers were kept.

The ambiguous evidence concerning the Kurliatev affair poses interesting questions for scholars. Why did the Smolensk commander seek to exculpate himself to the tsar by saying "he did not go by that road?" Where might he have gone from a fortress on the Lithuanian frontier? The obvious answer is that Kurliatev intended to flee from Smolensk to Lithuania, but prevented from doing so, tried to tell the tsar he had lost his way. Saying he did so accompanied by his entire staff and an armed entourage made the authorities highly suspicious and formed the basis of the charge made against the disgraced prince. This is why the tsar was justified in appending a list of the commanders of Smolensk and the number of men they had each year to the Kurliatev case and preserving it with Kurliatev's communication. This also explains why Kurliatev was sent to serve in Smolensk for a year but actually stayed there only a short time, until he was removed from office before the expiration of his tenure. The tsar hated the powerful boyar; he was confined to a remote monastery on Lake Ladoga and the rest of his family were tonsured.

Out of power but not crushed, the boyar opposition showed increasing interest in Lithuania, where those who could not stomach Ivan's autocratic tendencies hoped to find refuge and help to overthrow the tsar. The government's concern about connections the opposition had with that country grew as the struggle on the Russo-Lithuanian frontier steadily became more menacing. At last the tsar came to suspect his cousin, Prince Vladimir, of treason, and with good grounds. While the royal army and units from the Staritskii appanage were moving secretly against Polotsk a noble courtier, Boris Khlyznev-Kolychev, had deserted the tsar's staff and told the Polotsk commanders about Ivan's intentions. The renegade was close to Prince Vladimir and the tsar assumed he bore a communication from the latter to King Sigismund II. Fearing betrayal Ivan ordered a close watch on his cousin's family.

The intrigue of the Staritskii princes was revealed when their secretary, Savluk Ivanov, decided to inform the tsar about his master's plans. In an effort to dispose of the informer, Prince Vladimir imprisoned him, but Ivan brought Savluk to Moscow and learned a great deal about the plans of Vladimir and his supporters. Their guilt was so palpable that Ivan issued orders to confiscate the Staritskii appanage and bring its owner to trial. The fate of the tsar's cousin rested with the higher clergy. The boyar council took no formal part in the proceeding since the tsar did not wish to have boyars adjudicating his dispute with his relative, and the council contained many who supported Vladimir. Ivan read the clauses of the indictment to a church assembly in Prince Vladimir's presence. The metropolitan and bishops acknowledged their veracity but did everything in their power to end the dispute in the royal family and prevent a trial.

Purely family considerations finally resolved the conflict. Although the tsar despised his cousin's stupidity and weakness he made allowances, granted Vladimir a full pardon, and restored his appanage, but he surrounded his cousin with men of whose loyalty he entertained no doubts. Ivan disliked and was somewhat afraid of his aunt, the energetic, ambitious Princess Evfrosiniia, and showed personal animosity in his relations with her. Blaming her for all that had occurred he ordered the vigorous woman, then at the height of her powers, to take the veil. She adopted the name of Elder Evdokiia and went to reside near the Kirillov monastery in the Voskresensk nunnery, which she herself had founded. Although a nun living under displeasure, she was allowed to keep a servant and have boyar women as confidants. The servitors who looked after her were assigned thousands of acres near the nunnery. Evfrosiniia was not a prisoner at Voskresensk; occasionally she was permitted to go on pilgrimages to adjacent nunneries, and collected beautiful embroideries. The tapestries made in her workshop possessed considerable artistic merit.

The action of the Staritskii princes had provided the tsar with a splendid opportunity to get rid of the last powerful appanage in Russia, but he chose not to take advantage of it. No matter how threatening his dynastic pretensions, Prince Vladimir was too supine and improvident to acquire real popularity with the gentry and most nobles had no use for him, above all the Shuiskii princes of Suzdal, who had been responsible for the death of Prince Andrei Staritskii and had plundered his estate. The mild punishment Vladimir and the other princes received may perhaps be explained by the fact that Ivan's growing conflict with the numerous nobles of the Suzdal line was causing him increasing concern; he obviously had no wish to lose all support from close relatives when the throne was in jeopardy. With the tsar's approval the official chronicle made only short and deliberately vague reference to the charges against Prince Vladimir and to his trial. The account merely states that in 1563 Prince Vladimir and his mother were accused of impropriety and wrongdoing, but after a while Ivan himself removed the veil of secrecy that had shrouded this first trial of the Staritskii family. He later wrote: "Why should Prince Vladimir have come to the throne? He was born fourth from the royal line. What qualifications did he have to do so? What was his origin? (He had no claim) except your (boyar) treacherous support and his own stupidity . . . I could not brook such outrage. I stood up for myself." Ivan did not express his annoyance until much later. It might thus be assumed that once the trial was over the tsar desired to forget the distressing family quarrel, but such was not really his intention.

Ivan pardoned his cousin but he planned carefully to deal with him if a new crisis should arise. The unusual situation required an unusual solution. Ivan resorted to old chronicles and inserted in them a detailed account of the first conspiracy the Staritskii family had formed while the chosen council was in power. To understand his action one must remember that official chronicles were thought to possess exceptional significance. Muscovite rulers used to cite them in their disputes with Novgorod when it was independent, and diplomats drew arguments from them when negotiating with foreign courts. The chronicle work Ivan commissioned had a political, not a literary purpose; it was designed to expose Prince Vladimir's supporters who had escaped the punishment they had deserved.

Ivan began by studying the trial record of Prince Rostovskii, a leader of the boyar conspiracy in 1553. The catalog of the royal archive in the sixteenth century indicates the trial was elaborately documented and the record kept in a special box: "Box 174, in which is the flight and torture in the case of Prince Semen Rostovskii." Secretaries had made a notation in the margin of the catalog: "Given to the sovereign in the case of Prince Vladimir Andreevich July 20, 7071."[8] This means Ivan had studied the record of Rostovskii's conspiracy a week or two before he pardoned his cousin. Later turning to the chronicles, he inserted the names of boyar conspirators, taken from Prince Rostovskii's trial record in the box, into the compilation known as the Synodal Chronicle. The cursive marks indicate strikingly and precisely which boyars the tsar had chosen to implicate as conspirators after his cousin's inconclusive trial ended. They were the Kurakin princes, Prince Petr Shcheniatev, and Prince Dmitrii Nemoi, all of whom were indisputably close to the Staritskii family. Princess Evfrosiniia's maiden name was Khovanskaia and she came from the same family as Shcheniatev and the Kurakin princes. At the time of her trial Prince Petr Shcheniatev was a high officer in the boyar council; Princes Fedor and Petr Kurakin were in charge of Novgorod and Pskov, and Prince Ivan Kurakin administered the appanage of Uglich on behalf of the incompetent Prince Yurii Vasilevich.[9] The individuals implicated in the chronicle were among the most powerful boyars in the government.

Several recensions of the official royal chronicle, based on a rough draft of the Synodal Chronicle, have been preserved. The draft was corrected in Adashev's time, and final copies of the corrected text were made. One clean copy of the Moscow chronicle, called the Royal Book, was the principal chronicle, illustrated with numerous miniatures, and great resources were devoted to its preparation. Beginning with a description of the death of Vasilii III, the Royal Chronicle was supposed to embrace Ivan's entire reign, but work on it suddenly was suspended. Someone in authority has studded its pages with marks and insertions, the most remarkable of which are devoted to the trial of the Rostovskii faction, the same subject which had been inserted into the Synodal recension. The same conspirators, Princes P. M. Shcheniatev, D. I. Nemoi, and S. V. Rostovskii, figure in both interpolations, which thus may be assumed to have been based on the archival record of Rostovskii's trial. However, the editor of the Royal Book described the conspiracy in greater detail, including oral testimony from crown officials who came forward at the appropriate time to denounce the Staritskii faction. Fedorov, Master of Horse, asserted that when the tsar was ill in 1553 the conspirators tried to win him over, but he informed Ivan of their action as soon as the former recovered, although it is not clear whether this testimony comes from Ivan or Fedorov. The armorer, L. A. Saltykov, made a supplemental deposition. Such statements by loyal boyars, entered in the official chronicle, are valuable firsthand testimony.

Ivan was himself apparently the chief witness for the prosecution, and a more authoritative but prejudiced and partial one would be hard to find. He aimed to prove the Staritskii partisans had organized a conspiracy and provoked an open disturbance in council, which his personal intervention alone had averted. It may be recalled the chronicle asserts that on the day when the boyars were to swear their oath to the infant Dmitrii the stricken tsar addressed them in two long speeches. When the disaffected boyars refused to swear the tsar supposedly tried to restore them to their senses by saying: "You have forgotten your troth and refuse to serve me and my children. If you do not want us, then so be it!" Ivan next reproached the puzzled Zakharin family: "Why are you not frightened?" he is thought to have asked. "Do you think the boyars will spare you? You will be their first victims. You should be ready to lay down your lives for my son and his mother and not allow the boyars to insult my wife." Unwilling to rely solely on the Zakharin family the tsar made a desperate appeal to loyal members of the council: "It is the will of God whether I stand or fall. Remember what you have sworn to me and my son. Do not allow the boyars to destroy my son in any way. Take him to another country. God will show you the way."[10]

Ivan's speeches to the boyars are clearly based on what he actually said, but they contain an element of invention. The day of the disturbance the tsar was barely alive and unable, as has been noted, to be present when the boyars took the oath. The details of the conspiracy only came to light after Ivan recovered; prior to that he had no reason to make such formidable invocations. The tsar's appeal to the Zakharin family was out of place in the patriarchal atmosphere that prevailed during Silvester's administration, but appropriate to the time when the tsar made some of its members chief regents, responsible for his sons. The speeches, composed after the trial of the Staritskii group, well reveal Ivan's attitude at that time, when conspiracies against the throne were multiplying. The chronicle narrative shows Ivan's tragic situation better than any other source. Terrified for the future of his dynasty he appealed to the Zakharin family in panic, adjuring them to save his family by taking his children to another country in the event of disaster. The speeches also acknowledge indirectly that his efforts to remove the great boyars from power had failed. After ruling independently for three years Ivan had to reach the melancholy conclusion that his powerful vassals no longer required a God-annointed tsar or children of royal blood.

Any explanation of the source and nature of the clash between Ivan and the nobility must take into consideration the fact that the leading Muscovite boyars did not constitute a unified, homogeneous entity. The complex structure of the boyar group was a product of the unification of the Russian land. Appanage princes occupied the highest positions, but political centralization inevitably had undermined their former influence. No more than three or four hereditary appanages were left by the middle of the sixteenth century, and almost all belonged to former Lithuanian magnates separate from the native Muscovite nobility. The Suzdal nobles, who were the numerous progeny of the local dynasties in northeastern Russia, had been forced to yield primacy in the council and the army to the newcomers from Lithuania, but these nobles, the Shuiskii, Rostovskii, Yaroslavskii and Starodubskii princes, possessed far more political influence than the Lithuanian serving princes. Ivan's increasing hostility towards the Suzdal nobility was a major factor ensuring that the conflict within his own family was resolved peacefully.

On occasion powerful church leaders urged the tsar to avoid a definitive break with his mighty vassals. The aged Josephite, Metropolitan Makarii, always trying to strengthen the power of the Muscovite sovereigns, upheld the Josephite theory of autocracy and the official dogma that the ruler was of divine origin, but during the conflict used every opportunity to intervene on behalf of princes placed under displeasure. The affair of the Vorotynskii princes and the persecution of Adashev's relatives prove that his efforts were not always successful.

The tsar placed Adashev's relatives on trial after receiving information from Boyar M. Ya. Morozov, a former member of the chosen council. During the Polotsk campaign Morozov was serving in honorary exile as commander of Smolensk. After the capture of Polotsk he encountered a Lithuanian prisoner who told him the Lithuanians were hastily moving their forces towards the fortress of Starodub, because the governor had promised to betray it. Morozov at once told the tsar of these allegations and Ivan took his communication very seriously. The Starodub commanders were arrested and brought to trial. Their testimony chiefly implicated the governor, Prince Vasilii Funikov, but instead it was his deputy, Commander Ivan Shishkin-Olgov, belonging to the Adashev-Olgov family, who was punished. The government charged all the relatives of the late favorite with treason. Adashev's brother, Associate Boyar Daniel, and his son were executed, as well as his father-in-law, Petr Turov, and their relatives, the Satin family. The Starodub trial led to a massive persecution of those who had supported the fallen leaders. Contemporary testimony indicates that the authorities drew up long proscription lists containing names of Silvester's and Adashev's associates and even their friends and neighbors, who might or might not have known them.[11] Many arrested were tortured and exiled to remote frontier fortresses. The Starodub affair exacerbated the political climate and led to the first use of terror. The death of Makarii, occurring soon afterwards, deprived the church of a seasoned, authoritative leader, with whom the impetuous tsar and the boyar opposition both had been obliged to reckon, and freed Ivan's hands.

This wave of repressions contributed to the rise of a new man, Boyar Aleksei Basmanov-Pleshcheev, who came from a family that long had been close to the royal house. His father had been Vasilii III's chamberlain, and Aleksei had a splendid war record. He had distinguished himself at the siege of Kazan and at a crucial battle with the Tatars at Sudbishchi. Early in the Livonian war Basmanov with only meagre forces captured the impregnable fortress of Narva. An early supporter of the Baltic war, Aleksei won Ivan's favor and eventually became his chief advisor. Basmanov knew the Zakharin administration was coming to an end and sought to hasten its demise. When he filed a suit involving precedence[12] against Ivan Bolshoi Sheremetev and won it, it became clear the old government no longer possessed authority. Basmanov was unawed by the fact that Sheremetev, a close relative of the Zakharin family, had been a member of the tsar's intimate council for fifteen years, had performed considerable military service, and held exceptionally high precedence rank.

Basmanov's rise coincided with the start of further persecution of the nobility. The new favorite, a typical representative of the military, supported the use of force to put down boyar opposition. The Sheremetev princes were among his first victims. Boyars Ivan and Nikita Sheremetev were arrested as soon as the precedence suit was over. Ivan, one of the most popular members of the former chosen council, had rendered outstanding service. Ivan hesitated to execute him and merely confiscated his estate, but he was thrown into prison after enduring cruel tortures, and the tsar had his brother Nikita strangled in confinement. The Zakharin family was powerless to prevent these attacks on their relatives.

Early in 1564 the tsar learned that his army had suffered disaster in Lithuania, although the first reports of the defeat were greatly exaggerated because the commander-in-chief had fallen in battle and the extent of the catastrophe could not be determined. Suspecting that boyar opposition leaders had transmitted his war plans to the enemy, Ivan immediately ordered the execution of two suspected boyars. His attendants seized Prince Repnin in a church where he was performing a nocturnal vigil and killed him on the street. A few hours later Prince Kashin was slain at matins. Repnin and Kashin had fought heroically at the siege of Polotsk and their murder became the subject of an angry exchange between Kurbskii and the tsar. The former wrote with emotion of how Ivan spilt his commanders' victorious (sic) holy blood in God's churches. The tsar sarcastically replied that he had long heard nothing about holy blood in Russia, where there were no longer any martyrs for the faith, and it was improper to make martyrs out of traitors and fornicators. Unwilling to allow Ivan's attack to go unanswered, Kurbskii included a lengthy and extremely interesting parable about the victorious Commander Repnin and his martyr's death, in his *History*.[13]

After the Polotsk campaign the tsar, wishing to show friendship to his victorious commander, once invited him to a revel at the palace with jesters and mummers. When all were in their cups the tsar and his friends began dancing with the jesters. Apparently shocked by such impropriety, to everyone's amazement the pious man burst into tears and loudly upbraided and reproached Ivan: "Christian tsar, it does not befit you to behave like this." Trying to reason with the stubborn man Ivan said: "Enjoy yourself and come and play with us." but when he attempted to fit a mask on the unwelcome guest Repnin, forgetting his manners, trampled it underfoot. Citing his boyar rank he declared: "Do not urge me, a man of conciliar rank, to do insane degrading things."[14] In a rage Ivan ordered the recalcitrant boyar forcibly removed.

The parable of Repnin's exploit may be myth, but it suggests the relationship existing between the tsar and his proud great nobles shortly before Ivan organized the oprichnina. Fear could not silence them and they did not yet take seriously threats uttered by a man who had been under Silvester's tutelage. The princes continued to thwart and insult their autocratic sovereign as they had done in the days of Ivan III and Vasilii III. Ivan's enemies were fully aware that Basmanov was behind the recent executions. Soon after his flight to Lithuania Kurbskii indulged in unrestrained attacks on an unnamed flatterer of the tsar, who "behaves more evilly with his children than the priests of Kronus," an allusion to Ivan's young favorite, Fedor Basmanov.[15] Kurbskii wrote: "This deceiver whispers falsehoods in the ears of the tsar, sheds Christian blood like water, and has already destroyed the strong and noble in Israel." Kurbskii's letter, written the day after Repnin and the other boyars were executed, proves that Aleksei Basmanov was directly responsible for the death of the opposition leaders. Kurbskii called him "a glorious traducer, madman, and destroyer of the Old Russian land."[16]

Since the brutal executions caused great stir in Moscow the government did what it could to ensure the support of church leaders. After Silvester's fall Andrei, former archpriest of the Cathedral of the Annunciation and the tsar's personal confessor for more than ten years, was tonsured in the Chudov monastery in the Kremlin and took the name of Afanasii. The tsar chose him to be Makarii's successor because he desired a compliant individual in charge of the church. The new metropolitan enjoyed the exceptional honor of wearing a white cowl and the tsar granted him many exemptions and privileges which benefited the metropolitan treasury substantially. Such generosity was designed to strengthen cooperation between monarch and church.

Leaders of the boyar party condemned the alliance. In a missive to his sympathizer, Vasian Muromtsev of the Pechora monastery, Kurbskii asserted unequivocally that the Josephite church hierarchy had been bribed and corrupted; wealth had made holy men obedient government hirelings. No holy men were left in Russia to censure the tsar for his criminal acts or lament the bloodshed, nor anyone to quench the fierce conflagration or save the persecuted. Kurbskii was sure his criticism of the Josephite church would fall on sympathetic ears in the Pechora monastery, long a stronghold of the non-possessors, but he attacked the Josephites on political rather than dogmatic grounds in the hope that the influential Pechora monks might form an opposition group within the church.

Kurbskii's interesting communication is virtually the sole document openly to formulate the political program of the boyar opposition on the eve of the oprichnina. Its main demand was that attacks on boyars must cease immediately. Boldly challenging Ivan, Kurbskii charged that the autocratic ruler of Russia was bloodthirsty, neglected his realm, held unjust trials, impoverished the nobility, restricted merchants, and made landlords suffer—in short, the cause of all the misfortunes afflicting Russia.

Chapter Fourteen

KURBSKII'S BETRAYAL

The council was not the exclusive preserve of men hostile to the tsar, for many boyars enjoyed his confidence. Some, like Kurbskii, were personal friends, but the events that transpired after the Polotsk campaign soured Ivan's relationship with Prince Andrei. The tsar, claiming Kurbskii's association with traitors had offended him, inflicted a slight rebuke upon the prince by sending him to the fortress of Dorpat as governor of Livonia.

The Polotsk campaign, in which Kurbskii served with distinction, had just come to an end. Kurbskii had commanded the advance guard, an assignment usually reserved for the best field commanders, and faced considerable danger while in charge of siege operations before the walls of the enemy fortress. After the capture of Polotsk the successful army returned to Moscow, where it was received in triumph. Senior officers had the right to expect rewards and rest, but Kurbskii was denied such benefits; the tsar ordered him to collect forces and proceed to Dorpat within a month. It was generally recalled that this town had been the place to which Adashev was banished and less than three years had elapsed from the day Adashev, after his successful incursion into Livonia, went to serve in Dorpat, where he was imprisoned and died in disgrace.

Arriving there Kurbskii addressed his friends in the Pechora monastery: "Many times I beseech you to pray for a wretched man, for again many miseries from Babylon begin to burst upon us."[1] To comprehend the allegory contained in Kurbskii's words one needs to know that at the time Babylon meant the tsar's authority. Kurbskii anticipated further trouble with the tsar because this was the time Ivan was investigating the conspiracy of Prince Vladimir Andreevich, to whose house Kurbskii was related. The investigation implicated him. Ivan's envoys later stated in Lithuania that Kurbskii had betrayed the tsar long before he fled: "He had been undermining the sovereign's throne; he wished to have Prince Vladimir Andreevich as ruler; behind Prince Vladimir Andreevich stood his cousin, and eventually the affair of Prince Vladimir Andreevich became like your affair involving Svidrigailo and Jagiello."[2]

After a year in Dorpat Kurbskii fled to Lithuania. He used a rope to descend the high fortress wall at night, left his wife behind, and rode to Wolmar with a few trusted retainers. In his haste he abandoned almost all his property, including weapons, and books, which he prized highly. He moved precipitately because friends in Moscow secretly had warned him he was under imminent threat of the tsar's displeasure, Ivan confirmed that Kurbskii had good reason for alarm. His envoys informed the Lithuanian magnates that the tsar had investigated Kurbskii's treasonable activities and would have punished him had he not fled abroad. In a subsequent conversation with a Polish envoy Ivan acknowledged that he had decided to strip Kurbskii of his office and confiscate his estates, but he solemnly swore he never had any intention of condemning him to death. In a letter Ivan wrote to Kurbskii immediately after the latter had fled Ivan was not so forthcoming. He harshly assailed Kurbskii for believing the insinuations of false friends and seeking refuge abroad because of "one small word of tsaric wrath."[3] Ivan was dissembling, but even he did not know the full story behind his former friend's flight. The reasons for it have never been fully elucidated and historians are still unable to answer many questions pertaining to it.

After Kurbskii's death his heirs supplied a Lithuanian law court with documents pertaining to his departure from Russia. The court determined that protracted negotiations had preceded it. Kurbskii received informal secret letters without seals, one from the lord-lieutenant of Lithuania, Ju. N. Radziwill and vice-chancellor E. Volovich, the other from the king. When the parties reached agreement Radziwill sent an official letter under seal which promised appropriately to reward Kurbskii in Lithuania and the king also sent a letter with a similar offer. In view of the distance to the Polish capital, the unreliable transport and poor road conditions of those days, as well as the difficulty of crossing frontiers in wartime, it is reasonable to assume that negotiations in Dorpat had been under way for several months or perhaps more.

New documents pertaining to Kurbskii's flight recently have come to light, in particular a letter King Sigismund II Augustus wrote a year and a half before the defection. The king thanked a prince, who was commander in Vitebsk, for his good offices in the affair of the Muscovite commander, and asked him to transmit a letter to Kurbskii. The king observed: "Who knows what the result of this will be, but may God grant it to be a good beginning, since earlier I have received no information about any initiative on Kurbskii's part."[4] The king's letter reveals that a prince commanding in Vitebsk made a secret appeal to Kurbskii, and Lithuanian documents show this individual was Radziwill, whom the king allowed to send a letter to Kurbskii. His secret communication initiated covert negotiations between the Muscovite prince and the Lithuanians. Sigismund's statement about an initiative from Kurbskii may seem puzzling because it was written a year and a half before the Muscovite commander defected, but fierce battles were raging on the frontier and the king's army had experienced numerous reverses, so the king naturally would welcome any initiative from Kurbskii and express the hope that something good might come from it. He had obviously calculated correctly.

New documentary evidence requires reexamination of the references in Lithuanian chronicles to Kurbskii's activities while governing Russian Livonia. F. Neustadt's well-known chronicle relates that a certain Count Arts, governor of Swedish Livonia for Duke John, sought help from the Poles after Erik arrested John, and then went to Kurbskii and secretly offered to surrender the fortress of Helmet to him. They signed and ratified an agreement to this effect, but the conspirators were betrayed to the Lithuanian authorities and Count Arts was conveyed to Riga, where he was broken on the wheel late in 1563. The Lithuanian chronicler portrayed the negotiations with Arts in a light favorable to Kurbskii, but in good conscience also reported rumors circulating in Livonia that Kurbskii had betrayed the governor of Swedish Livonia. He writes: "These discussions aroused the grand prince's suspicions of Prince Andrei Kurbskii, for he felt that the latter might be plotting evil against him with the Polish king."[5] The reports of Kurbskii's secret negotiations with Lithuania show that the tsar's suspicions were abundantly justified.

The Riga archives contain a transcript of testimony Kurbskii gave the Lithuanian authorities directly after his flight from Dorpat. After detailing his secret negotiations with the Livonian knights and the people of Riga Kurbskii continued: "I also negotiated with Count Arts, urging him to come over to the grand prince with the fortresses held by the grand duke of Finland. I knew a good deal about these matters, but forgot them when I made my dangerous flight."[6] The unexpectedly laconic nature of Kurbskii's statement, in which he alleged forgetfulness, indirectly confirms the rumors current in Livonia that he was involved in Arts' death. In Lithuania he took one of the deceased count's retainers into his service and often commiserated with him over his master's death, which he might have done in a desire to shift suspicion of betrayal from himself.

Upon initiating secret negotiations with the Lithuanians Kurbskii apparently rendered them valuable services. After his flight he told them the tsar had intended to send an army of 20,000 men to invest Riga but was persuaded by the former governor of Livonia, Master of Horse I.P. Fedorov, to alter his plans. The Russian army assembled in Polotsk proceeded towards the Lithuanian frontier. Meanwhile the man with whom Kurbskii had been negotiating, Prince Ju. N. Radziwill, who evidently possessed exact information about the army's movements, arranged an ambush and defeated the Muscovite commanders. This event occurred three months before Kurbskii fled to Lithuania.

As soon as news of the defeat reached Moscow the tsar ordered the execution of two boyars he suspected of maintaining secret relations with Lithuania. The executions had a devastating effect on Kurbskii. He wrote at the time: "The autocratic tsar has savagely tortured and brutally murdered those who wished him well." His agitation was understandable, for his own position again had become precarious, but once more the threat abated and nothing happened to him. Nevertheless, Kurbskii now began preparing to flee, as the letters he wrote from Dorpat reveal.[7] Anxious to justify to his friends his decision to forsake his native land, Kurbskii heatedly exposed the misery of various elements in Russian society—gentry, merchants and landowners—declaring that the gentry had nothing to eat and the landowners suffered from relentless taxation. A few words of sympathy for the peasants fell from his lips unexpectedly; Kurbskii never again said anything about them in any of his numerous writings.

The circumstances surrounding Kurbskii's defection may help explain his financial situation. In Dorpat he appealed for loans from the Pechora monastery, but a year later he arrived at the frontier with a purse full of gold, and his wallet contained a sum in foreign currency enormous for that time—30 ducats, 300 gold pieces, 500 silver thalers, as well as 44 Muscovite rubles. Kurbskii complained that the treasury confiscated his estates after his flight and he received nothing from the sale of his lands. He did not remove the military treasury from Dorpat, for Ivan would surely have mentioned it had he done so. The only plausible assumption is that the king paid Kurbskii generously to defect. It may be noted in passing that gold coins did not circulate in Russia. Ducats had replaced orders; when a retainer received a Hungarian ducat for his service he would carry it in his cap or his sleeve.

Historians have noted the paradox that Kurbskii arrived at the border a rich man but soon afterwards directed another lachrymose appeal for assistance to the Pechora monks. An explanation for this may be found in the original acts of the Lithuanian *Metric*,[8] which records a decision by a Lithuanian court that Kurbskii was robbed when he arrived. The hearing rehearses his flight in minute detail. Leaving Dorpat at night Kurbskii reached the Lithuanian border fortress of Helmet by morning. Here he was supposed to have met a guide to conduct him to Wolmar, where officials from the king awaited him, but Germans in Helmet seized the fugitive and stole all his gold. He was conveyed like a prisoner to the fortress of Armus, where the local gentry submitted him to crowning indignity by taking away his fur hat and appropriating his horses.

Kurbskii, who now had lost everything, on reaching Wolmar was obliged to ponder the fickleness of fate. The day after the robbery in Helmet he sent a reproach to the tsar: "I have lost everything and you have driven me from God's land." Kurbskii's statement should not be taken literally. He had long been engaged in treasonable negotiations with Lithuania; it was fear of discovery that drove him from his own country, for he had never experienced overt persecution even to the moment of his flight from Russia. When he arrived abroad neither the king's safe-conduct nor the oaths the Lithuanian magnates had sworn sufficed to protect him. He failed to receive the rewards he had been promised, suffered despite, was robbed of his possessions, and lost simultaneously his high position, power and gold. The catastrophe moved Kurbskii involuntarily to lament forsaking "God's country," his native land.

The fugitive boyar first announced that he considered it his duty to inform the king about Moscow's intrigues, which should be halted without delay. He told the Lithuanians about all of Moscow's partisans in Livonia with whom he had negotiated, and named Moscow's spies operating at the king's court. He also sent his loyal servant, Vaska Shibanov, to Dorpat with instructions to remove certain writings from beneath the stove in the commander's headquarters and transmit them to the tsar or the Pechora elders. After many years of humiliating silence Kurbskii was filled with desire to hurl angry charges at his former friend and justify his defection to the world. Furthermore, Shibanov was told to ask the Pechora elders for a loan. The secret courier failed to execute his commission. Shibanov was apprehended and brought as a prisoner to Moscow. The tradition that shows Shibanov bravely handing the tsar a provocative letter on the Red Porch in the Kremlin is legend, the only trustworthy component of which is that the arrested servant refused to denounce his master even when tortured and loudly sang his praises while standing on the scaffold. Kurbskii sent two brief notes to the tsar and the Pechora elders from Wolmar, both of which ended with exactly the same phraseology. Threatening both the elders and his former friend with God's judgment he sought to frighten them by vowing to take his indictments against them to the grave.

Kurbskii was not the only one to seek haven in Lithuania. Thither fled the fusilier captain Timokha Teterin (called Kurbskii's wicked sympathizer), who had slipped away from a monastery, as well as others. Formation of a group of Russian political emigres in Lithuania had important consequences. For the first time in many years the opposition had a forum from which it could express openly its views and oppose its demands to those which were proclaimed officially. The extensive trade and diplomatic relations that existed between Russia and Lithuania enabled the emigres to maintain unbroken contact with sympathizers at home, and people in Moscow eagerly listened to and scrutinized every rumor and report originating abroad. Emigre protests assumed increasing significance as conflict between the ruler and his aristocratic opposition intensified.

Ivan's quarrels with council and the challenge posed by opposition leaders aroused him to take pen in hand and reason with his refractory subjects. During the next several weeks, while in Aleksandrovskaia Sloboda and Mozhaisk, he prepared his celebrated reply to Kurbskii. Basmanov accompanied the tsar to Mozhaisk; thus, it is safe to conjecture that the tsar's new favorite was one of the first to read Ivan's letter and probably had a hand in composing it. The sweeping, resonant epistle constituted an entire book by the standards of the time, an original manifesto of autocracy, which contained much stilted rhetoric and bombast together with some sound ideas, and stated assumptions as facts. The main issue which concerned the tsar was the relationship between the monarchy and the nobility. Ivan craved unlimited power. He asserted: "Godless pagans do not rule their

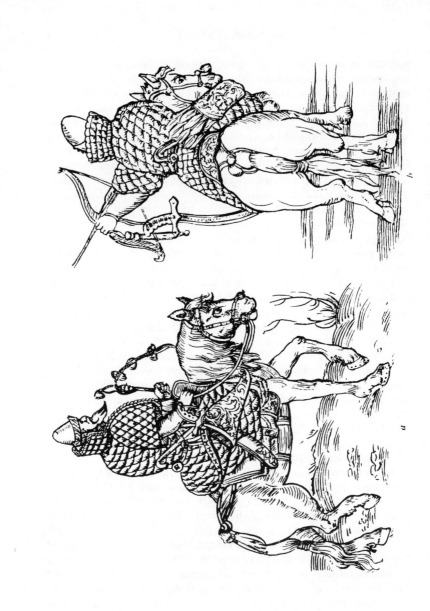

Sixteenth Century Russian Horsemen
(Herberstein, *Commentary on Russian Affairs,* Basel, 1556)

realms; they rule as their slaves bid them, but the Russian realm has always been ruled by its sovereigns, not by boyars or nobles." God Himself had placed the ancestors of Kurbskii and other boyars in bondage to the rulers of Moscow, and high noblemen are not the tsar's "brothers," as Kurbskii had dubbed himself and the rest of the princes; they are his slaves, and "we are free to reward our slaves and free to punish them."

The image of the mighty ruler projected in the tsar's epistle often has led historians astray: the facts contradict the veracity of his portrait. Ivan longed for total power, but by no means possessed it, and he was acutely conscious of his dependence upon his powerful vassals. What the tsar said about boyar disobedience, known from the chronicle interpolations, leaves no doubt on that score. It was fear for his safety at the hands of the boyars and a depressing awareness that they had no need of him that lay behind Ivan's cavalier assertion that the boyars were his slaves. The tsar had no wish to display his weakness to Kurbskii, but the epistle was unable to conceal his fears. He wrote: "What makes the boyars so hostile to us that they always long to dispatch us to the other world? These new traitors have defied their sworn oath in order to reject their tsar, whom God gave to them and who was born to rule, and have done all the evil they possibly can with words, deeds, and secret conniving."

Ivan generally expressed his remarkably frank concerns and doubts through the medium of historical tales about the past, since he hesitated to provide his enemies with occasion for satisfaction by discussing contemporary issues. Refusing to admit that his rupture with the boyar council was growing more serious, he wrote Kurbskii: "Our boyars all agree with us, save only your friends and advisors, who now, like devils, work in dark of night to accomplish their insidious schemes." It is easy to divine at whom the tsar's arrows were aimed. Considering Kurbskii and his supporters to be partisans of the Staritskii faction and participants in their conspiracy, he unabashedly threatened them with reprisal. Moving from the present to the past, the tsar found abundant examples to illustrate the boyars' treachery. In the interpolations he made in the Royal Chronicle Ivan had tried indirectly to implicate Silvester and Adashev as abettors of the Staritskii interest, and now by a single stroke of the pen his letter to Kurbskii made them leaders of a conspiracy against the dynasty. The treacherous boyars, Ivan wrote, "arose like drunkards with Priest Silvester and your chief, Aleksei," to destroy the heir, his son Dmitrii, and hand the throne to Prince Vladimir.

The arguments in Ivan's epistle depend upon the thesis that the boyars were monstrous traitors. He wrote that they were demanding that individual autonomy should replace the power of the crown, although in a country where the ruler's subjects refuse to obey him internecine strife is incessant, for all kingdoms where criminals go unpunished collapse in disarray and internal struggle. The tsar attempted to contrast unlimited monarchical power confirmed by God with boyar arbitrariness. Ivan rang various changes on the theme that boyars should be persecuted for disobedience and treachery, and looked for and found many reasons to proceed against the nobility. His writings paved the way for the oprichnina. The tsar lavished harsh epithets on Kurbskii and his entire clan. The fugitive boyar, as Ivan put it, made his charges "with spiteful, cur-like intent, like a barking dog, or a viper spewing forth venom." Kurbskii had incidentally threatened never again to show his face to Ivan until the Day of Judgment. The tsar retorted: "Who would want to see such an Ethiopian face? When you find a righteous man, does he have grey eyes?"[9]

The tsar's screed reached Kurbskii after the latter had fled to Lithuania and been granted large estates by the king, when his desire to conduct a polemic with Ivan had begun to wane. He composed a short argumentative reply but did not send it. From now on the quarrel with Ivan could be settled only by force of arms, and Kurbskii devoted his energies to intrigues directed against the "God's country" he had abandoned. At his advice the king stirred up the Crimean Tatars against Russia and moved forces against Polotsk. Kurbskii participated in this incursion and again crossed the Russian frontier with a Lithuanian contingent a few months later. Recently-discovered archival documents reveal that since he knew the terrain well, Kurbskii was able to surround a Russian unit, drive it into the swamps, and destroy it. This easy victory turned his head. He begged the king to give him an army of 30,000 men to capture Moscow. To allay lingering suspicions Kurbskii offered on the march to be chained to a wagon surrounded by fusiliers with loaded rifles, who could shoot him on the spot if they saw him hesitate.[10] He would ride ahead in this wagon, further surrounded by mounted men to increase his danger, to direct and guide the army which he vowed to lead to Moscow if it would but follow him. Kurbskii was compromised by his defection. Even his friends, the Pechora elders, announced they had broken with him It would soon appear whether the tsar's triumph was complete.

In Lithuania Kurbskii had reproached the tsar for indulging in lascivious conduct with Fedor Basmanov. The Basmanov family generally was loathed and despised at court; many covertly reviled its members, and at last a man expressed this view openly. A nobleman, Commander Prince Fedor Ovchinin, quarreled with Fedor Basmanov and upbraided him for his vile relationship with the tsar, and Basmanov went in tears to Ivan to relate the insult. Enraged at such impudence Ivan summoned Ovchinin to the palace and after a revel ordered him to descend to the wine cellar to conclude the festivities. The tipsy prince, failing to discern the threat contained in the ruler's words, repaired to the cellar, where he was smothered by kennelmen. Prince Fedor Ovchinin-Telepnev-Obolenskii, son of Regent Elena's famous favorite, belonged to the high nobility and had distinguished himself on the battlefield. His murder made even those loyal to the tsar protest. An informed contemporary states that the metropolitan and some boyars approached Ivan to ask him to end the carnage.

Not knowing why the metropolitan had come forward, others were disposed to explain his action in terms of the great authority Ovchinin was presumed to have exercised in Moscow, but in point of fact Ovchinin's fall was little more than an excuse for further intervention by the influential forces that earlier had changed the government's course and put an end to terror. The outwardly respectful appeal by the tsar's subjects was markedly different from Kurbskii's angry emigre philippics, but in essence it was identical. The clergy and boyar council firmly requested Ivan to stop unjustified repressions. Kurbskii's letters imply that the demand to end the executions was also meant to exclude Aleksei Basmanov, who was primarily responsible for the terror, from the government. The involvement of the latter's son in Ovchinin's murder gave the opposition an excellent opportunity to insist on removal of the hated favorite. The nobility openly condemned the tsar's cruelty: when the latter ordered Kurbskii's servant, Vasilii Shibanov, executed and his corpse exposed to instil fear, Boyar Vladimir Morozov immediately told his servitors to take up and bury the body. Ivan did not forgive Morozov; he was charged with maintaining secret relations with Kurbskii and thrown into prison.

The opposition of the boyars and higher clergy placed the tsar in a difficult position. Even those advanced after Adashev's removal to become the tsar's executors were unwilling to trust him further. One member of the future regency council, Prince P.I. Gorenskii, was commanded to leave home and report to a field army. On reaching the mustering point he attempted to flee abroad, but was overtaken at the Lithuanian frontier. Gorenskii was conveyed to Moscow in chains and speedily hanged. Ivan manifested distrust of some influential figures in the Zakharin administration and briefly placed his executor, Boyar I.P. Yakovlev-Zakharin, under arrest. Earlier Ivan had regarded the Zakharin family as the potential savior of his dynasty, but now it too had fallen under suspicion. The Zakharin administration, formed after Adashev's removal, only lasted four years. Its acknowledged head, Daniel Romanovich, died late in 1564, and its decline allowed the tsar's new favorites to appear.

The number of those advocating harsh measures against and repression of the boyar opposition was actually very small and did not include a single influential member of the boyar council, except, of course, A.D. Basmanov, whose closest coadjutors were now Afanasii Viazemskii, the energetic transport commander who had attracted the tsar's attention during the Polotsk campaign, the minor courtier Petr Zaitsev, and a few others. The protest by the metropolitan and the boyar council had isolated those who espoused the new course, but it was precisely their estrangement which aroused them to extreme measures. Without support from most of the prominent boyars and church leaders the tsar could not continue to govern the country in the usual way, and he could never cope with the mighty aristocratic opposition without the cooperation of the gentry, whose support might be acquired in two ways. The first was to increase their corporate rights and privileges by implementing the program of reform. Ivan chose the second way. He refused to become dependent upon the gentry at large and decided instead to create a separate police unit, a special bodyguard, formed from a relatively small number of genry whose members would enjoy substantial privileges, to the detriment of all the rest of the service ranks.

Traditional administrative practice in the army and chanceries, precedence, and other institutions, which guaranteed the political predominance of the boyar aristocracy, were not susceptible to reform because moves in that direction were fraught with dangerous consequences. The monarchy was simply not in a position to destroy the foundation of the nobility's political power and reorganize the gentry. The privileges accorded the tsar's bodyguard aroused great dissatisfaction among other serving men, and thus the oprichnina reform in the last analysis contributed to narrowing the social basis upon which the administration rested, and this in turn ultimately led to the use of terror as the sole means of resolving the conflict that had arisen.

Chapter Fifteen

THE OPRICHNINA DECREE

Poland-Lithuania refused to accept the loss of Polotsk and the king dispatched a large army to regain it in the fall of 1564. Russian units were transferred hastily to the northwestern frontier when the Crimean Horde, perfidiously breaking its agreement, invaded Russia. The forces stationed on the Oka river were unable to check the Tatar incursion, but Khan Devlet-Girei, deciding not to march on Moscow, turned towards Riazan, where the garrison was small and the fortifications in deplorable condition. Basmanov chanced to be in the area, after resting on his estate. He immediately raised a force, fell upon Tatar reconnaissance groups, seized their men, and entered Riazan. All the Crimeans' efforts to storm the fortress ended in failure and they quickly withdrew to the steppe. The Polish army, which had remained inactive a few miles from Polotsk, retreated across the Daugava river soon after the Tatars left Riazan. The attacks on the Russian frontiers had been repulsed, but the military situation precipitated a crisis. Moscow's inability to prevent the coalition of its most dangerous antagonists meant that it had sustained a serious diplomatic defeat and henceforward war on two fronts was inevitable. Ivan had undertaken his first campaign against Kazan fifteen years earlier, and since that time wars had occurred every year, inflicting hardship on the people and devastation on the country.

The failures in foreign policy led the tsar's counsellors to urge him vigorously to establish a dictatorship and use violence and terror to smash the opposition, but no major political decision could be taken without confirmation by the boyar council, and the known position of the council and church leaders did not augur well for the success of such an endeavor. This is the reason why the tsar was forced to perform a singular action. In an attempt to impose his will on the council of mighty feudatories he announced his abdication. He calculated that such a move would enable him to compel the council to accept proclamation of a state of emergency.

Dramatic events preceded Ivan's abdication. Early in December, 1564 the tsar's family began preparing to leave Moscow. Ivan visited churches and monasteries, where he prayed passionately. To the intense dissatisfaction of the church hierarchy he ordered venerable icons and other holy objects collected and transferred to the Kremlin. On Sunday, December 3, Ivan attended service in the Cathedral of the Dormition. At the end of the service he said a moving farewell to the metropolitan, members of the boyar council, secretaries, courtiers, and merchants. Hundreds of loaded wagons, guarded by several hundred armed courtiers, were standing in the square before the Kremlin. The royal family left the capital, taking with it the holy objects of Moscow and the state treasury. The church's resources and treasury were in a sense pawned to Ivan. His mode of departure was unprecedented. Close associates accompanying Ivan were told to bring their families. Boyars and clergy left behind in Moscow had no knowledge of the tsar's intentions and they were "filled with doubt and despair at such an unusual move by the great sovereign, and had no idea of the road he would follow."

The tsar and his entourage made their way through the environs of Moscow for several weeks until they reached the fortress of Aleksandrovskaia Sloboda. Early in January the tsar sent word to the metropolitan and council that "in great sorrow of heart" he had left his kingdom and decided to settle in the place "where God enjoins his highness."[1] During his wanderings the tsar composed a rough draft of a new will, in which he openly stated his reasons for leaving Moscow: "God's wrath has descended upon me for my many trespasses. In their imperiousness the boyars have driven me out; I have forsaken my patrimony and will wander throughout the world until God finds a place for me." The tsar's will included a long confession, filled with keen avowals of guilt. Ivan repented of innumerable sins and ended his display with pathetic words: "Although I am alive I am more vile and stinking in God's eyes for my loathsome deeds than a corpse . . . wherefore I am hateful to all."[2] The tsar himself had said what his subjects dared not utter.

Lamenting his exile in far countries, Kurbskii recently had reproached the tsar for his ingratitude: " . . .Me you have requited evil for good, and returned irreconcilable hatred for my love." Now Ivan, another exile, used the same language: "My mind is covered with scabs; my body had grown feeble; my spirit is infirm, my physical and mental scars multiply and no doctor can cure me. I expected someone to be sorry for me, but no one has been. I have found no one to console me. They have requited me evil for good and returned hatred for my love."[3] A scant few months earlier Ivan had hurled at Kurbskii proud phrases about the free Russian autocrat, but now

came the sad finale. His slaves, the boyars, had expelled God's annointed ruler from his patrimony. Abdication was no trivial matter
to a man utterly convinced of the divine origin of his power. Ivan experienced a severe nervous crisis; he lost almost all his hair, and when
he returned to Moscow from the Sloboda many had difficulty recognizing him, so greatly had he altered. His complaints that his body
had grown weak and his physical and mental scars had multiplied
were obviously not mere rhetorical exercises.

The tsar sent a courier to Moscow from the Sloboda with letters
for the council and the people. While the council members and bishops were meeting in the metropolitan's residence to hear that their
ruler had placed them under displeasure, crown secretaries assembled
large crowds in the square to inform them Ivan had abdicated. In his
proclamation the tsar asked the people not to worry, for he was not
angry with them and would not place them under displeasure.[4] By
disgracing those in power the tsar was in effect appealing to the people in his longstanding quarrel with the boyars. He spoke scathingly
of the oppression and insults the treacherous boyars had inflicted on
the populace. The boyar council of course contained opponents of
Ivan who possessed considerable influence, but the universal indigna-
tion against those declared to be traitors prevented any of them raising his voice. The crowd in the palace square increased hourly and its
attitude grew more menacing. Representatives of the commons and
merchants admitted to the metropolitan's chambers declared they
would adhere to their oath, ask the tsar to protect them from the
powerful, and were ready to deal with traitors.

The pressure of events induced the boyar council to reject Ivan's
abdication and display its loyalty. Representatives of the metropolitan and boyars lost no time repairing to the Sloboda, where the tsar
declared at an audience with the clergy that his decision was final,
until he was persuaded to yield by the tearful entreaties of his close
friend Levkii, archimandrite of the Chudov monastery, and Pimen,
archbishop of Novgorod. The leaders of the boyar council then were
admitted to the Sloboda, which looked like an armed camp, and escorted to the palace under heavy guard like prisoners of war. They
begged the tsar to lay aside his wrath and rule the country as he saw
fit.

Taube and Kruse,[5] foreigners who served in the oprichnina, report
the tsar's reply in detail. They merit no great credence as a source,
but they do reflect many themes found in Ivan's authentic epistle to
Kurbskii. He told the boyars that they had tried previously to destroy

his glorious dynasty and were ready to do so again. Ivan was obviously alluding directly to the conspiracies in support of the Staritskii interests, although he mentioned no names because he had pardoned
his cousin. As in his letter to Kurbskii, the tsar dwelt insistently on
the lawless boyar regimes that had existed during his childhood, but
made new charges that had not appeared in his epistle. He claimed
that after his father died the boyars had tried to rob him of his birth-
right and set one of the Gorbatyi-Shuiskii princes on the throne, and
now daily he had to associate with such people in conducting the
business of government. Ivan ended his tirade by charging that traitors
had murdered his wife and had tried to kill him too until God had
intervened to expose their wiles, and so he had himself been forced
to move in order to avoid imminent disaster. Those present fully
grasped the purport of the tsar's speech. The older members of the
Shuiskii clan had died long ago, except for Prince A. B. Gorbatyi,
who was the man the tsar meant when he said he was forced to meet
such people daily in council, although Gorbatyi had performed merely minor duties during the Shuiskii regency and had only become a
person of importance during Adashev's administration. This was the
cause of his downfall, and the boyar council proved unable to protect
its recognized leader.

Alleging his need to combat conspiracy, the tsar demanded that
the boyars confer exceptional powers upon him, and they humbly
consented. He kept a few of them in the Sloboda to work out details
of his agreement with the council and sent the rest back to Moscow
the same day. To split council ranks in this way was what Basmanov
and the tsar's other associates had desired. It took more than a month
to devise the statute to establish the oprichnina, but by mid-February
Ivan had returned to Moscow and gave the protocol to the boyar
council and the ecclesiastical assembly for ratification. In a speech to
the assembly Ivan said that he intended to create an oprichnina in his
realm, with its own court, army and territory, to protect his person.
He further announced he was transferring authority over the rest of
the Muscovite state (the zemshchina) to the boyar council and invest-
ing himself with unlimited powers, including the right to pronounce
official disgrace upon, execute, and confiscate the property of disobedient boyars without the advice of council. The tsar insisted that
abuse of power and other injustices must be stopped, and, paradoxi-
cally enough, this theory was one of his main arguments for the
oprichnina. The government easily obtained approval of the decree,
for the council members were bound by the oath they had sworn
during the dynastic crisis. All they now could do as loyal subjects was
to thank the tsar for his concern for the country.

The oprichnina, organized like an appanage fief, was under the tsar's personal rule and administered by its own boyar council, over which the appanage prince Mikhail Cherkasskii, the young Kabardian brother of the queen, nominally presided. In reality council decisions were taken by members of the Pleshcheev family, Boyars Aleksei Basmanov and Zakharii Uchin, the steward Fedor Basmanov, and their friends, Viazemskii and Zaitsev. The appanage utilized several of the large royal estates to furnish its court with necessary supplies, and large northern districts like Vologda, Ustiug Velikii, Vaga and Dvina, in which wealthy trading towns were located, provided its treasury with essential revenue. Financial concerns also motivated the new governmental entity to take control of major centers of the salt trade like Staraia Rus, Kargopol, Sol Galitskaia, Balakhna, and Sol Vychegodskaia. Monopoly of the salt trade soon became a valuable financial device for the oprichnina to exploit the country.

Chapter Sixteen

THE OPRICHNINA MENACE

The tsar placed the regions of Suzdal, Mozhaisk, Viazma, and some ten smaller areas in the oprichnina, and summoned the gentry inhabiting them to Moscow for examination. The oprichnina council, headed by Basmanov, questioned each man closely about his origins, his wife's antecedents, and his friends. Low-born gentry with no ties to the boyars were enrolled in the oprichnina. Aristocrats despised these new lords, calling them beggars, clumsy peasants, and vile creatures. Even the tsar, still prone to aristocratic prejudice, bitterly lamented that he was forced to hold converse with peasants and slaves. He wrote to Vasilii Griaznoi, a member of the oprichnina who later fell from favor: "For my sins it came to pass (and we cannot conceal it) that our father's princes and boyars tried to betray us and so we and you, base beings that you are, had to come together, for we desired service and righteousness from you."[1] Ivan believed an oprichnina army composed of non-noble gentry would prove a reliable instrument in his struggle with the feudal aristocratic opposition. On enrolling in the ruler's appanage each man took an oath to expose dangerous plots threatening the tsar and to inform about any evil he might discover, and he was forbidden to have anything to do with the zemshchina. These minions of the tsar wore dark clothing made of rough cloth and attached a broom to their belts, next to a quiver of arrows, a distinctive sign symbolizing their determination to sweep treason from the land. A squadron of one thousand men was formed to serve as the tsar's personal privileged bodyguard. Service in the oprichnina promised a splendid career for low-born gentry, who received grants of land, but only a comparatively small group acquired real privileges.

To ensure holdings for the members of the new oprichnina the government confiscated lands belonging to landowners in Suzdal, Mozhaisk and elsewhere who had not been accepted into it. Expulsion of nobles from districts taken into the oprichnina and confiscation of their patrimonial estates have led some historians to regard the oprichnina as a major reform mechanism. The distinguished historian S. F. Platonov asserted that when the oprichnina systematically absorbed almost all concentrations of princely lands it shattered this type of land ownership. Platonov considered the oprichnina a conscious, deliberate reform of the government, but his hypothesis has been completely disproved by Academician S. B. Veselovskii, who showed that the oprichnina was largely comprised of districts in which service-tenure landholding had developed, and where scarcely any hereditary princely patrimonial estates existed. His discovery enabled Veselovskii to assert that the oprichnina destroyed individuals but did not change the existing order and declare that to consider that the institution was directed against the great feudatories, boyars and princes, was an outmoded concept. Both Platonov's hypothesis and Veselovskii's conclusions are essentially based on analyses of the territorial composition of the oprichnina. However, the key to solving the riddle of the oprichnina cannot be found through consideration of territorial issues. The discovery of new archival material offers a different solution to the problem.

In the first days of the oprichnina Moscow witnessed brutal executions. The tsar ordered Prince Gorbatyi, his fifteen-year-old son, and his father-in-law, Associate Boyar P.P. Golovin, beheaded. The conqueror of Kazan possessed a harsh, uncompromising nature and did not hesitate to contradict the tsar. This was his basic fault, for charges concerning conspiracy seem contrived. Ivan had reason to correct the official history of his reign. The chronicles take the place of missing investigative reports implicating many prominent partisans of the Staritskii family, against whom the repressions Ivan took were comparatively mild.

Boyar Princes I.A. Kurakin and D.I. Nemoi-Obolenskii, whom the chronicle interpolations depict as leaders of a conspiracy in favor of the Staritskii family, were tonsured and shut up in a monastery. The cashiered boyar, Prince S.V. Rostovskii, who once had been sentenced to death, was seized and murdered while serving as commander of Nizhnii Novgorod. Ivan's minions brought the dead man's head to Moscow and gave it to him. Prince Ivan, brother of the boyar Yurii Kashin, who had been killed earlier, and Prince Dmitrii Shevyrev, two noble courtiers, were the oprichnina's next victims. The latter endured a painful death. He was impaled on a stake, and it is reported he died slowly. Affecting not to feel the excruciating pain he sat on the stake as though it were a throne and sang hymns, but such tales are likely legendary.

The official reports convey an impression that the chronicler was describing the first moves of the oprichnina in a summary manner, leaving much out and omitting important events. It is difficult to believe that complex activities such as organizing the separate new army, sequestrating the tsar's holdings, and so forth, were undertaken solely to remove five boyars from the council. The discussion of the oprichnina's purpose can never be settled without new data, which are hard to find when one is following a path trodden by innumerable predecessors! Success will depend upon the direction of the investigation, and the chronicle narrative suggests one approach.

The official account of the establishment of the oprichnina states that after the traitors were executed the tsar disgraced several courtiers and lesser boyars, some of whom were exiled with their wives and children to Kazan. The entry is obscure, but it raises the question of which courtiers were exiled to Kazan and what became of them. The lists of the military records office provide assistance. One of them notes: "That year (1565) the sovereign in his regal displeasure sent the Yaroslavl and Rostov princes, and many other princes and courtiers, to live in Kazan."[2] The military registers definitely state that the victims banished were not ordinary courtiers, but titled nobles, yet, like the chronicle, they too are vague.

Veselovskii was the first to analyze this question in greater detail. He identified approximately sixty exiles and saw that the overwhelming majority of them were minor court figures. This led him to the highly significant conclusion that the tsar regarded the oprichnina as a break with his court, not just boyars and princes. The results of Veselovskii's research, which he had done in 1945, were not published until 1963, and form part of his book, *Studies in the History*

Torture at the Rack. Sixteenth-century miniature. State Historical Museum, Moscow.

of the Oprichnina. Three years earlier, independently of Veselovskii, I completed my study of the Kazan exiles, based on new archival sources.[3] My discovery resulted from a fortunate and extremely simple guess that missing data should be sought in tax records, or cadastral books, rather than in literary materials, and once the goal was properly defined the archival research produced success that surpassed my wildest hopes. The cadasters of the Kazan region have been preserved in their entirety, a stroke of good luck in view of the condition of sixteenth-century archives. The first pages in the books refer to the year 1565, when the oprichnina came into existence. It soon became clear that the tsar's command to banish the disgraced courtiers to the eastern regions of the country was the circumstance that led to compilation of the Kazan cadastral books.

The Kazan cadastral books need not be considered tendentious. The scribes were very careful to observe protocol when listing the names of disgraced princes and lesser boyars, "whom the sovereign has ordered sent to his Kazan patrimony to live," and given estates on service-tenure. The cadastral books indicate that some 180 persons were banished.[4] This means the exiles were three times as numerous as Veselovskii had assumed. He did not realize that the oprichnina attacked the upper level of the aristocracy (some two-thirds of the exiles had princely titles), rather than courtiers in general.

Giles Fletcher was one of the most perceptive writers of the sixteenth century. He vividly described the means the tsar employed to undermine the power of the noble appanage princes after he formed the oprichnina. Fletcher believed that Ivan's technique was to exchange lands on service-tenure, located at considerable distances and in various parts of the country, for the princes' hereditary estates and lands, of which the tsar took control.[5] Taube and Kruse, who saw the early phase of the oprichnina, noted that its members systematically terrorized inhabitants of princely enclaves. Disgraced princes were seized and sent into exile and their families were driven from their homes. The princes had to make their way to the places to which they were banished as best they could, and since they were forbidden to take their effects with them some survived en route only through charity.[6]

The government had no wish to maintain the exiles; this was the reason for assigning them lands in their places of banishment on the eastern frontier. Associate Boyar N. V. Borisov, sent from Moscow, prepared a list of land available in the Kazan area in 1565-1566, including that belonging to Tatars, Chuvash, Mordva, and the court. The distribution of estates was carried out by local authorities, at the head of which Ivan placed the most influential and noble exiles, so that in effect the exiles assigned themselves estates in Kazan. The land made available in the Kazan and Sviiazhsk districts was inadequate to provide suitable maintenance for the disgraced courtiers. The chief commanders of the Kazan area, Boyar Princes P. A. Kurakin and A. I. Katyrev-Rostovskii, though they were granted more than some 1300 acres, obtained no more than 160 to 175 acres of arable and fallow land; the remaining princes had to be content with even smaller amounts, and several courtiers received no land at all. Twelve princes of the Gagarin family received one tiny allotment.

The cadastral surveys make it possible to draw up a roster of those exiled to Kazan with confidence, but they fail to solve the more important question, which has not been investigated, of what became of the estates that previously had belonged to the disgraced. The sources indicate the exiles received land in Kazan to compensate for, not to supplement, their former holdings. The authors of the official chronicle definitely assert that the courtiers banished to Kazan had their estates confiscated: "The ruler took the holdings of courtiers and lesser boyars who fell under his displeasure and whom he disgraced." The accuracy of the chronicle account is confirmed by original chancery documents from the period. Immediately after the introduction of the oprichnina, Assistant Secretary Maksim Trifonov confiscated the estates of the Starodub princes in Starodub and Riapolovskii in 1565.[7] He also visited the Yaroslavl district, where authentic monasterial documents of 1565 show he confiscated the hereditary estates of the Yaroslavl princes. The tsar specifically mentioned them in his will: "The patrimonies we have taken from the princes of Yaroslavl are for my son Fedor."[8] The confiscation elicited a strong protest from Kurbskii, who came from Yaroslavl: "He completely ruined the princes of the house of Yaroslavl because they possessed great patrimonies; it was for this reason he destroyed them."[9]

The Ushatyi princes, to whom Kurbskii was referring, were the richest branch of the house of Yaroslavl. Prince S. Yu. Menshoi-Ushatyi was the proprietor of an estate comprising almost 11,000 acres of land and could field 25 armed retainers. When he was exiled to Kazan all his lands passed to the treasury. The Sitskii princes, who were close relatives of Queen Anastasiia, also possessed great wealth. Prince D. Yu. Menshoi-Sitskii had an estate of some 6,000 acres, which he lost when he was banished to Kazan. The distinguished commander Prince Troekurov-Lvov, Kurbskii's associate, was sent into exile, as were A. F. Alenkin-Zheria, whose ancestors had been grand princes in Yaroslavl, brothers of the boyars Shestunov and Sitskii, seven nephews of the aged armorer Shchetinin, numerous Zasekin princes, and others. Kurbskii had reason to be angry with the oprichnina, for it had deprived some forty princely families related to him of their land when they were exiled.

The oprichnina dealt similarly with the lands belonging to the princes of Rostov. Boyar Prince A. I. Katyrev, the last representative of his line in council, his cousin, I. Yu. Khokholkov, the sons and nephews of the court boyar Yu. V. Temkin, the son of Boyar V. I. Temkin, who had served the Staritskii family, members of the Yanov family, who had been the tsar's chamberlains, eminent commanders from the Bakhteiarov-Priimkov family, members of the house of Lobanov, and others were all sent to the eastern borderlands. More than twenty Rostov princes were disgraced, and this list cannot be considered complete because data from the Cheboksarai district, which also served as a place of exile, are lacking. Shortly before establishing the oprichnina the tsar executed Boyar D. I. Khilkov, so that the Starodub princes no longer were represented in council. Soon after that the brother of Boyar Prince A. I. Strigin-Riapolovskii, three Romadanovskii princes, four Pozharskii princes, and dozens from the Kovrov, Gundurov, and Krivoborskii families were exiled to Kazan.

The information concerning the exile of several hundred princely families supplied by the cadastral registers of the Kazan region in 1565-1566 finally solves the riddle of the oprichnina. In the first place, any notion that the tsar placed only districts containing princely estates in the oprichnina definitely must be rejected. The princely holdings confiscated were not part of the territory in the oprichnina at all. The official chronicle relates that when the oprichnina was established five individuals were publicly executed. However, military activity in the oprichnina went far beyond what was necessary; the tsar could have executed these men, no matter how influential they may have been, without dividing the country and forming a special guard. The banishments to Kazan are the key to the paradox. The tsar needed his own army because he planned widespread confiscation of princely estates. The authorities understood that seizing patrimonial estates, which always was considered illegal, without hearings at which landowners might offer a defense, was bound to produce intense dissatisfaction, and they were prepared to crush the nobility's opposition by force.

There were historical reasons for the repressions undertaken by the oprichnina. When the ancient duchy of Rostov-Suzdal broke up, the princes of Suzdal, Moscow, Rostov, Yaroslavl and Starodub superseded the regional dynasty. The rise of Moscow and unification of the Russian land brought the Suzdal princes into the service of Moscow. Leaving their grand duchies and appanages, the princes came to Moscow in order to rule conjointly. These younger brothers of the Muscovite rulers, filled with envy of the ruling dynasty, formed a firm wall around the throne, and the monarchy became a captive of the aristocracy.

Ancient custom powerfully protected the nobility's privileges, and when the system began to change in the sixteenth century opposition was inevitable. The pro-gentry reforms of the 1550s failed to eliminate the influence of the Suzdal nobility. In Adashev's time the four princely houses of Suzdal, the Shuiskii, Rostovskii, Yaroslavskii and Starodubskii families, exercised enormous influence on the political course the country followed. They had the largest number of members in the boyar council (seventeen boyars and associate boyars) and as many as 265 of them served at court. Enjoying exceptional privileges, many (119) members of these four families performed service at their own recognizance. The Suzdal princes possessed powerful enclaves in the territory that formerly had been their grand or appanage duchies and continued to own a great deal of land. Unlike the small group of appanage princes mainly of Lithuanian origin, the native Suzdal nobility had strong ties with the gentry.

The Russian autocrats greatly feared the political ambitions of the Suzdal nobles and they naturally came under attack at the time Ivan was striving to acquire unlimited authority. These first repressions, which were carefully planned, showed strong animus against the princes. Banishment to Kazan was disastrous for the Suzdal nobles, and the oprichnina destroyed the old system of princely landowning. The damage was so extensive that no subsequent amnesties nor partial restoration of hereditary estates could reverse the trend.

Chapter Seventeen

THE LAND ASSEMBLY

During the second year of the oprichnina military activity declined first on the western and then on the eastern frontier of Russia. A great embassy from Poland arrived in Moscow to undertake peace negotiations. The envoys proposed a truce based on the *status quo,* but Moscow countered with a demand for the cession of the port of Riga, and the negotiations faltered. At this juncture the government urgently summoned a land assembly, composed of members of the boyar council, clergy, numerous representatives of the gentry, chancery people, and wealthy merchants, to meet in Moscow. The members of the assembly opposed making concessions in Livonia and assured the government they were prepared to make further sacrifices to achieve victory.

Land assemblies as a device to represent the various groups in society had existed long before the oprichnina, but it was an irony of fate that the first genuine representative assemblies were convoked after it came into existence. The assembly of 1566 was composed of 205 representatives of the nobility and gentry, and 43 crown secretaries and under secretaries, although none of them was elected and all had been designated by the government. The nobility exercised preponderant influence on the assembly's deliberations; in addition to members of the boyar council, almost one half the participants classified as gentry belonged to the high titled and old Muscovite nobility. The middle gentry were represented by approximately 260-270 men, but the petty provincial gentry had virtually no representation.

The reason for convoking a representative body in Moscow was the financial difficulties of the government, which wanted the zemshchina to agree to new taxes. The tsar hoped to manipulate the assembly in order to make the zemshchina assume all military expenditures and the entire burden of the Livonian war. Calculations of this sort led the government to invite leading merchants as official representatives of the third estate, but although merchants accounted for one fifth of the assembly's numbers, they were the least influential element in it. It is strange that the dark oprichnina period was conducive to the flowering of a tender plant—a representative assembly—in Russian soil, but there was a reason: the assembly was an attempt to explore possibilities for political compromise.

Long-awaited changes occurred in the spring of 1566. Executions abated and the government proclaimed that the disgraced were forgiven. Intervention by zemshchina leaders persuaded Ivan to bring Prince Mikhail Vorotynskii back from exile and restore his ancestral appanage, containing the fortified towns of Odoev and Novosil. On the first of May a courier came to Kazan to inform the exiles of the ruler's clemency; he would pardon many of the disgraced princes and gentry and generously allow them to return to Moscow. His concession was ambiguous, for the most prominent exiles were left behind. Nevertheless, the amnesty led to a fundamental change in oprichnina land policy. The treasury had to find new lands for the returning princes to replace the ancestral patrimonies they had lost, but the land available did not remotely approximate the extent of their lost patrimonies. First in individual instances and then on a larger scale the treasury restored them to their own ancestral estates, which had been neglected after the owners were sent to Kazan. In effect the authorities had been forced to abandon the policy they had instituted when the oprichnina was established. Oprichnina land policy had lost its anti-princely orientation. This circumstance may be explained by the fact that confiscation of princely patrimonies had aroused opposition among the nobility, and the monarchy possessed neither sufficient independence nor adequate force to sustain for long a policy running directly counter to the interests of the powerful aristocracy. Furthermore, the authorities believed banishment to Kazan had achieved the basic purpose of shattering the power of the Suzdal princes.

The decline of the princely nobles inevitably advanced ruling boyars who had stood one rank lower, a group including such old Muscovite boyar families as Cheliadnin, Buturlin, Zakharin, Morozov and Pleshcheev, who long had served the Muscovite court and possessed large hereditary estates around Moscow. They had once held leading positions in the boyar council but subsequently had been forced to yield them to the titled nobility. Lost in the crowd of princes, these ancient servants of the Muscovite rulers nevertheless had managed to retain such important branches of the administration as the stable and treasury chanceries, the chief revenue bureau and a number of regional bureaus, and for all practical purposes administration of the zemshchina fell to them after the oprichnina was established. Princes Belskii and Mstislavskii were the titular leaders of the zemshchina council, but actually it was controlled by the Master of Horse, I.P. Cheliadnin-Fedorov, the courtier N.R. Yurev, and the treasurers. Whenever the tsar was absent, administration of Moscow devolved upon a regency council composed of I.P. Cheliadnin, V.D. Danilov, and some other persons. The zemshchina leaders were in a difficult position, for the role the oprichnina favorites had assigned them was obviously not to their liking. The mean and petty tutelage exercised by the oprichnina council, which had established a regime of arbitrary violence in the country, was bound to lead to new conflicts between the tsar and his boyars.

The land redistribution carried out by the oprichnina had harmed the gentry holding estates in Suzdal and Viazma who were not taken into its service. They lost their lands not because they were disgraced but because their towns were reclassified. They were made to accept service-tenure holdings of equal value in regions controlled by the zemshchina, but the government did not have enough land containing peasants or effective means to compensate the gentry it uprooted for the hereditary estates its members lost. Zemshchina gentry were particularly concerned that the tsar might at any time invoke the charter and absorb new districts into the oprichnina, as this would be bound to lead to further confiscation and resettlement. The zemshchina disliked the arbitrary actions of Ivan and his supporters. A chronicler declares that after creating the oprichnina the tsar "also divided the towns and sent away many from the ones he took into the oprichnina, and from their patrimonies, and their ancient service-tenure estates . . . and there was hatred for the tsar felt by all the people."[1]

The old Muscovite boyars and leading elements in the gentry were the monarchy's strongest political supporters, so when it clashed with them, limited repression was certain to escalate into massive terrorism, but this did not yet appear likely in the spring of 1566. The decrease in executions and the concessions offered by the government encouraged the disaffected and aroused hope that the oprichnina might be abolished. Leading clergymen supported the opposition. On May 19, 1566, during the tsar's absence, Metropolitan Afanasii deliberately renounced his office and retired to the Chudov monastery.

Ivan hastened to the capital and, after conferring with the zemshchina, bestowed the office of metropolitan upon German Polev, archbishop of Kazan. The story goes that Polev took up residence in the metropolitan's palace but was there only two days. Since he opposed the oprichnina, the archbishop sought to influence the tsar, reproving him with mild and modest counsel. When the oprichnina council learned of these conversations its members insisted Polev be removed from office at once. The zemshchina and boyars were offended by the oprichnina's unceremonious intervention in church affairs. Disagreement with the ecclesiastical authorities, who enjoyed substantial influence, placed the tsar in an awkward position and forced him to make concessions in choosing a new candidate. Filipp, abbot of the Solovetskii monastery (whose secular name was Fedor Stepanovich Kolychev), a scion of a very old Muscovite noble family, who had strong ties with the boyars, was summoned to Moscow. He was a distant relative of the Master of Horse, I. P. Cheliadnin, who headed the group that at the time enjoyed substantial influence in the zemshchina, and it was apparently these people who advanced Filipp's candidacy.

Kolychev was well informed about the attitude of the zemshchina and on his arrival in Moscow soon came to understand his new situation. The zemshchina opposition acquired in him one of its most vigorous and energetic leaders. When Kolychev agreed to serve as metropolitan he categorically insisted the oprichnina be dissolved, and his conduct drove Ivan into a frenzy. The tsar might have handled Filipp as he had Archbishop German, but he hesitated to do so because he realized the clergy was greatly irritated because of Polev's dismissal. The fact that Kolychev's cousin was a member of the oprichnina council may have influenced the outcome. On July 20, 1566 Filipp was required publicly to abandon his demands, pledge not to interfere with the oprichnina or in the tsar's personal affairs, and leave the office of metropolitan under the oprichnina's jurisdiction.[2] He was confirmed soon afterwards.

Many signs indicated that Polev and Kolychev did not stand alone and that more powerful political forces were behind the church opposition. Two different sources convey the information that zemshchina serving-men asked the tsar to abolish the oprichnina after it had been in operation for a time. A Muscovite chronicle states that the tsar had brought down a curse upon his head and "they had petitioned, and tendered him a petition about the oprichnina, saying it was improper for such a thing to exist."[3] Albert Schlichting,[4] a servant of the tsar's physician, said that men of the zemshchina had gone to the tsar to protest the excesses perpetrated by his bodyguard, which had mortally affronted the zemshchina. The gentry, alluding to its members' loyal service, demanded that the oprichnina be abolished immediately. The serving-men's appeal could not lightly be dismissed: more than 300 leading members of the zemshchina had subscribed to it, including court boyars. Schlichting thought the opposition stated its case in 1566.

A well-known student of the oprichnina, P. A. Sadikov, was the first to advance the hypothesis that those invited to the land assembly in Moscow were the ones who made this protest against oprichnina excesses. The protest and the assembly occurred in the same year, and those who made it and the members of the assembly, leading elements among the zemshchina gentry, were identical. Sadikov's conjecture is justified.

Schlichting asserts the tsar rejected the intervention of the zemshchina gentry and used the extraordinary powers conferred upon him by the oprichnina statute to punish them. He incarcerated 300 petitioners, but the government could not keep the flower of Moscow's gentry locked up and released almost all the prisoners within six days. The acknowledged leaders, fifty in number, were beaten in the square. Some had their tongues cut out and three were beheaded. The three who were executed, Prince V. F. Pronskii, I. M. Karamyshev, and K. S. Bundov, had taken part in the land assembly.

The gentry's move against the government created so great a sensation that the tsar's diplomats were called upon to explain it abroad. They made the following statement about the execution of members of the land assembly: "The tsar had determined that these evil persons were wickedly plotting against the sovereign and the sovereign's realm, and the sovereign, having determined their guilt, ordered them executed."[5] This was the official position. The government considered the demand made by the zemshchina serving-men to abolish the oprichnina to be an attack on the security of the tsar and his realm.

These repressions alarmed the higher clergy, and Filipp appears to have intervened with the tsar on behalf of a majority of those who had signed the petition, who were released unharmed after a brief imprisonment. In relating this incident Schlichting conveys the valuable information that a short while later the tsar had second thoughts about the men he had released and placed them under displeasure. This action facilitates making a more precise estimate of the composition of the opposition, for soon after the assembly's dissolution many who had attended it were persecuted or executed. Boyar I. P. Cheliadnin, the Master of Horse, was one. When the oprichnina was established the Master became one of the chief leaders in the zemshchina council. Contemporaries believed the tsar considered him the wisest of the boyars, and Ivan let him govern Moscow in his absence. During the oprichnina's first year Cheliadnin presided over the council of seven that administered Moscow and later, under a mandate from the tsar, he effected an exchange of land in connection with the confiscation of the Staritskii appanage. Cheliadnin was one of the richest men of his time, but was honorable and refused to take bribes, a characteristic that endeared him to the people. His career can be traced on a monthly and even a weekly basis until the stormy dissolution of the land assembly, which decided his fate. He was removed from leadership of the zemshchina and sent to command the border fortress of Polotsk. The Polish-Lithuanian government lost no time secretly offering him refuge, and implied the tsar intended to destroy him. Cheliadnin was obviously in danger of meeting the same fate as Pronskii, Karamyshev and Bundov. Joining the appeal of the zemshchina gentry to abolish the oprichnina nearly cost him his life.

The government was dumbfounded because the zemshchina opposition was so intense and the protest emanated from loyal council members and church leaders. Their action made a deep impression on the tsar. It was not now merely the case that Ivan was unable to endure criticism; at last he was forced to realize that offering concessions had failed to stabilize the situation and the social base on which the government rested was continuing inexorably to contract.

Although efforts to find a political compromise had met with no success and hopes of reforming the oprichnina had to be abandoned, the period of compromise had a lasting effect on Russia's political development. Beset by financial difficulties, the government had invited gentry, chancery people, and even merchants, genuine popular representatives, to an assembly which initially assumed characteristics of a convention of the estates. Its members were willing to accommodate the government's wishes and approve extraordinary taxes to continue the war, but in return they asked the tsar for the political concession of abolishing the oprichnina. Their petition upset the government's calculations. New oprichnina violence put an end to further development of land assemblies.

Chapter Eighteen

DESTRUCTION OF THE ZEMSHCHINA OPPOSITION

The government rejected the appeal of the assembly members to abolish the oprichnina and set about strengthening it. Incorporating the Kostroma district the tsar carried out a muster, which brought approximately two-thirds of the local gentry into the oprichnina. The guard was raised from 1,000 to 1,500 men. The government increased the amount of territory in the oprichnina and began feverishly building blockhouses and forts in its main centers. At first Ivan intended to construct a special headquarters within the Kremlin, but later decided to move his residence to the part of Moscow that was in the oprichnina;[2] —"outside the town," in the contemporary phrase. In a year and a half a strong castle, surrounded by stone walls twenty feet high, was built near the Kremlin on the other side of the Neglinnaia river. The gate which led from it to the Kremlin was sheathed in iron and adorned with the figure of a lion, his raised paw pointing towards the zemshchina. The ramparts, decked with two-headed black eagles, constantly were patrolled by several hundred archers.

The departure of the head of state from the Kremlin gave rise to ominous rumors. To counter them the ambassadorial bureau officially announced that the tsar had built the residence for his royal relaxation. If foreigners should say that he had decided to get rid of the boyars he had disgraced, diplomats were supposed to refute such charges by stating categorically that the sovereign had no plans to get rid of anyone.[1] Ivan did not consider his fortress on the Neglinnaia a safe refuge. Ill at ease in Moscow, he created a plan to build a separate oprichnina capital in Vologda, where he thought to construct a huge fortress resembling the Kremlin. His wish was translated immediately into action. Over the next few years a main southeast wall, ten towers and an elaborate Cathedral of the Dormition inside the structure were erected. Some 300 cannon, cast in a Moscow factory, were delivered to Vologda, where they piled up in disarray. Day and night 500 fusiliers patrolled the walls. Enrolling gentry in the oprichnina army, building a castle near the Kremlin, constructing an elaborate fortress in the wooded Vologda region remote from the frontiers, and other military activities were not undertaken to strengthen the country's defenses against foreign foes. The tsar and his men feared domestic revolt and were preparing to crush the powerful zemshchina boyars if they should attempt it.

The apprehensive autocrat viewed the future with alarm. The spectre of revolt made him anxious about his personal safety and he felt obliged to explore all avenues to achieve it in the event of the real possibility he might be forced to abdicate. Ivan was strongly attracted to the idea of becoming a monk. On a pilgrimage to the Kirillov monastery he invited several elders to a remote cell, where he revealed his innermost thoughts under pledge of secrecy. Seven years later he reminded the monks of this unusual event: "Holy fathers, you must remember how once it happened that I came to your habitation and how, overcome by dark and gloomy thoughts, I discovered a small ray of God's light and told some of you, brethren, secretly to meet in one of the cells, where I too came, fleeing the disturbance and dissidence in the world. During our long conversation I, sinner that I am, informed you of my desire for tonsure; my vile heart and abandoned soul rejoiced when I found refuge in God's help for my incontinence and a haven of salvation."[2] The proud ruler fell on his knees before the abbot, who blessed his resolve. "And it seems to me, accursed as I am, I am already partially a monk." Thus the tsar ended his account of his visit to the Kirillov monastery.

To convince the monks his intentions were serious, Ivan gave them a large sum of money to prepare a special cell for him in a wall of the monastery. They did so at once, but the tsar considered even this gesture he had made to be insufficient. He decided to start preparing for monastic life without delay, and this is the source of a practice which puzzled contemporaries considered aberrant. Leaders of the oprichnina were attired in monastic habits and a monastic regimen prevailed at Aleksandrovskaia Sloboda on days not occupied with other pursuits. Returning from punitive raids the oprichnina brethren engaged in an enthusiastic parody of monastic life. Early in the morning, holding a lantern the tsar would go to the belltower, where the bellringer, Maliuta Skuratov, awaited him to ring the bells summoning the rest of the monks to church. The tsar-abbot laid a curse upon brothers who failed to appear for prayers at four in the morning. Services lasted, with a brief interruption, from four to ten o'clock. Ivan and his sons prayed earnestly and sang in the church choir. Next everyone proceeded from church to the dining room, carrying a spoon and a dish. Their abbot stood humbly beside the brethren while they ate. The men removed food they had not eaten from the table and distributed it to the poor as they left the dining room. Ivan would play the monk for several days and then return to the tasks of government. In spite of his best efforts to keep secret the substance of his discussions at the Kirillov monastery, rumors concerning the tsar's intentions reached the zemshchina, where they made a strong impression, for the monastic regimen at the Sloboda underscored their seriousness. Influential zemshchina leaders considered Ivan's tonsure the best solution to their problems, because they no longer harbored any illusion that the oprichnina would be abolished unless Ivan ceased to rule.

The Lithuanians were preparing for a new campaign against Russia. They had no hope of winning on the battlefield, but counted on taking advantage of the domestic difficulties in Muscovy. Informed that hostility between oprichnina and zemshchina was intensifying, they attempted further to arouse disaffection by directing secret appeals to the zemshchina leaders Cheliadnin, Belskii, Mstislavskii and Vorotynskii. The tsar had spared Vorotynskii's life but had imprisoned him. He had just regained his freedom, and so the Lithuanians had high hopes he might lead an armed uprising. The king promised to send armies to help and allow Vorotynskii to control any territory he might wrest from the tsar. To hasten the process the king sent an old retainer of the Vorotynskii family, who earlier had fled to Lithuania, to reconnoitre. He had no difficulty reaching Polotsk, which Cheliadnin commanded, and the spy transmitted the king's letters to him. The Lithuanians had planned meticulously for an armed uprising, but the intrigue depended upon a successful outcome of their secret negotiations with the Master of Horse. Whether Cheliadnin would use his great authority to win over other zemshchina leaders, or refuse to take part in the affair and hand the spy over to the government would determine the future course of events.

The commander of the border fortress could easily escape to Lithuania, as the king earnestly urged Cheliadnin to do, but the latter, unwilling to follow Kurbskii's example, surrendered the spy, apparently in person. When Ivan learned of the arrest he left Vologda for Moscow to investigate. His inquiry revealed that no grounds existed to charge the boyars with treason. Two months later the tsar assured Jenkinson, the English ambassador, that at first he had been furious with the boyars but later decided to ignore the intrigues of the Polish king, who was merely trying to arouse suspicion and cause a charge of treason to be brought against the tsar's servitors. Ivan had reason to believe Kurbskii was responsible for the letters. The polemical exchange with Kurbskii, that had greatly aroused the tsar before he set up the oprichnina, had ended, but this affair afforded an opportunity to revive the quarrel, and the tsar had no intention of overlooking it. He ordered the boyars to reply to the secret Lithuanian overtures and apparently told them how they should compose their letters, which reflected the tsar's favorite ideas about the descent of the Muscovite dynasty from Caesar Augustus and the divine nature of the autocratic power possessed by Muscovite sovereigns, who succeeded to the throne and were not elected to it. The chief boyars pretended to accept Lithuanian citizenship and ironically proposed to divide Lithuania up among themselves, so that they and the king might eventually come under the control of the great sovereign, who ruled independly as tsar and autocrat, and Ivan Vasilevich could protect all of them from the Turks and Tatars. Cheliadnin was the only one who composed and signed his letter without the tsar's help. Avoiding the offensive phrases in which the letters of the other boyars abounded, the master sarcastically mocked the Lithuanian nobles for trying to meddle in Russian affairs: "You nobles are not capable of ruling your tiny domain, to say nothing of the Muscovite tsardom."[3]

Apparently not satisfied with a mere exchange of letters, Ivan decided to send the spy back to Lithuania to communicate verbally the abuse the letters could not contain, but he was not fated to return, for the Lithuanians made a desperate attack and routed forces commanded by Petr Serebrianyi 40 miles from Polotsk. The defeat produced a painful reaction in Moscow, and the arrogance pervading the letters the boyars had supposedly written vanished. The tsar lost interest in hostile exchanges with the king, put down his pen, and reached for his sword to chastise his neighbor. He never sent the harsh replies, and the spy was impaled on a stake.

The oprichnina council reverted to its previous violent mode of governance, but showed vacillation and hesitation. The incautious and ambiguous statements the tsar had made in the Kirillov monastery were discussed widely in the zemshchina and encouraged the opposition. Everyone remembered Ivan's first abdication, so now the principal question agitating the zemshchina was who would ascend the throne if the tsar became a monk. The opposition had no wish to see young Ivan, the heir, thirteen years old, mount the throne, for then his father would be free to reassert control at any time. The person with the strongest claim next to the heir was Vladimir Andreevich, grandson of Ivan III. The boyars considered this weak, obtuse individual an acceptable candidate, calculating that under him they could regain the influence they previously had enjoyed in affairs of state.

Ivan had never trusted his cousin and had done all he could to guard against his intrigues. He had confined Vladimir's ambitious and energetic mother, Princess Evfrosiniia, to a nunnery, appointed boyars who were above suspicion to serve in Vladimir's appanage, and finally deprived his cousin of his ancestral seat in Staritsa, exchanging it for Dmitrov and a few other towns. Evfrosiniia's relatives were expelled from the boyar council. One, Boyar P. M. Shcheniatev, entered a monastery but was removed from it and roasted to death in a large iron pan. Boyar Ivan Kurakin was tonsured, and Petr Kurakin sent to the eastern borderlands. The chronicle interpolations took pains to designate these boyars as vigorous abettors of the conspiracies fomented by the Staritskii family.

These persecutions eliminated the Staritskii faction from the council, and the support of his personal faction was not enough for Prince Vladimir to become tsar. Now more than ever the fate of the country depended upon the powerful boyars who led the zemshchina. Whenever an interregnum occurred, the administration devolved upon the boyar council, over which the masters of horse, its senior representatives, presided. Tradition assigned the masters the role of guardian until a new sovereign mounted the throne. The split between tsar and boyars and the rumors that Ivan might become a monk obviously aroused fears of a dynastic crisis, when the master, Cheliadnin-Fedorov, would be the central figure in the struggle. Sympathizers kept Ivan informed of zemshchina attitudes and the hostile remarks circulating in council. The tsar subsequently inserted into the chronicle a detailed narrative about the boyar conspiracy on behalf of Prince Vladimir, ending with the significant sentence: "And thence great enmity arose between the sovereign and Prince Vladimir Andreevich, and turbulence and dissent among the boyars, and the tsardom grew wasted."[4] The turbulence and dissent among the boyars became more menacing after the land assembly. The danger of revolt was genuine, for the oprichnina had provoked universal discontent.

Rumors about a zemshchina conspiracy seriously alarmed Ivan, who contemplated flight with his family. He had formulated such plans before, but now he acted. Early in September, 1567 he summoned Jenkinson to the palace. The meeting took place in great secrecy; the ambassador came attired in Russian dress and was conducted to the royal apartments through a secret passage. Afanasii Viazemskii was the sole counsellor present. What the tsar asked Jenkinson to communicate to the English queen was unprecedented; hence, severe restrictions were placed on the way in which it was to be divulged. The ambassador was forbidden to take notes and Ivan requested him to memorize secret issues of great import, which he should impart to the queen by word of mouth only, but Jenkinson disobeyed instructions and compiled a written account of his discussion after he returned to London. According to his report the tsar asked the queen to provide him with a refuge in England "to save himself and his family . . . until the danger was over; God will not dispose otherwise."[5] Refusing to compromise his dignity Ivan insisted that the agreement should be reciprocal, but the diplomatic formula deceived no one. A few years later the tsar reminded the English of his appeal, which, he said, was occasioned by his genuine apprehension concerning the mutable and dangerous position of rulers, who were as much exposed to the winds of change as their humblest subjects.

The negotiations with the English court could not remain secret for long. English merchants made frequent journies to Russia and rumors were bound to reach Moscow, which assumed fantastic forms in the provinces. The Pskov chronicler wrote that a certain evil warlock, an English heretic, told the tsar to slay all the boyars and flee to England.[6] Ivan's pusillanimity alarmed members of the oprichnina, who knew what would happen to them if the ruler should flee. Serving-men, who longed for abolition of the oprichnina, were anxious to believe the rumors were true.

Ivan was also busy with military preparations. Early in autumn he mustered the zemshchina and oprichnina forces for another invasion of Livonia, but the campaign barely had begun when he abruptly cancelled it, left the army and returned precipitately to Moscow. His hasty departure was occasioned by a report that a conspiracy had formed in the zemshchina, the information about which is confusing and contradictory. Many contemporaries had heard of it, but only two, Staden[7] and Schlichting, were actual witnesses.

For some years Staden served as an interpreter in one of the chanceries, knew personally, and enjoyed the favor of the Master of Horse, Cheliadnin, the chief conspirator; thus, his statements concerning the attitude of zemshchina leaders must be accepted. Staden claims they had lost patience, decided to elect Prince Vladimir Andreevich to the throne, eliminate the tsar and his men, and sealed their covenant by a special document. However, it was Prince Vladimir himself who informed the tsar about the conspiracy and told him of the zemshchina leaders' plans and dispositions. Schlichting also worked as an interpreter, not in a chancery, but for the tsar's personal physician. He and his master used to visit the oprichnina court and Schlichting translated conversations the doctor had with Afanasii Viazemskii, who was directly responsible for investigating the conspiracy. Schlichting knew a great deal, but after twice alluding to the conspiracy he offered two opposing and mutually exclusive versions of events. In his *News from Muscovy* he portrayed Cheliadnin as a wicked conspirator, but in his more detailed *Narrative* said the master, who never thought a base thought, had been the victim of a tyrant.

Depending upon their conception of the oprichnina, historians have utilized Schlichting's account to support one or the other version. Which should be considered more reliable can be determined only by inquiring into the circumstances surrounding Schlichting's decision to set down his narratives. He composed the *News* as soon as he crossed the Lithuanian border, mentioning facts he knew which he thought were important; hence, this is a valuable source. He wrote the *Narrative* later at the express instance of the Polish government. After scrutinizing Schlichting's observations about Muscovite affairs the king's officials decided they would be useful for diplomatic forays against Russia. The pope had sent an envoy to urge the tsar to attack the Turks. Detaining the papal legate in Warsaw, the king gave him Schlichting's *Narrative* in an effort to stop him from proceeding to Moscow. The pamphlet then was transmitted to Rome, where it produced a marked impression. The pope at once ordered diplomatic ties with the tyrant of Muscovy severed, and Schlichting's work, subsidized by Polish gold, achieved its purpose. Responding to the instructions he had received, Schlichting vilified the tsar and indulged in open calumny. The *Narrative* deliberately falsified what Schlichting knew of Cheliadnin's conspiracy, but, refusing to sacrifice the truth entirely, Schlichting drew attention to his falsehoods in a way those without special knowledge would fail to grasp. When describing the sack of Novgorod he parenthetically made the remarkable observa- tion: "And if the Polish king had not withdrawn from Radoshkovich and ended the war, all would have been up with the tyrant's life and power." This statement has nothing to do with the Novogorod cam- paign and refers to Cheliadnin's conspiracy. The tsar called off the Livonian campaign and the armies dispersed at the moment when the king went to Radoshkovich and was waiting for the conspirators to hand over the tsar. These words prove that even in the *Narrative* Schlichting preserved his original version of a zemshchina conspiracy.

Historians long have wanted to know whether the conspiracies that caused the oprichnina to resort to terror were fictitious or genu- ine. Now it has been shown that two contemporary witnesses testi- fied that one conspiracy was real. Should their views be accepted? Should not the sources they used first be determined? The answer is not difficult. Schlichting and Staden served in the oprichnina and obtained their information from people connected with it, whose semi-official outlook was colored and biased. The opposite view is found in unofficial chronicles of zemshchina origin. Unlike members of the oprichnina, their authors insisted no conspiracy existed in the zemshchina, whose members' sole fault was to have made unguarded remarks. The disaffected were disposed favorably towards Prince Vladimir Andreevich; malicious persons relayed their observations to the tsar, and they perished "though they were guilty of no more than words."

No one will ever determine where dissent ends and conspiracy be- gins. An historian can do no more than make a tentative reconstruc- tion of events. The zemshchina was unquestionably disaffected. Its dissatisfied members had exhausted all legal means to combat the oprichnina, and the persecutions had convinced them the tsar had no intention of abolishing the institution. Ivan's opponents next moved to discussing his removal from office, and eventually they were bound to include Prince Vladimir Andreevich in their plans, since he was the sole candidate possessing a legal right to the throne. Feeling compro- mised, the latter naturally gave information in an effort to save him- self. During the Livonian campaign he told the tsar about conversa- tions disaffected boyars had held in his presence. Ivan believed they implied a direct threat to him and portended the outbreak of the boyar revolt he had long feared and expected. Prince Vladimir's com- munication was probably imprecise, and constituted inadequate grounds to bring Cheliadnin to trial. The master was very popular in the council and the capital, and thus Ivan made no move to execute him for a year after the conspiracy was uncovered.

Lacking proof, the tsar tried to provoke the conspirators. He told Prince Vladimir to visit the unsuspecting Cheliadnin and ask him in a friendly way to draw up a roster of men whose support he could count on. The master listed thirty persons who had been striving to place Vladimir on the throne. The operation was conducted in great secrecy and no one apprehended danger. After cunningly unmasking the dissenters in this way Ivan decided to eradicate the conspiracy. His aides forced Cheliadnin to pay an enormous sum of money, exiled him to Kolomna, and executed many of his associates on the spot, thereby inaugurating a reign of terror by the oprichnina which lasted three years. Muscovite chronicles fell silent. Ivan had rough drafts of them conveyed to Aleksandrovskaia Sloboda and apparently never returned them to the ambassadorial bureau. A long cultural tradition thus came to an end. The oprichnina destroyed the institution of chronicle-writing in Russia.

Chapter Nineteen

TERROR

Few credible details have survived from the next dark period of the oprichnina, and historians must rely on tendentious memoirs and reports by foreigners, the best-informed of whom served in the oprichnina before fleeing abroad, where they tried to enhance their reputations by elaborating projects to destroy barbarous Muscovy and frighten readers with tales about the evil deeds of the tyrant of Muscovy. The dearth of native sources renders it difficult to criticize tales told by foreigners.

The destruction of the oprichnina archives also has complicated study of the period of the terror, although traces may be found in a few contemporary documents, above all in one of the most complex sixteenth-century sources, the *synodical,* or memorial list of the executed, which Ivan ordered compiled towards the end of his life. The synodical has long intrigued historians, but until Veselovskii no one had analyzed it systematically as a source. Veselovskii elucidated its origin and demonstrated its historical value. He proved that the surviving lists were based on an official register a chancery had compiled from authentic court records and testimony by members of the oprichnina. Secretaries carrying out the tsar's behest followed available sources closely and made no insertions or alterations of their own. Veselovskii took the first step towards explaining the synodical, but he failed to follow his research to its logical conclusion. In order to validate the source, an original text, as close as possible to its original, had to be established, but this task was fraught with difficulty. Unable to solve the problem, Veselovskii abandoned his efforts to establish such a text and arranged the list of disgraced persons in alphabetical order. Thus revised, the document was no longer an historical source and the puzzles it contained remained unresolved, so that Veselovskii's overall estimate of the synodical was not an advance over that of his predecessors. He wrote: "The surviving synodical lists contain neither a chronological nor a complete list of those executed; they incompletely enumerate persons who perished during the period when executions took place, which lasted more than fifteen years. The list was not made at the time when events occurred, but was subsequently drawn up in haste from different sources." Veselovskii's assertion that the synodical was incomplete and haphazard obviously contradicts his conclusion that it was based on original sources.

Since historiographical analysis is impossible without a dependable text, I undertook the complex task of reconstructing the synodical. The extant texts differ greatly from one another, and this presents a serious textological problem. The history of the synodical's compilation is briefly as follows: shortly before he died the tsar ordered monks to pray eternally for all those he had executed. He decided to forgive them, although heretofore even their names had been consigned to oblivion and it had been strictly forbidden for many years to mention them. Acting on Ivan's orders, secretaries went to the archives and drew up a detailed list of the slain, copies of which then were distributed to all monasteries. The monasteries entered names of the disgraced in their own synodicals from this chancery list, which was known as the sovereign's book, or royal rescript. No original sovereign's book of the 1580s has survived, or, at any rate, has been found. Surviving monastery records resemble the chancery list only remotely. The monks made no effort to copy the sovereign's book closely. It was of little use for memorial purposes, because the secretaries working on archival documents seldom found the Christian names of the slain, but church rules required people to be remembered to have names. Nevertheless, fearing the tsar's wrath the monks prayed for them, reinforcing their prayers with references to omnipresent God: "O Lord, remember 1505 persons. Their names, O Lord, Thou Thyself knowest." Most often the elders simply listed forenames of the disgraced in their commemorative books, omitting surnames and irrelevant details of their execution.

Monastery synodicals soon wore out from extensive use. Names were erased; wax from candles damaged the text, and pages were confused and lost. Those rendered unfit for use were recopied, when they were abbreviated further and distorted. As the dread days of the oprichnina receded into the past monks showed less enthusiasm for copying old synodicals than they had while Ivan was alive. Archival research has turned up a few lists not known to Veselovskii; at present some fifteen copies are extant. The bulk of them comes from the seventeenth century and later copies exist, belonging to the eighteenth and nineteenth centuries. Only one goes back to Ivan's reign.

The Nizhegorod-Pechorskii monastery compiled a commemorative book in 1552 and kept supplementing it until Ivan died. The names of the disgraced were recorded on its last pages, but the monk who transcribed the royal rescript merely listed names and numbers of the disgraced, omitting virtually all other details. As a result, this synodical initially appeared to be no more than a monotonous enumeration of people known to God ("Remember, O Lord, Ivan, Petr, Anna, Semen," etc.), useless for historical research. However, it was the Pechorskii list that enabled me to reconstruct the original synodical, for it accurately reflected the sequence of names of the disgraced that had been copied from the lost royal rescript of the 1580s. Using it as a guide I managed to reconstruct the other monastery texts. In each of them I had to locate an essential sequence of "Ivan, Maksim, Semen," etc. (to take one example) among thousands of names in order to restore the original order, after I had identified these fragments of the shattered and confused mosaic. To recognize and replace transposed pages required only patience and care, but it proved no mean task to read some of the synodicals I had thus restored.

The greatest discrepancies in all the lists were found in three from the Bogoiavlenskii monastery in Moscow, where the sequence of names was entirely different from that in the Pechorskii and other synodicals, and the Bogoiavlenskii lists could not be ignored, because they contained far more surnames of the disgraced than any others. I was able to take advantage of these unique synodicals after I had determined the method the copyist had used. When copying the monk divided the text into units, perhaps corresponding to individual pages in the synodical. He selectively transcribed names of the disgraced from each unit, returned to the start of the section, and copied all the remaining names. A schematic construction of the Bogoiavlenskii lists looks like this:

Pechorskii list	Bogoiavlenskii list
A B V G D E Zh	1) A B D Zh Z L
Z I K L M	2) V G E I L M

Each unit preserved a sequence of names in abbreviated form. Copies made in the seventeenth and eighteenth centuries contained misplaced pages, which further confused the names, but once a pattern emerged the text of the Bogoiavlenskii synodicals could be established.

It was a long time before all the thousands of the disgraced were entered properly in these thick ledgers. Reconstructed texts of these lists were entered in two parallel columns, and when compared, it became clear that a single royal rescript formed the basis for all of them. The lists abounded in errors, but since each transcriber made his own, it was possible to correct them. This was the work I did in order to reestablish Ivan's original chancery list of disgraced persons.

The reconstructed text permits important conclusions to be drawn about the primary source. Contrary to Veselovskii's view, it becomes clear that the chancery list recorded the disgraced in chronological order. The first pages contain those who perished late in 1567, the month of March, July 6, and September 11, 1568, and January, April, and October, 1569, January, 1570, and so forth. Such a sequence at first appears incomprehensible, but an explanation can be found. In the archives the secretaries, fearing to be thought derelict in the task the tsar had enjoined upon them, wrote down the names of those executed in sequence from trial records and reports by members of the oprichnina. Whether the lists the secretaries compiled contained all the names, and in sequence, depended upon how fully the records were kept and how systematically they utilized them. Proceeding from one document to another they listed the disgraced in the order they were mentioned at the trials. The reconstructed synodical shows that its compilers conscientiously studied the data concerning the conspiracy involving Prince Vladimir Andreevich, the main political trial held during the period of the terror, which lasted three years (1567-1570) and provided nine-tenths of the names in the synodical. Ivan's supporters executed approximately 3200 of the 3300 persons listed in the synodical over the Staritskii affair.

Material on the first wave of executions in 1565, the Staritskii affair, and the second appearance of the oprichnina in 1575 was kept in proper order in the archive. Records of executions that took place before and after the time of the oprichnina apparently have been lost or, at any rate, the secretaries did not use them in preparing the chancery list. The synodical makes no reference to the execution of D. F. Adashev (1563), M. I. Vorotynskii (1573), and a few others, but these omissions are not major. Veselovskii's conclusions notwithstanding, the chancery list was surprisingly complete, especially for the epoch of the terror. The chancery people who industriously excerpted the trial records never thought the archives would be destroyed and their summaries would prove of priceless value to historians. The reconstructed chancery list is truly a chronicle written in blood, which accurately and impartially described the activity of the oprichnina day after day, and month after month. The disputes about the aims and results of the terror that have lasted for ages will soon no longer be necessary.

The tsar, anxious to justify the inglorious conclusion of the Livonian campaign of late 1567, gave problems in the transportation corps, which failed to deliver cannon to the frontier on time, as the reason for cancelling it. The corps was commanded by a treasury secretary, Kazarin Dubrovskii, who was notorious for taking bribes. The tsar heard complaints against him, and Dubrovskii was convicted and executed. The synodical accords him the following entry: "Kazarin Dubrovskii, and his two sons, and ten men who came to his aid."[1] Ivan next attacked the nobles against whom Prince Vladimir Andreevich had laid information. His men slew one of the prince's uncles and some others. The uncle must have been incautious enough to hint that power might pass to his nephew.

The higher clergy sharply protested the new round of executions. Metropolitan Filipp visited the tsar and conversed at length with him privately. Convinced it was fruitless to intercede, he waited until Ivan and his entourage attended service in the Cathedral of the Dormition in the Kremlin, at which before a large assemblage he called for abolition of the oprichnina. The Novgorod chronicler described the situation briefly but accurately: "On March 22, 1568, Metropolitan Filipp quarrelled with the sovereign in Moscow about the oprichnina."[2] The quarrel shattered the decorum of the service and its outcome was disagreeable for Ivan. Without waiting for the metropolitan's blessing the tsar dashed his staff on the ground and threatened him and the zemshchina with harsh punishment, supposedly saying: "I

have been too lenient with you, but now you are my enemies."[3]
Next day all Moscow was talking of the confrontation between the
tsar and the metropolitan. The church enjoyed great authority in the
government and with the turbulent lower classes. By stirring up fanatical monks and holy fools the church astutely played upon popular
sentiment, and the people were already agitated by the incident.
Filipp's protest showed that the tsar had lost all prestige in the zemshchina, and his acolytes strongly urged him to activate the terror machine, for any sign of vacillation might have disastrous results, in view
of the severe domestic crisis that now existed.

Filipp had broken his oath not to interfere with the oprichnina,
which was bound to provoke reprisal. Ivan's minions attacked boyars
in the metropolitan's service and beat them to death with iron rods
as they led them through the streets of Moscow, a fact the synodical
reflects by recording the names of such elders as Leontii Rusinov,
Nikita Opukhtin, and others. In addition to the metropolitan's counsellors, the synodical also lists close associates and servitors of Cheliadnin, the Master of Horse. The dispute with the metropolitan obviously had aroused Ivan to issue orders he had long held in readiness
to proceed against the conspirators.

The official version holds that Cheliadnin was planning a revolt,
aided by his numerous servitors and tributaries, who supposedly knew
his plans. Ivan's henchmen naturally were merciless in destroying the
master's armed retainers and other supporters. The tsar's guard made
several punitive raids on Cheliadnin's estates, and the synodical registers provide a detailed picture of these sweeps. Maliuta Skuratov ravaged the estates Cheliadnin owned near Moscow. The services this
brutal man rendered were appreciated; this action was the beginning
of his swift rise through the ranks of the oprichnina. Once Cheliadnin's
central estates were destroyed the attack spread to those he owned
on the periphery. One of the wealthiest men of his time, the master
owned huge tracts of land in Bezhetskii Verkh, near Tver, where the
tsar went in person with the entire oprichnina army, razed Cheliadnin's residence, slew his retainers, herded the rest of his servants
and domestics into a hut, and blew them up. The synodical entry on
these executions laconically runs: "In Bezhetskii Verkh 65 of Ivan's
(Cheliadnin) men were dispatched, together with twelve who died
when their hands were cut off." The sack lasted several months, from
March into July. That summer Ivan's men supplied a distinctive account of how they had spent their time after the conspiracy was discovered. The synodical reads: "369 persons have been dispatched, all

of them by the sixth of July."⁴ Some 300 of the slain were Cheliadnin's servants and slaves, who perished during the raid on the master's estates.

The prolonged bloodbath exacerbated the conflict between the
tsar and the church. Following Metropolitan Afanasii's example, Filipp abandoned his residence in the Kremlin and ostentatiously moved
to a monastery in the capital, but unlike his feeble predecessor, refused to lay down his office. The open quarrel with the head of the
church put Ivan in a difficult position. He withdrew to Aleksandrovskaia Sloboda, where he busied himself preparing a case against Filipp.
His associates immediately summoned Archbishop Pimen, a close
supporter of the tsar, from Novgorod, and sent a special commission
composed of oprichnina members and churchmen to Solovki. The
commission investigated Filipp's conduct at the Solovetskii monastery
and by using threats and bribery forced a few monks to make deposi-
tions damaging to their former abbot. The testimony the commission
extracted was so suspect that Bishop Pafnutii, its most influential
member, refused to sign the report. Pafnutii's opposition threatened
to abort Filipp's trial, leaving the outcome in the hands of the boyar
council, many of whose members sympathized with the metropol-
tan.

As the conflict entered a critical phase Ivan decided to strike
first at the council. On September 11, 1568 executions recorded in
the synodical were carried out in Moscow: "Slain. Ivan Petrovich
Fedorov. Mikhail Kolychev and his three sons slain in Moscow. Prince
Andrei Katyrev, Prince Fedor Troekurov, Mikhail Lykov and nephew,
slain in various towns." These executions of council members, mentioned in the synodical, were almost as numerous as the first wave
had been. The senior boyar in council, I. P. Cheliadnin-Fedorov, Associate Boyars M. I. Kolychev and M. M. Lykov, and Boyar Prince
A. I. Katyrev-Rostovskii all mounted the scaffold simultaneously.
Eradicating Cheliadnin's conspiracy caused greater loss of life than
had occurred during the first months the oprichnina had existed. The
synodical reveals that as many as 150 noblemen and chancery people
and double the number of their servants and slaves perished with the
master. The arrests followed no consistent pattern. Cheliadnin's
friends and acquaintances, surviving partisans of Adashev, relatives of
noblemen who had fled abroad and the like, as well as anyone daring
to protest the oprichnina, were all apprehended indiscriminately.
Many of the disaffected refused to remain silent. M. S. Mitnev, a

nobleman listed in the synodical, attended a party at the palace and boldly reproached the tsar to his face: "Accursed tsar, in truth you make us drink mead mixed with the blood of our brothers, which you are drinking."[5] Ivan's henchmen killed him on the spot. Mitnev, from Viazma, had reason to protest. He had been banished from his district and deprived of his estates when the oprichnina was established.

Besides the nobles who were transferred, those exiled to Kazan, who were ruined when their patrimonial estates were confiscated, also voiced the dissatisfaction. Amnesty was now out of the question; some princes pardoned earlier were put to death, including Boyar A. I. Katyrev, three members of the Khokholkov family, F. I. Troekurov, D. V. Ushatyi, and D. Yu. Sitskii. But the execution of princes seemed to be an after-thought; the majority so treated belonged to the non-titled nobility.

The leading figures convicted at the trial of the zemshchina conspirators were members of the noblest old Muscovite non-titled houses: the Cheliadnin, Kolychev, Shein-Morozov, Saburov, and Karpov families, Fedor Danilov, Kh. Yu. Tiutin, a treasurer, several prominent crown secretaries, and B. N. Borisov, B. I. Kolychev, and F. R. Obraztsov, former Staritskii retainers. It is impossible to believe that all the men who were executed had been part of one conspiracy. The original Staritskii partisans mentioned in the chronicle interpolations were no longer politically active, and the chronicle accounts show that Cheliadnin opposed Prince Vladimir in 1553 and had been instrumental in exposing his initial conspiracy. Associate Boyar M. I. Kolychev, who also had demonstrated his loyalty at the time of the Staritskii affair, had been specially chosen to keep watch on Evfrosiniia in the Goritskii nunnery after she took the veil.

The charges alleging relations with the contentious Prince Vladimir were actually mere pretexts for attacking the powerful boyars who were genuinely able to oppose the oprichnina. The authorities used torture to make the false charges stick. They compelled those arrested to name their associates, and men so indicted were executed without trial, except for I. P. Cheliadnin and M. I. Kolychev, who were found guilty after a quick hearing. The tsar summoned council members and Moscow nobles to a public room in the great Kremlin palace and had the accused brought before him. He ordered Cheliadnin to array himself in royal robes and sit on the throne. Bending his knee, Ivan ironically mocked the unfortunate man: "You desired to take my place; now you are grand prince. Rejoice in the dominion you craved."[6] At a given signal his minions killed the master, dragged his body from the palace, and threw it into a ditch. The farce of pretending Cheliadnin had intrigued to acquire the crown showed that Ivan's government had failed to prove its charges against the master. His principal associates, M. M. Lykov, commander of Narva, Katyrev, commander of Sviiazhsk, and Troekurov, commander of Kazan, were executed without semblance of trial. The investigation was conducted in strict secrecy and the death sentences were not carried out in the prescribed manner, as might have been expected. The condemned were slain in their homes or on the street, and a short note was left on the body to bring the conspirators' crimes to general attention.

Cheliadnin's fall sealed Filipp's fate. The investigative commission returned from Solovki and presented evidence to the boyars to substantiate a charge that the metropolitan had led a corrupt life. The opposition in the council no longer had a leader and no one ventured openly to express doubts. Obedient to the tsar's will, the council agreed to try the leader of the church. To frighten the metropolitan Ivan sent the head of his cousin, Associate Boyar M. I. Kolychev, sewn up in a leather bag, to Filipp's monastery. Filipp was tried by the council and higher clergy. The chief witness against him was Paisii, abbot of Solovki and Filipp's former pupil, who had been promised the rank of bishop for his treachery. Filipp denied all the allegations and sought to curtail his trial by proclaiming his intention to resign his office voluntarily, but the tsar refused to allow him to do so. Ivan had not forgotten the insults he had endured and wanted to humiliate the disgraced head of the church publicly. Filipp was forced to hold service after the court had passed sentence upon him, and members of the oprichnina burst into the Cathedral of the Dormition in the middle of it, where, to everyone's embarrassment Basmanov read out the council verdict, which found the metropolitan guilty. Filipp was stripped of his cowl and mantle, thrown into a sleigh, and carted off to Bogoiavlenskii monastery. Since Filipp had been convicted of turpitude, church law provided that he might be burnt at the stake, but Ivan commuted his sentence to perpetual confinement in a monastery.[7]

The disaffected in the zemshchina fell silent, and gloom overspread the realm. The conspirators, and anyone suspected of sympathizing with them, had been severely punished. The oprichnina leaders were triumphant. However, the events that occurred next showed that their triumph was premature. Within a year the terror, as it intensified, had swallowed up both the opponents of the oprichnina and those who were intimately associated with it.

Chapter Twenty

ONSET OF RUIN

For twenty years, ever since the first campaigns against Kazan, Russia had been chronically at war. The gentry was constantly under arms, and landholders had to appear for campaign with horses, men and weapons. Such service required large financial outlays, and the gentry had somehow to recoup its losses. Its members acquired land for tillage, which they worked with slave labor, while increasing their exactions from the peasantry. The Novgorod subservience charters strikingly illustrate the change in the peasants' status. Composed in the tsar's name, they required peasants to obey their landlords. Early charters had directed peasants to hearken to their landlords "in everything, and furnish them as of old with money, grain, and the small things you used to give your landlords in the past." In time the subservience charters assumed a new form: "And all you peasants must obey your landlord, plough the land he holds, or pay the quitrent he lays upon you."[1] Some scholars have claimed that the introduction of oprichnina practices into Novgorod was the cause of the change in the formula in the subservience charters, but the new formula had appeared long before the oprichnina was established there; it merely reflected the new conditions which had developed. Ever since the Kazan campaigns landlords everywhere had been revising and raising quitrent.

Alarmed by the growing rural decay the government frequently sent officials to different sections of the Novgorod region to make inspections and conduct investigations. They carefully recorded the population's views, which unanimously reflected the peasants' complaints about the unbearable and ruinously high taxes. During the boyar regimes the Novgorod peasants had paid low imposts and rendered the state all sorts of services in kind. After the wars with Kazan and Livonia started, the state often raised the taxes levied on the peasants. The increased tax burden, combined with exploitation by landlords, had a disastrous impact on small peasant farming, although taxes were not the only cause of the rural decline which set in during the 1570s and 1580s. Great natural disasters ravaged the country three years in a row and caused catastrophe. Bad weather in 1568 and 1569 twice ruined the harvests. The price of bread rose five or ten times by early 1570 and famine stalked towns and villages. When the oprichnina sacked Novgorod, on bitterly cold winter nights the starving citizens stole and ate the bodies of the slain, sometimes salting the flesh in barrels. Witnesses testified that twice as many people died of starvation in Tver as had died in the sack. The same was true of Novgorod.

A plague, coming from the West, broke out on the heels of the famine and was reported in eighteen towns by fall, 1570. The epidemic carried off 600 to 1,000 people a day in Moscow. In early fall the people of Novgorod gathered up and buried 10,000 corpses in common graves. Plague spread to the remote northern and eastern borderlands, attacking Vologda and Ustiug. A local chronicler wrote: "12,000 are said to have died in the town quarter of Ustiug, apart from visitors, and only six priests are left in the quarter."[2] The plague lasted a whole year, and the authorities took draconian measures to arrest it. Military checkpoints were set up on highways and all attempting to leave infected areas were seized and burned in large bonfires, along with their goods, horses and wagons. In the towns patrols walled up infected houses containing corpses and healthy persons alike, but none of these measures had much effect.

Hundreds of thousands died during the three-year famine and the plague, and murderous Tatar raids completed the ruin. Russia had never experienced such disaster. Less than half the land in the Shelon district of Novgorod was under cultivation. Some trading depots were unoccupied. Scribes who visited one wrote: "There is no one in this depot to ask about the land, because no priests or lesser boyars or peasants are here." Faced with ruin, masses of peasants began moving to the uninhabited borderlands.

Chapter Twenty-One

THE SACK OF NOVGOROD

The tsar did not stay long in the fortress he built near the Kremlin. After the quarrel with the metropolitan Ivan abandoned Moscow and moved to Aleksandrovskaia Sloboda, surrounded by thick woods and marshes, where he dwelt in seclusion behind the strong high walls of the fortress, which had been rebuilt. An augmented guard protected the approaches to it, and no one could enter the tsar's residence without a permit. The oprichnina council members lived there with the tsar, received ambassadors, dealt with important affairs of state, and played monk in their spare time.

To explain the striking changes in the Muscovite administration diplomats were instructed to tell foreigners the Russian tsar wished to spend time in his holiday residence for relaxation; it was located near Moscow, and thus the tsar was able "to rule his realm whether he was in Moscow or at the Sloboda."[1] In reality, Ivan was not at leisure; he had hidden in the Sloboda through fear of a boyar uprising. His concern led him to request his sons to send large sums of money to the Kirillov monastery to construct cells so that all the royal family could take refuge behind the walls of the monastery, situated in a dense forest, if necessary. On his regular visit to Vologda Ivan decided to speed up construction of the fortress he was erecting there, and ordered a shipyard built adjacent to it. Vologda carpenters assisted by English craftsmen, built boats and barges to transport the tsar's treasure to Solovki, from which it would go by sea to England. These practical preparations for going abroad were undertaken after Ivan had successfully negotiated with Randolph to provide his family refuge in England.

Closely watching developments, Ivan and his associates detected signs of imminent disaster everywhere. He was convinced that only chance had saved him from becoming a prisoner in Lithuania. Meantime the king continued his covert war against Russia, assisted by the emigres. Early in 1569 a small Lithuanian detachment occupied the impregnable fortress of Izborsk, an important defense position in the northwest. The circumstances of its capture were unusual. In the middle of the night Teterin, a Russian turncoat, disguised as a member of the oprichnina ordered the guard to open the gate in the name of the oprichnina. On retaking Izborsk Ivan's forces ordered its assistant crown secretaries executed for cooperating with Teterin, as the synodical shows, and beheaded secretaries in fortresses near Izborsk in Russian Livonia. The betrayal of Izborsk implicated the chancery administration and the people of Pskov and Novgorod. Indications of disaffection multiplying everywhere made Ivan suspect that Pskov and Novgorod would emulate the example of Izborsk if the situation deteriorated further. In anticipation of potential treachery the authorities issued orders to resettle malcontents in Novgorod and Pskov; 500 families were removed from the latter and 150 from the former. Some two to three thousand men, women and children were driven into exile. Ivan's transfer of population recalled similar measures taken by his grandfather, but Ivan III had expelled members of Novgorod's privileged elite, whereas his grandson proceeded against the commons. The massive resettlement of the inhabitants of Pskov and Novgorod, the two cities the administration regarded as capable of fostering social discontent, speaks volumes about the way in which the oprichnina regarded society.

Shortly before this happened his envoys had given Ivan detailed information about a *coup d'etat* in Sweden, which had overthrown his ally, King Erik XIV. This greatly alarmed the tsar, for the parallel was striking. The envoys told him Erik had executed many prominent courtiers and then grew afraid that his nobles might kill him. Fearing revolt, he secretly asked the tsar's envoys to escort him to Russia just at the time when Ivan covertly was preparing to flee to England. This information, which Ivan learned at Vologda, apparently had an affect on his investigation of the Izborsk affair. In his eyes the situation in Pskov uncannily resembled the one in Sweden. The envoys told Ivan that just before the rising Erik XIV had asked them "to find out about the people of Stockholm and their treachery; they were trying to betray their king and surrender the city to his brothers." Betrayal by the people of Stockholm was what finally ruined the Swedish king.

The oprichnina leaders, frightened by the events at Izborsk, assumed that the people of Pskov and Novgorod were prepared to follow Stockholm's example and support a rising against the government. Prince Vladimir Andreevich could play the role of the rebellious Swedish dukes; like his father, he maintained a residence and retainers in Novgorod where, as a neighbor, he enjoyed support. The Novgorod chronicler, well acquainted with local attitudes, observed that many of the population wept for Prince Vladimir when he died. The suspicion that Staritskii and Novgorod might concert an agreement was strengthened further by the fact that Novgorod landholders had figured prominently in the conspiracy of the Master of Horse, I. P. Cheliadnin-Fedorov, which Ivan had just crushed.

The suspicions and fears occasioned by the Izborsk affair and the reports from Sweden determined the fate of the Staritskii cause. The tsar was determined once and for all to eliminate the danger of a rising by his cousin. Such a decision involved a moral issue. In ancient times the church had canonized Boris and Gleb in order to stop feuding among the princely families. Fratricide was considered a heinous crime and the tsar hesitated to take such a step, for Vladimir's previous transgressions seemed inadequate to justify condemning him to death. More serious charges were needed, and they were soon forthcoming. Ivan's judges alleged that Vladimir had tried to assassinate the tsar. Their story, which made no allowances for the temperament of the individuals involved, was implausible, but contemporaries who observed the proceedings noted that the witnesses at the inquiry were the tsar's intimate flatterers, hangers-on, and executioners, which effectively guaranteed the desired result. [2]

After the fall of the master, Cheliadnin, Prince Vladimir was assigned to the forces at Nizhnii Novgorod. Members of the oprichnina were determined to prove the disgraced prince had been plotting to poison the tsar and his family. They arrested the palace cook, who had gone to Nizhnii Novgorod to procure salmon for the royal table, and charged that he and Prince Vladimir had entered into a criminal conspiracy. A powder, declared to be poison, and a large sum of money, which Vladimir allegedly had given him, were found in the cook's possession. In proceeding against the Staritskii family the authorities officially proclaimed that Prince Vladimir and his mother had tried to debauch the tsar and his children.[3] This false charge of an attempted assassination of the tsar was a pretext for indulging in unusually brutal persecution and massacre.

Believing his aunt, Evfrosiniia, was behind all the intrigues against him, Ivan decided to remove her from the Goritskii nunnery as quickly as he could. The longstanding family feud reached a savage climax. No real proof connected her with the Nizhnii Novgorod conspiracy, and as he wished to avoid meeting her for the last time, Ivan had the disgraced princess poisoned by gas when she was being brought by boat along the Sheksna river to the Sloboda.

Prince Vladimir was ordered to leave Nizhnii Novgorod to report to the Sloboda, but at the last posting-station before it his camp suddenly was surrounded by oprichnina forces. Maliuta Skuratov and Vasilii Griaznoi appeared as judges in his tent to proclaim that the tsar regarded him as an enemy, not his cousin. After a confrontation with the palace cook and a brief trial, Vladimir Andreevich was sentenced to death. Hypocritically citing ties of kinship Ivan refused to order his cousin executed and compelled him to commit suicide. The helpless Vladimir, terrified and morally shattered, drank a cup of poisoned wine. He had been married a second time to a cousin of Kurbskii. The tsar vengefully poisoned her too, along with her nine-year-old daughter, but spared Vladimir's older children, his heir, Prince Vasilii, and the two daughters of his first marriage. Later he restored the ancestral appanage to his young relative.

The synodical lists permit a detailed reconstruction of the end of the Staritski family. They show that the chief witnesses, the cook Moliava, his sons, and some fishermen, who were supposed to have participated in the Nizhnii Novgorod conspiracy, were killed before Vladimir's trial ended, and contradict Taube and Kruse, who assert that the witnesses secretly had cooperated with the judges and were tortured only for show. An assistant secretary of Novgorod, Anton Sviiazev, was executed with the witnesses. His deposition widened the investigation of treason in Novgorod. The royal archive has preserved "the Novgorod affair, involving Assistant Secretary Anton Sviiazev and his associates, which was sent from Novgorod at the request of Pavel Petrov by Vasilii Stepanov." This means Sviiazev was implicated by a denunciation originating in the zemshchina, which was laid before oprichnina authorities by the zemshchina secretary Stepanov, who outlasted Sviiazev by no more than six months.

The sack of Novgorod, carried out after Prince Vladimir was executed, dumbfounded contemporaries. Scarcely anyone knew the cause of the tragedy, for the affair was shrouded in secrecy. The oprichnina council adopted a resolution to march on Novgorod in December, 1569. The tsar summoned his forces and announced that the people of Novgorod had grossly betrayed him. The army set out immediately and Ivan reached the city on January 8, 1570. The clergy, carrying crosses and icons, met him on the bridge over the Volkhov river, but the celebration was over in a few minutes; the tsar called Pimen, the local archbishop, a traitor and refused to receive his blessing. However, as a pious man he felt he must attend service, and the clergy had to say mass amid scenes of general disorder. After the service Pimen invited his guest to break bread at his palace, but the inauspicious gathering was of short duration. Shouting angrily, the tsar ordered the guard to arrest his host and plunder his residence. The soldiers stripped St. Sophia cathedral, carried off valuable church ornaments and icons, and wrenched the ancient Korsun gate from the altar. They also arrested people indiscriminately throughout the city and took them to the royal camp at Gorodishche.

The anonymous author of *The Tale of the Destruction of Novgorod*, which forms part of the Novgorod chronicle, closely described the violence that ensued, but certain details in his account seemed doubtful. The winter of 1570 chanced to be unusually severe, but the chronicler stated soldiers threw women and children bound hand and foot into the Volkhov, while others travelled along the river in a boat, forcing those who came to the surface down again with axes and pikes. However, the doubts appear unfounded, for a newly-discovered German source, based on testimony of witnesses to the sack of Novgorod who fled abroad and published in 1572 in Frankfurt-am-Main, describes events much in the same way as the chronicle.[4] The origins of the two sources are different; hence, their credibility is enhanced by the fact that the information in both of them corresponds.

The judges employed cruel tortures to conduct their inquiries. The Novgorod source asserts that some were excruciatingly tortured and roasted over fires, and the German source adds that others were strung up by their hands and had their eyebrows singed off. Both state that wretched people were tied by long ropes to sleds, dragged through the city to the Volkhov, and thrust under the ice. The families of those suspected of treason were also killed. The German account narrates the massacre on the Volkhov bridge, when women and children were bound, hurled into the water, and pushed under the ice.

The chronicle has identified accurately the persons summoned to Gorodishche for examination. Ivan's men interrogated boyars from the archbishop's court, and many serving-men, lesser boyars, merchants and traders. They killed in sequence; first assistant secretaries with families, and their wives and children, and then unmarried men in the Novgorod chanceries, who appear in the synodical under the general heading: "Unmarried assistant secretaries of Novgorod." The rich Syrkov family of merchants and many other prominent citizens perished in Gorodishche. The court condemned some 200 gentry, more than 100 servants, 45 secretaries and chancery people, and a like number of their families.

The central episode of the campaign was the trials, held in the tsar's camp, of the principal figures charged with treason. No matter how expeditiously investigators and judges worked they could not interrogate, torture, confront, transcribe the testimony of, and finally execute several hundred people in two or three weeks. The trials likely lasted three or four weeks, to the end of January, when the Novgorod affair entered its second phase. After describing the violence at Gorodishche the local chronicler observed: "After this the sovereign and his soldiers began visiting the monasteries of Great Novgorod."

Assuming monks too were guilty, the tsar decided to tour prominent monasteries in the suburbs, not as a pilgrim but personally to superintend removal of their treasures, which his men had already conveniently impounded. Staden, who accompanied him, wrote: "Every day he mounted and moved to another monastery, where he indulged his savagery." His men took money, ransacked cells, tore down bells, destroyed equipment, and slaughtered cattle. They beat abbots and elders on their heels with sticks from morning to night, demanding extra from them. The sack ruined the monks, and the priceless artifacts of St. Sophia cathedral went into Ivan's fisc. The Novgorod chronicles also affirm that he confiscated treasure in twenty-seven of the oldest monasteries. Ivan visited some in person. His tour took at least several days, probably a week. Those who participated in the sack and people in Novgorod who saw and wrote about these events declared that the inhabitants of the city went normally about their business while the tsar was occupied with the trials at Gorodishche and the monasteries. Markets functioned as usual and soldiers even sold goods they had seized in them, but the situation altered once the trials and the tour of the monasteries came to an end.

Careful scrutiny of the sources refutes the traditional view that Ivan's soldiers pillaged Novgorod for five or six weeks. The tsar ended trials involving monks a few days before he departed for Pskov, and his men were able to assault the city at large only during this interim. They plundered the market place, divided booty that was valuable amongst themselves, and piled up goods like tallow, wax and hemp and set them on fire, destroying quantities of merchandise destined for trade with the West. The soldiers also ransacked homes of ordinary inhabitants, broke down gates, burst open doors, and smashed windows. Citizens who tried to resist were slain on the spot. The poor were treated with especial harshness. Famine had driven a host of paupers into Novgorod, but in the depth of winter the tsar ordered them expelled from the city, and many perished from cold and hunger. Two considerations dictated the attack on the townspeople: the need to fill the royal treasury, and to terrorize the lower levels of the city population in order to stamp out disaffection among them and lessen the danger of popular revolt. The sack of Novgorod is the most repulsive episode in the brutal history of the oprichnina. The cruel, senseless slaughter of innocent people made oprichnina synonymous with lawlessness and excess.

After settling accounts with Novgorod the tsar's army proceeded to Pskov, whose inhabitants were quick to show their submission by placing tables with bread and salt along the streets through which the tsar was to pass. Ivan did not spare Pskov, but he directed his wrath at the clergy. He beheaded the abbot of the Pechora monastery, who came to greet him with crosses and icons. His soldiers pillaged the churches of Pskov mercilessly, tore down cathedral bells and carried them off to the Sloboda, and seized church decorations. Before he left the tsar told his men to sack the city, but they failed to complete the task. Legends grew up around the abrupt end of the sack of Pskov, even in Ivan's lifetime. Participants in the campaign asserted that Ivan supposedly encountered a holy fool, Nikola, who advised him to leave the city at once to avoid great misfortune. Churchmen embroidered the legend of the tsar and the fool with imaginary details. The simple man told the tsar "in awesome tones to desist from terrible bloodshed and not presume to pillage God's holy churches."[5] Refusing to listen to him Ivan had the bell removed from Trinity cathedral, and just as he did so his horse fell beneath him. Nikola's prophecy had come true, and the tsar fled in terror.

The deranged holy fool of Pskov was one of the few who dared assail Ivan openly and it is conceivable his words hastened the departure of the tsar's forces, for Ivan was highly susceptible to the superstitions of the age, but Nikola's prophecies were powerless to check the measures Ivan took against the church. The tsar did not leave Pskov until he had ruined the clergy. Historians have long failed to grasp the reason why Pskov escaped Novgorod's fate, which did not become clear until the synodical was reconstructed. Shortly before the campaign the authorities had moved several hundred families suspected of treason from Pskov and resettled them around Tver and in Torzhok. Acting under the tsar's orders his minions slew 220 of the exiles from Pskov, with their wives and children. Fully satisfied with their action, the tsar decided to spare the rest of the city's inhabitants. Ivan went from Pskov to Staritsa and then to the Sloboda. The punitive raid was over.

Who was responsible for so gruesome a tragedy? Even many who saw or took part in it were confused. Not daring to impugn the pious ruler, the people of Novgorod invented a legend about a spiteful vagabond, Petr Volynets, who, planning vengeance on Novgorod, wrote a letter falsely accusing its people of treason, and when the tsar received it he authorized the sack of the city. When shown Petr's note people in Novgorod hysterically exclaimed: "We cannot deny the evidence of our signatures, but we never thought of nor intended becoming subjects of the Polish king." During the sack of Novgorod the Venetian abbot Gerio came to Moscow and managed to collect valuable information about contemporary events. He claimed the tsar destroyed Novgorod "after intercepting a courier bearing a treasonable letter."[6] It is easy to detect a resemblance between the contemporary reference to interception of a courier and the subsequent tradition about the vagabond Petr, who was actually a Lithuanian scout from Volynia. Another source alludes to the treasonable letter: the original description of the royal archive of the 1570s, which refers to an enigmatic document, a submission "from Novgorod, from Secretaries Andrei Beznosov and Kuzma Rumiantsev, concerning the Polish note." Although the secretaries themselves informed the tsar they had received a note from Poland they soon were executed for their presumed betrayal in the Polish interest. After the sack the ambassadorial bureau drew up detailed instructions for Russian diplomats in Poland. If the Poles should ask about the executions in Novgorod their question should be testily countered by questions: "How do you know?" and, "since you know, what is there for us to say? You used scouts to concert this vile deed with traitors to our country, but God revealed this treason to our sovereign, and thus he dealt with the traitors."[7] As can be seen, scouts delivered a provocative letter (the Polish note) to Novgorod; the secretaries lost no time informing Moscow, but the suspicious tsar considered their action proof that his subjects were traitors, and the instructions from the bureau show how blind he was. It appears that Ivan and his associates had been hoodwinked. The Lithuanian secret service used false documents to compromise the people of Novgorod and was completely successful. Losing trust in his subjects the tsar sent armies, which should have been used against Poland, to destroy his own people, and to free forces for this purpose hastened to conclude a truce with the enemy and had his envoys sententiously tell the Poles that God Himself had revealed their collusion with the people of Novgorod.

The irony of fate has obliterated the name of the leader of the Novgorod conspirators. Among contemporaries only Schlicting inadvertently has alluded to him in a vague account that runs essentially as follows: a certain Vasilii Dmitrievich (whose last name Schlichting did not know) was using Lithuanian prisoners to man cannons. They tried to escape but were apprehended, and under torture declared their commander was aware of their intention. Ivan's men put Vasilii Dmitrievich on the rack, and he acknowledged he had had treasonable dealings with the Polish king. Schlichting attached no significance to the death of an obscure Vasilii Dmitrievich, but Russian documents show he overlooked what was most important. The original description in the royal archive contains the first reference to this incident. Among other investigative materials the archive has preserved a report "to the sovereign on the affair of Vasilii Dmitrievich and the runaway cannoneers, the Mishki." The report, confirming Schlichting's account, supplied the tsar with his first information about the fugitive cannoneers in Vasilii Dmitrievich's service. The synodical takes matters further. It lists Vasilii Dmitrievich among those executed at the time of the trials in Gorodishche; "Vasilii Dmitrievich Danilov; Secretary Andrei Beznosov; two Germans among Vasilii's men; Maksim, a Lithuanian; Rop, a German, and Rumiantsev from Kuzmin's people," and so forth. This synodical list goes to the heart of the formidable political affair known as the treason of Novgorod and makes it possible to show that Vasilii Dmitrievich Danilov, an eminent zemshchina boyar during the time of the oprichnina, was the leading figure. The synodical links him with the first secretary of Novgorod, Beznosov, servants of the second secretary, Rumiantsev, and, finally, "Boyar Danilov's people," which meant the Lithuanian prisoner Maksim (in Russian transcription "cannoneer Mishka"), whose deposition destroyed Danilov, although he shared the same fate.

Careful juxtaposition of the sources reveals many facts that were previously unknown. Petr Volynets, the mythical vagabond, becomes the historical Boyar Danilov. It now becomes clear that the Novgorod affair was essentially an expanded replay of Cheliadnin's conspiracy. In the one case it was the metropolitan and Master of Horse who were destroyed; in the other, the archbishop of Novgorod and Boyar Danilov. In both cases the government hunted for conspirators among the ancient Muscovite non-titled nobility, and this led to the deaths of V. A. Buturlin, Grigorii Volynskii, and members of the Pleshcheev family in Novgorod. Those who established the oprichnina had designed it to combat the princes, but by now it had lost its original impulse. The Novgorod affair brought about a second change of boyar leaders in the zemshchina.

Participants in Danilov's conspiracy were indicted on two counts: "to hand Novgorod and Pskov over to the Lithuanian king, and with evil intent to remove Tsar and Grand Prince Ivan Vasilevich of all Russia and set Prince Vladimir Andreevich upon the throne."[8] It is easy to see that the official version embraced two incompatible charges. If the people of Novgorod hoped to place Vladimir Andreevich, a person useful to them, on the throne, why should they subject themselves to Lithuania and the authority of a foreign ruler? However, such a simple question presumably did not trouble Maliuta Skuratov and his friends in charge of the investivation.

Contemporaries claimed that as few as 20,000 or as many as 60,000 people were slain during the sack of Novgorod. A century ago using figures given in the chronicle historians began trying to refine the dimensions of the tragedy, and estimated the soldiers killed an average of 1,000 persons a day for five weeks, which gives a total of 40,000. This figure is unacceptable, because it is based on erroneous data. The chronicler's claim that 1,000 persons died per day is clearly a product of his imagination, as is his assertion that the townspeople were pillaged for five weeks. Apart from all else, Ivan minions could not have killed 40,000 people, because even in the city's best days the population of Novgorod never exceeded 25,000 to 30,000 inhabitants, and during the sack a severe famine forced many people to leave the city in order to avoid starving to death.

The synodical supplies data about the sack of Novgorod. Its compilers included an authentic report by Maliuta Skuratov, who was in charge of the punitive raid. The list has even preserved the rough jargon he used: "According to his report, during the Novgorod campaign Maliuta dispatched 1490 (by cutting off their hands) and shot 15 persons." The majority of the "Orthodox Christians" Maliuta slew belonged to the lower stratum of the townspeople. His men could not be bothered to record their names because they were more interested in the gentry, the names and nicknames of several hundreds of whom, with their servants, are found in the synodical. A summary of these data leads to the conclusion that no more than two or three thousand persons died in Novgorod. The sack did not affect the rural population, which had grown impoverished long before Ivan's henchmen appeared. Their activities aggravated the situation, but were not the sole cause of the decline in the Novgorod region.

The needs of the state treasury were mainly responsible for the attacks on the church, rich merchants, and artisans in Novgorod, for constant war and the costly ventures undertaken by the oprichnina required enormous outlays at a time when the treasury was empty. Financial pressure caused the authorities to cast covetous eyes on the church, which was extremely wealthy, but the clergy had no intention of giving up its property. The trial of Metropolitan Filipp had damaged the church's prestige, and the government took advantage of this to appropriate ecclesiastical resources in Novgorod. The charge of treason served as a handy excuse to rob the archbishoprics of Novgorod and Pskov, but the oprichnina had no wish to undermine the church's authority and dared not touch church lands, the main source of its wealth. The sack greatly harmed the townspeople of Novgorod, Pskov, Tver and Ladoga. Novgorod's trade with western Europe was suspended for many years. However, the attacks on town dwellers were of comparatively short duration and were designed to terrorize, not destroy the population.

A view exists that the sack of Novgorod was motivated by the crown's need to eliminate the last survivals of decentralized autonomy. This is hardly accurate. After Moscow conquered the republic of Novgorod, by the end of the fifteenth century the government had expropriated the lands belonging to local feudatories, including boyars, merchants and prosperous farmers, and settled them with gentry from Moscow on service-tenure. Measures to ensure unification were resolutely carried out in Novgorod, and Muscovite practices had been firmly established before the formation of the oprichnina. Moscow always designated or changed the personnel of the chancery and church administrations and controlled the allotments of service-tenure estates. Abolition of the office of governor in the early 1560s significantly enhanced the local authority of church and chancery people. The Novgorod chancery apparatus, totally dependent on the central authority, loyally supported the monarchy, and the same was true of the church. During the oprichnina years Archbishop Pimen performed many valuable services for the tsar and his confederates. The Novgorod administration was unquestionably loyal to the oprichnina, but Ivan and his supporters for various reasons placed little trust in and were hostile to the people of Novgorod and their city.

As the cleavage between oprichnina and zemshchina grew more serious the tsar's council viewed with increasing concern the attitude of Novgorod's seasoned troops, whose numbers were twice as great as the forces at the disposal of the oprichnina. The political influence of the Novgorod gentry was so substantial that at times of crisis any faction contending for power tried to secure its support. During the boyar regimes the people of Novgorod by and large refused to support

Andrei Staritskii, and so his rising was put down. A few years later the city supported the Shuiskii boyars, who were thus able to bring off a *coup* and seize power. The coming of the oprichnina fostered dangerous symptoms of dissatisfaction among the zemshchina gentry. The tsar barred its members from serving in the oprichnina, and they experienced its excesses at first hand. It is not surprising that people from Novgorod figured in the earliest oprichnina trials.

Longstanding commercial and cultural rivalry between Moscow and Novgorod was one reason why the oprichnina proceeded against the city, but growing social conflicts in the Novgorod region, caused by the economic decline of the late 1560s, were incomparably more significant. Earlier, when Novgorod and Pskov had been independent feudal republics, social contrasts were extremely marked, and the massive resettlement carried out in the late fifteenth century had no effect on the basic layer of the city population, the common people, who kept the democratic traditions of Old Novgorod alive and maintained a high level of hostility to Moscow, which was nurtured by abuses perpetrated by those in power. The Muscovite administration in Novgorod had long rested on a precarious foundation, as can be seen in the *Tale of Towns,* a well-known work of Novgorod origin. It states that Novgorod was a scene of shocking disorders, of which the disobedience and contentiousness of the common people was the worst. The boyars "cannot control them, and the commons will not listen to the boyars; the people are foulmouthed, vile, and drink heavily and with abandon. Only God preserves them in their folly." This passage from the *Tale* refers to an earlier time, but it had not lost its relevance in the oprichnina years. The notorious Novgorod separatism was merely a byproduct of deep social clashes. The famine which struck the Novgorod region shortly prior to the oprichnina campaign fanned the flames of discontent. Recognizing the danger, the authorities tried to combat it with savage massacres and intensified terrorism against the commons.

Chapter Twenty-Two

VICTORIES AND DEFEATS

When military activity resumed on the western frontiers, Russian diplomats tried to bring England and Sweden into a coalition against
Poland, but after King Erik XIV was overthrown the Swedish government denounced the alliance it earlier had concluded with Russia. In
meetings in Vologda with the English ambassador, Randolph, Ivan's
diplomats drew up a treaty between England and Russia, but England
refused to ratify it. Russia had to continue fighting the Livonian war
alone under highly unfavorable conditions. The Union of Lublin made
Poland and Lithuania a single state, the Rzeczpospolita, and a peace
treaty Poland signed with Turkey threatened to bring about a broad
anti-Russian coalition, save that both the Rzeczpospolita and Russia
needed peace; the two countries agreed to a three-year truce in 1570.
Ivan's diplomats meanwhile had devised a scheme to create a puppet
kingdom in Livonia under Russian auspices. Duke Magnus of Denmark, the tsar's vassal who was promised the throne of Livonia, supported by a large Russian army equipped with siege artillery tried to
expel the Swedes from Reval, but he could not take the city, and the
tsar's commanders withdrew after a protracted siege.

Sweden was anxious to avoid war with Russia. The new Swedish
king, John III, sent envoys to the frontier, but the couriers riding
ahead of them were detained in Novgorod. One of the couriers, who
expressed a desire to enter Ivan's service, said the Swedish envoys
possessed full powers to make peace with Russia under any conditions, no matter how onerous, even if it meant ceding Reval. The tsar
rushed authorization to admit the envoys, but it was too late. Sweden
had come to terms with Denmark; Ivan's commanders had suffered a
defeat south of Moscow, and Sweden now refused to discuss the question of ceding Reval. Oprichnina diplomacy had sustained a major
defeat, for it had failed to take advantage of an unique opportunity
to end the contest for Reval peacefully. The incompetence of the
oprichnina leaders was the cause of the failure; the ambassadorial bureau of the zemshchina already had lost its most authoritative and
perceptive leaders.

The difficult situation that had arisen on the southern borders prevented the Russian command from dispatching adequate forces to resolve the Baltic conflict. The danger that the Tatars might unite under the aegis of the Ottoman empire, which had haunted the Russians since they began the war with Kazan, now became a reality. In spring, 1569 Turkey massed 100 divisions, amounting to 17,000 men, in Azov to capture Astrakhan and expel the Russians from the lower Volga region. In summer the Turkish army advanced from Azov towards Astrakhan, linking up en route with a force of 40,000 Crimeans, and the Nogais, who had risen in revolt. The Turks stayed two weeks on the narrow stretch of land between the Don and Volga rivers, through which they tried to dig a canal but failed in the attempt. They were unable to drag galleys holding heavy artillery overland to the Volga and then bring them back along the Don to the Black sea. Leaving the stretch of land the Turks and Tatars reached Astrakhan, but they could not take Hare Island, on which the fortress was situated. The disorderly Janissaries refused to winter in the Volga area, and ten days later the Turkish army began to retreat to Azov. Making their way through the arid steppes of the northern Caucasus by the Kabardian highroad the Turks suffered heavy losses from hunger and thirst, and only a pitiable remnant of their large and powerful army managed to reach Azov. However, the destruction of the Turkish army did not mean an end to Turkish and Tatar expansion at Russia's expense. The Crimeans savagely devastated the area around Riazan in 1570.

The following year 40,000 Crimeans, the Greater and Lesser Nogai Hordes, and Circassian detachments marched on Moscow. Taken by surprise, the Russian command could muster no more than 6,000 men on the Oka river. The zemshchina army moved vigorously to close the fords at Serpukhov, and the tsar with the oprichnina army followed it to the frontier. However, the Tatars moved west, circumventing the Oka fortifications, and crossing the Ugra river managed to outflank the royal army. Ivan was convinced the Tatars had not crossed the Oka, but his advance guard was suddenly attacked and routed by an overwhelming Tatar force. Ivan abandoned the army at this critical juncture and fled to Rostov. The swift Tatar cavalry meantime pressed on to Moscow and threatened to cut the small Russian armies off from their northern escape route. Lacking sufficient forces to contain the Tatars, the commanders withdrew and took refuge behind the walls of the Kremlin in Moscow. The khan reached the capital at the same time as the commanders and destroyed their camp near Kolomenskoe. The Tatars plundered unprotected villages and set several fires in Moscow's suburbs. It was a clear, calm, wind-less day, but then a gale arose and flames engulfed the city. All the bells rang when the conflagration broke out, but later one after an-other fell silent as fire destroyed them. Soon tremendous explosions shook the city to its foundations when powder magazines in some Kremlin towers and Kitaigorod blew up.

When the Tatars appeared the adjacent population sought refuge inside the fortress walls. Fleeing the flames, inhabitants and refugees alike converged upon Moscow's northern gate. A huge crowd piled up there and in the narrow streets leading to the gate: "Three rows of people were heaped on top of one another; those above suffocated those below."[1] Anyone who managed to save himself from the fire perished in the frightful crush. The army penned in Moscow also suf-fered heavy losses. Detachments became disorganized in the narrow streets and mingled with people fleeing from burning areas. The com-mander-in-chief "hid from the intense heat."[2] Moscow burned to the ground in three hours, and Tatars trying to loot perished in the flames. Next day the Tatars withdrew into the steppe by the road through the Riazan area.

The government admitted the prostrate country could not fight such strong foes as Turkey and the Crimea. The tsar let the Crimeans know he was willing to cede Astrakhan to the khan if the latter would conclude a military alliance with Russia, but the Crimeans consider-ed the tsar's concessions inadequate and rejected his offer. After Moscow burned down, the Crimea, encouraged by Turkey, formulat-ed a plan of campaign to destroy Russia and reduce it to tributary status.

Chapter Twenty-Three

THE MOSCOW AFFAIR

During the sack of Novgorod Ivan told Metropolitan Kirill that the archbishop of Novgorod was a traitor. The metropolitan and bishops at once publicly condemned those sacrificed to the oprichnina and informed the tsar they had decreed "at an assembly to deprive Archbishop Pimen of his rank for his offense against the royal charter," which meant that Pimen had been consigned to the mercies of the oprichnina. But the higher clergy had gone too far in seeking to accommodate the secular authorities. In another message to Kirill the tsar forbade Pimen be deprived of his office "without a thorough investigation and a decree of council."[1]

Ivan anticipated no opposition from the cowed clergy, but before the trial he took further steps to warn disaffected churchmen. His minions beheaded an archimandrite in Riazan and imprisoned several members of the ecclesiastical assembly. Everyone remembered how Pimen had presided over the assembly that had condemned Filipp, and now he found himself in the same position. Obediently executing the tsar's mandate the higher clergy deprived Pimen of his rank and sentenced him to life imprisonment in a small monastery near Tula, where he soon died. Pimen's associates arrested in Novgorod were held several months in the Sloboda while a full investigation was conducted. Ivan shared duty with Maliuta Skuratov and spent days and nights in the dungeons, where the disgraced were subjected to horrible tortures and confessed to any crime. The investigative report states: "In this affair, after torture (!) many spoke in reference to the treason against Novgorod, Archbishop Pimen, and against his counsellors, and against themselves."[2] The information extracted in torture chambers implicated many highly-placed persons in Moscow.

The brutal sack of Novgorod aggravated the split between the tsar and the zemshchina leaders. After his return Ivan had held a long discussion with Ivan Viskovatyi, the Keeper of the Seal. Risen from the common people, Viskovatyi's keen intellect and remarkable capacities enabled him to carve out a distinguished career. He had been in charge of the ambassadorial bureau since the beginning of the war with Kazan, and it was said in Moscow that Ivan loved his old counsellor like himself. Viskovatyi ventured to ask the tsar for an explanation after Ivan's henchmen had arrested, cruelly tortured, and executed his brother, and strongly urged the ruler to stop the bloodshed and not to destroy the boyars. In reply Ivan fulminated: "I have not yet annihilated you; I have only begun, but I shall keep on trying to root you all out, until not even a memory of you will remain!"[3]

Viskovatyi openly expressed the position of the zemshchina, and this alarmed Ivan. Opposition from upper chancery officials, who had won entry into the boyar council, came as an unpleasant surprise to the tsar and his confederates. To eliminate such dissent Viskovatyi and some other zemshchina secretaries were arrested and charged with having been Pimen's advisors; in this way the Novgorod affair became the Moscow affair. The trials of the group in Moscow lasted only a few weeks, and on July 25, 1570 the condemned were led into the square popularly known as the Foul Pool. Ivan arrived at the place of execution attended by 1500 mounted fusiliers. The preparations for the executions and the appearance of the tsar and his men caused panic among the inhabitants of the capital, and people dispersed to their homes. The tsar was puzzled, and exhorted them to approach and watch closely. The panic abated somewhat and crowds filled the market square. Turning to them the tsar loudly inquired: "Am I right to wish to punish my traitors?" Cries were heard in answer: "Long life, most noble tsar. You do well to punish traitors for their deeds."[4] It was, of course, a fiction that the whole people approved the actions of the oprichnina.

Guards brought out some 300 disgraced persons, divided into two groups. About 180 were led aside and consigned to representatives of the zemshchina; the tsar magnanimously proclaimed he had spared them. Then a secretary read out the guilt of the remainder and the executions commenced. Viskovatyi, lashed to beams shaped like a cross, was told to admit his guilt and beg the tsar for mercy, but the proud man refused: "A curse upon you, you bloodsuckers, and your tsar!" These were his last words, for he was immediately cut to pieces. The treasurer Nikita Funikov also refused to admit guilt and was boiled alive. Next the executioners dispatched head secretaries of the zemshchina chanceries in Moscow, boyars in the service of Archbishop Pimen, Novgorod secretaries, and more than 100 Novgorod gentry and their servitors.

The execution of the Moscow secretaries was but the first round of the Moscow affair. The boyar nobility stood behind the chancery people. Viskovatyi and Funikov owed their rank to the Zakharin boyars, who had controlled the zemshchina and managed the court of Ivan, the heir, who was related to them on his mother's side. The oprichnina was preparing to sack Moscow as it had Novgorod. The day Viskovatyi was executed the tsar told the people he "had intended to slay all the inhabitants of the city but had laid aside his wrath." The thought that what had happened in Novgorod might be repeated in Moscow frightened the zemshchina leaders. It is possible the Zakharin family attempted to use its influence with the heir to dissuade the tsar and limit the monstrous terror.

Execution of Boyars in Moscow. Sixteenth-century miniature. State Historical Museum, Moscow.

Relations between the tsar and his son were strained, and the hot-tempered, despotic father often struck him. Young Ivan was seventeen and displayed a temperament as harsh as his father's. The tsar had long distrusted the Zakharin family and feared its members might involve his son in court strife. The tsar's suspicion of hidden intrigues by the boyars attending his son was so great that a month before the Moscow executions he publicly proclaimed his intention to deprive his son of the succession and confer it upon Magnus, king of Livonia. Perceptive contemporaries realized Ivan was merely trying to frighten the zemshchina boyars and intimidate his refractory son, but his impetuous utterance in the presence of boyars and envoys irritated those close to the heir.

Popular tradition has preserved a folktale of how the terrible tsar became enraged with his son. Bards handed down orally an old story of how Tsar Ivan Vasilevich, after rooting out treason from Novgorod and Pskov, was pondering how to extirpate it from Moscow, the city of stone. Then wicked Maliuta Skuratov told the sovereign he could never be rid of traitors as long as an enemy (his son) sat opposite him. Believing Maliuta, Ivan ordered his son executed, but Boyar Nikita Romanovich intervened: "O Maliuta, you Maliuta Skurlatovich. You are biting off more than you can chew, and it will be the ruin of you." His uncle's intercession saved the tsar's son.[5]

The editors of the folk tale considered this song, *Ivan the Terrible's Wrath,* a fable but they were wrong, for it was based on fact. When the servant of the tsar's personal physician, who knew court secrets, fled to Poland he told the Poles that discord arose in the royal family after the Novgorod campaign: "A great difference of opinion and a split occurred between father and elder son; many influential nobles favored the father, many the son, and a trial at arms took place." [6] The tsar prevailed and severely punished his son's partisans. Novgorod trial records note that traitors in Novgorod "referred to Moscow . . . to the keeper of the seal, Ivan Mikhailovich Viskovatyi, and to Semen Vasilev, son of Yakov . . . ."[7] Ivan's henchmen killed Boyar S.V. Yakovlev-Zakharin, who was related to the heir, and his son Nikita. The Moscow affair also implicated Boyar V.M. Yurev-Zakharin. Yurev had died a few years earlier, but the tsar vented his rage on members of his family. He put Yurev's daughter and grandson to death and refused their bodies Christian burial, and the execution of his cousin must have served as an ominous warning to young Ivan. Oprichnina Boyar V.P. Yakovlev-Zakharin for many years had been a confidant and courtier at the heir's court. He and his brother, the zemshchina boyar I.P. Khiron-Zakharin were beaten to death with clubs. The distinguished zemshchina boyar, I.V. Bolshoi-Sheremetev, closely related to the Zakharin family, saved himself from the tsar's wrath by becoming a monk in Beloozero.

The Moscow affair was like previous political trials, but this time the victims were non-titled nobility and the higher chancery bureaucracy. After the Suzdal nobles were crushed the boyar leaders of the zemshchina were frequently changed, and so only one group of boyars, those who controlled the oprichnina, maintained positions of power, and it was this group that felt the final lash of the terror. The circle of political development was thus closed.

The Moscow and Novgorod events disturbed those in the oprichnina who were not simply careerists and had not lost the ability to reflect intelligently on their actions. It was obvious to them that the charges against Archbishop Pimen were senseless. The Novgorod archbishop had been outstanding among church leaders for his loyalty to the oprichnina and his devotion to the tsar, and had enjoyed friendly relations with the oprichnina leaders Viazemskii and Basmanov. Members of the oprichnina council were afraid the attack on Pimen would increase their unpopularity, and they were growing concerned for their own safety, which was by no means secure if massive repressions should again take place. They had unleashed the terror, but now they were less and less able to control it.

Some oprichnina leaders had tried to prevent the attack on Pimen. Viazemskii, the armorer, secretly forewarned him of his danger, but since he did not openly object to the tsar's plans he was able to accompany Ivan on the Novgorod campaign. The oprichnina government contained men of more independent judgment and action, whose authority was based on genuine service. The eminent commander, Boyar A.D. Basmanov, was one of them. By all accounts he did not approve of the sack of Novgorod and was excluded from the punitive raid. When the tsar realized that Viazemskii had maintained covert relations with Pimen he became convinced that treason was abroad among his closest associates in the oprichnina. Ivan's imagination suggested a vast conspiracy, which would unite zemshchina and oprichnina leaders against him. Investigative reports claimed that Pimen, when preparing to surrender Novgorod and Pskov to Lithuania, had conferred with his confederates in Moscow, Boyar A.D. Basmanov and his son Fedor, Armorer Viazemskii, zemshchina Boyar Yakovlev, and some secretaries.

The Basmanov family, the original force behind the oprichnina, had brought the entire Pleshcheev clan into it, and now catastrophe overwhelmed them. The synodical states that Ivan's henchmen executed "Aleksei Basmanov and his son Petr; Zakharia Pleshcheev and

Iona." Basmanov and Z.I. Ochin-Pleshcheev had been oprichnina boyars and I.I. Ochin had commanded oprichnina detachments. The
tsar treated Basmanov with extraordinary savagery. He had his
younger son Petr beheaded, and spared his older son, Fedor, but the
tsar's favorite, a steward in rank, had to pay a frightful price to save
his life: he had to behead his own father in order to show his devotion to the tsar. Fedor's crime did not save him; he was exiled to
Beloozero, where he died. Viazemskii was arrested, beaten about the
shins, and banished to the town of Gorodets on the Volga, where he
starved to death in prison. After the great Moscow fire the tsar purged
the oprichnina council, executing the appanage prince M.T. Cherkasskii, the boyar courtier L.A. Saltykov, Boyar V.I. Temkin, Privy
Councillors P.V. Zaitsev and I.F. Vorontsov, and the steward F.I.
Saltykov. Maliuta Skuratov-Belskii and Vasilii Griaznoi, who were in
charge of the investigative arm of the oprichnina, undoubtedly intrigued to bring about the fall of the old leaders. These individuals
were typical representatives of the petty gentry who rose in the
oprichnina. Unlike Basmanov and Viazemskii they had taken no part
in establishing the institution, but when they uncovered treason in
Novgorod they were able to acquire minor conciliar rank, eliminate
the old influential cadres, and become leading figures in the oprichnina.

Chapter Twenty-Four

NOVGOROD UNDER THE OPRICHNINA

The personnel changes among the oprichnina leaders did not at first
lead to any shift in policy. After the Novgorod affair the oprichnina
undertook its last major territorial expansion. In an effort to strength-
en its military and social base the tsar took parts of Novgorod into it.
The commercial section and the Bezhetskii and Obonezhskii districts
passed under the rule of his secretaries and the oprichnina army enjoyed its single greatest increase when more than 500 members of
the Novgorod gentry entered it. Distrusting the original oprichnina
leaders, the tsar hoped this new force might serve to counterbalance
the old guard troops. The officials sent to Novgorod at once set about
strengthening their section of the city. Opposite the zemshchina

Kremlin the tsar proposed to build an oprichnina fortress like the one in Vologda, and the authorities razed 227 residences in the commercial quarter to clear a site for it. However, when the Tatars burned Moscow the treasury had to allocate all its available resources to restore the capital and oprichnina construction in Novgorod, Vologda, and Aleksandrovskaia Sloboda automatically ceased.

During the sack Ivan's minions had robbed many rich merchants, and now the tsar's representatives systematically exploited Novgorod's trade. Three weeks after they arrived his secretaries issued a decree on customs dues, imposed higher tariffs on zemshchina merchants in the Sofia quarter and ordained severe punishment for violations. Close supervision and regulation were features of the new commercial policy. The tsar's men had established a special relationship with the English merchants, members of the largest foreign trading company in Russia. Shortly before he raided Novgorod the tsar had granted the English the right of free trade everywhere in Russia, and the privilege of minting Russian coins from foreign silver money. Such generous subsidies and privileges inevitably attracted English merchant capital. In need of military supplies, Ivan's government was anxious to increase production and permitted the English to prospect for iron in the north and "wherever they are successful in finding deposits, to build a facility for processing such iron." The English also were given permission to rebuild and expand their rope factory in Vologda, and some accounts assert they manufactured textiles and processed flax. Curiously enough, the oprichnina government was the first in Russia to offer concessions to foreign capital, which were operative in the territory it controlled.

Trade and industry were not the only areas of economic concern; the tsar's secretaries were interested in farming in the Novgorod region, and attracted peasants by offering generous subsidies. They employed unusual methods to set up and populate a trade and industrial center in the Kholyn district. A proclamation was read out all over Novgorod to indentured and monastery serfs, and to all persons: "Whoever you are, you should come to the sovereign's village of Kholyn, and the sovereign will give each man five rubles regardless, and an exemption for five years."[1] Serfs responding to the call who came to the royal village were declared legally free of indenture. The government's unusual action may be explained easily. Famine and devastation had led many landlords to refuse to maintain household slaves and indentured serfs, who were forced to ask for alms and live as vagabonds. Ivan's new administration badly wanted to attract this social group.

The oprichnina acquired Novgorod when the area's economy had collapsed. Patrols reported that crop failures and unreasonable taxes were the cause, but the administration refused to accept the statements of its agents and strictly collected taxes and arrears from the peasants and townspeople, regardless of ability to pay. When the people of Ladoga failed to meet their obligations and did not pay "the sovereign's usual fish," officials known as enforcers appeared in the town. They drove many people out, beat two to death, and finally extracted the arrears. Ladoga suffered less in the sack than it did during the oprichnina. Since it was impossible for the impoverished people to pay their taxes in cash the authorities increased the imposts in kind. For several months the people of Novgorod had to go and build a bridge over the Volkhovets river, shore up and sweep roads for the ruler all over the region, build a castle, and provide carters and wagons to haul artillery and supplies. At first the administration's efforts to collect money and increase imposts substantially augmented the oprichnina treasury, but the profit soon turned to loss. The requisitions ruined the very source that provided revenue and the impoverished people deserted the cultivated areas en masse.

All the people of Novgorod, including those living in the zemshchina section, experienced the burden of the oprichnina. The tsar once sent a courtier to make a list of "jolly people," or jesters, and trained bears. He performed his mission and a month and a half before Ivan's marriage to Marfa Sobakina a courier escorted a troop of jesters and a host of bears to Moscow. Before he left, the agent decided to divert himself in the zemshchina area. Going with a band of revellers over to the Sofia side he introduced bears into the headquarters of the zemshchina secretaries. Terrified assistant secretaries jumped out of the window, and Secretary Bartenev was beaten to a pulp and mauled by a bear. Having finished with him the gang continued to make mischief everywhere in the Novgorod Kremlin, beating passers-by and egging the bears on to attack and harm them. The chronicler noted: "And at that time many people were injured."[2] The authorities in the zemshchina section of Novgorod were victims of oprichnina abuse, but the common people suffered even more. The Pskov chronicler wrote that the oprichnina authorities levied heavy fines, listened to slanderous anonymous denunciations, and "many people were reduced to penury and wandered about foreign lands."

From time immemorial hostile observers had criticized the people of Novgorod; they were "foulmouthed, vile, and drank heavily and with abandon."[3] The morals of the fractious city became the concern of Ivan's representatives, who tried to prevent all dealings in wine except in state taverns by "forbidding wine merchants to trade, and whenever they caught one with wine in his possession, or a drunken man, they had them beaten with a knout and thrown off the great bridge into the water."[4] This directive was implemented during the last weeks of winter; it is small wonder that immersion in the icy waters of the Volkhov turned out so badly for many topers. Those who suffered most from the oprichnina's concern over morality were the commons: apprentices, idlers, slaves, and the poor; in short, all who were called "wicked persons" because they showed disrespect to the authorities. The steps taken to regulate the wine trade inevitably provoked the turbulent Novgorod commons, as well as increasing revenues in the state taverns.

The authorities displayed keen interest in security measures. Novgorod's critics were exasperated because the city lacked walls and a gate: "Anyone who wishes may come and go; there is no guard." But Ivan's men soon put a stop to this. They forbade people to cross the Volkhov in boats and placed a guard and a barrier on the bridge, so that henceforth the secretaries could regulate intercourse between the two sides of the city. The Volkhov became the boundary of the oprichnina district. In the heat of summer the secretaries forbade citizens to light stoves in their homes and told them to cook their food in safe open places. The regulation was designed to reduce fire hazard, but it caused much trouble and inconvenience. The oprichnina administration in Novgorod was able to make the populace comply strictly with its decrees, but its authority was based on enforced coercion and harsh compulsion.

Chapter Twenty-Five

THE LAST OPRICHNINA GOVERNMENT

Although natural disasters and Tatar raids had wrought indescribable havoc, the people considered the oprichnina worse than the Tatars. The tsar had sought to justify such an institution on the grounds that the crimes committed by the boyar regimes must be stopped, but the oprichnina regime itself had perpetrated monstrous abuses. Contemporaries noted that judges in the zemshchina were handed an ordinance by the tsar which introduced a new principle into the administration of justice. It reads: "Judge rightly, but among our men there are no guilty." Following this concept judges no longer could proceed against thieves and robbers who happened to be in the oprichnina. Political denunciations had never been so widespread. A member of the oprichnina might inform on a member of the zemshchina, alleging the latter had defamed him and the oprichnina, and in such an instance the member of the zemshchina would go to prison and his property to the informer. Oprichnina excesses reached their height during the sack of Novgorod. The country was ravaged by plague and famine; paupers and beggars roamed the highways, and the towns could not bury their dead, but Ivan's henchmen kept on robbing and murdering with impunity. One of them, Staden, observed that although the tsar had not given them licence to do so, they ransacked the country and caused death and destruction in the zemshchina. [1] Ivan and his confederates were not, of course, advocating highway robbery, but in conferring privileges on the oprichnina they endowed it with legal sanction and equated brutal violence with official policy; thus they were responsible for the lawless raids and violence which at last seriously demoralized members of the oprichnina themselves.

The fall of the original leaders destroyed the system of mutual guarantees that had bound members of the oprichnina council together. Its membership was augmented by men from the zemshchina, many of whom previously had suffered at the hands of the oprichnina. The new council members seem to have recognized the dangerous demoralization of the guard. Staden relates that the oprichnina had wrought such harm in the zemshchina that the grand prince himself at last declared, "enough." The execution of Basmanov meant that a whole cycle in the history of the oprichnina had ended. The tsar disgraced those who had established it, received complaints by zemshchina gentry, and investigated flagrant abuses.

Justice in the oprichnina had come full circle. One of its members, Boyar Prince V.I. Temkin, was brought to trial because he had borrowed a large sum of money from one of the metropolitan's secretaries, refused to repay it, and killed the secretary's son in order to escape his creditor. The court punished Temkin by confiscating one of his estates, and the tsar, pleased at the strictness, approved the sentence. Ivan was probably moved to punish members of the oprichnina in hopes of winning back trust in the zemshchina. The trials and executions shook the oprichnina government and paralyzed its administration, which formerly had functioned vigorously and effectively. Staden was struck by the attitude prevailing at its main headquarters in Moscow after he visited it: "When I came to the oprichnina residence everything was at a standstill . . . the boyars who used to live in oprichnina houses had been expelled, and everyone, mindful of his treason, was anxious only about himself." Efforts to end the most flagrant abuses did not initially affect the basic structure of the oprichnina but, carried out with Ivan's typical decisiveness and ruthlessness, they aroused great discontent. Staden avers: "At that time the grand prince decided to proceed against the leaders of the oprichnina."[2]

The oprichnina court needed fresh faces and the tsar sought to adorn it with members of the most aristocratic families of Russia. During the first days of the oprichnina he had sent Boyar Prince A.B. Gorbatyi to the scaffold; now in its final days Boyar Prince I.A. Shuiskii became president of the oprichnina council, and noblemen of the highest rank served on it with him: Appanage Princes F.M. Trubetskoi and N.R. Odoevskii, Boyar Princes P.D. and S.D. Pronskii, Boyar Prince V.A. Sitskii, Associate Boyar Prince D.M. Shcherbatyi, Prince A.P. Khovanskii, and others. Almost all these men or their relatives had been harassed in Basmanov's time, but in preparation for a showdown with the guard Ivan was trying to win the support of those who had suffered most under the oprichnina. However, these moves did not mean that the high aristocracy finally had succeeded in taking control of the oprichnina. Taube and Kruse described the last oprichnina government accurately when they observed that the only people remaining close to the tsar were inveterate scoundrels or young simpletons. These representatives of the high titled nobility who entered the oprichnina fall into the second category; most of them were young and were there merely for show. The real council rulers were the brutal Maliuta Skuratov and his confederates, who ran the investigative arm.

The tsar, living in constant terror of imaginary conspiracies, trusted Maliuta blindly and saw him as his savior. Skuratov had helped Ivan deal with the old oprichnina guard. The nobles hated Maliuta Skuratov-Belskii as much as they did Basmanov-Pleshcheev, founder of the oprichnina. Kurbskii fiercely upbraided Ivan for advancing "vile parasites and maniacs; the stinking, God-loathed Belskii family and their comrades," and "oprichnina bloodsuckers."[3] Skuratov was remarkable for his humble birth even among members of the oprichnina who were not of noble origin. His name came last in lists of oprichnina privy councillors. He was not made court commander until shortly before the oprichnina finally was abolished, when his influence was at its height, for such a post was reserved for representatives of the pedigreed boyar nobility. The tsar's favor alone is not enough to explain Skuratov's rise. His appointment to this high office evidently came about because he had arranged for Ivan to marry Marfa Sobakina and thus became related to the royal house, and this connection removed the stigma of humble birth. One of his daughters married the tsar's cousin, I.M. Glinskii, another, the future tsar, Boris Godunov, and the third, Prince D.I. Shuiskii, the future tsar's cousin.

Privy councillor Vasilii Griaznoi assisted Maliuta in the investigative branch. He also had sprung from a humble family and began his service with one of the Staritskii boyars, "little above the huntsmen with dogs." After Vladimir Andreevich's suite was disbanded Griaznoi was enrolled in the oprichnina and advanced from kennelman to royal councillor. Maliuta and he were both investigators and judges in the affair of Prince Vladimir, and presided over the sack of Novgorod. Griaznoi's position was weakened by the purge of the guard, when his cousins were executed, but the protection of his friend Maliuta saved him from their fate. When Skuratov died Griaznoi was deprived of conciliar rank and banished to a small fortress on the Crimean frontier, where he was captured by the Tatars. His letters from the Crimea reveal the temperament and accomplishments of Maliuta's chief confederate. An unquenchable bottle companion of the tsar, who won approbation by making jokes at table, Griaznoi possessed the characteristics of jester and executioner combined. He was amazingly boastful, vain and thoughtless. To explain how he had been captured, he seriously told the tsar that the bowmen under his command fled on sight of the Tatars and left him alone to grapple with 200 enemy soldiers. Vasilii claimed that when forced to the ground "he bit six men on top of him to death and wounded twenty-two." Held prisoner by the Crimeans he somehow or other managed to "bite all the traitorous dogs, suddenly (!) did for all of them, so that only one dog, Kudeiar, was left, and he, for his sins, was a little humbled." He closed his letter from captivity to the tsar with the words: "You, O sovereign, are like God, and you dispose of great and small alike."[4] Historians have considered his words a manifesto of the low-born gentry, but, perhaps, they are rather the servile utterances of a favorite who had fallen from grace.

The privy councillor Roman Olferev-Nashchekin, who came to prominence during the last phase of the oprichnina, was much like Belskii and Griaznoi. Although illiterate, the tsar's favor made him Keeper of the Seal, in charge of the oprichnina chancery apparatus.

Once Olferev filed a precedence suit against the zemshchina treasurer, Prince Mosalskii, and with no trace of embarrassment wrote in his petition to the tsar: "I, your slave, do not know why the Mosalskii princes exist or who they are." The treasurer swallowed the insult and humbly observed: "Roman is a great man, and I am a little man."[5] The precedence suit depicted the illiterate Keeper of the Seal as an imposing figure in the oprichnina.

No description of the oprichnina would be complete without mention of Tsar Ivan. Contemporaries exaggerated the influence Ivan's whims and caprices had upon events, but the historian would be going too far if he tried to maintain the tsar's actions had no effect upon the history of the sixteenth century. Ivan's numerous writings furnish an excellent source to judge his personality. They show him as a man of natural ability, and his capacities, including political sensitivity and a bent for publicistics, and his education, were rare in his generation. However, contemporaries were also aware of the strange blend of opposing qualities in Ivan's nature, and expressed amazement as they described his impetuosity, mistrustfulness, intelligence, ferocious brutality, liking for war, pride, and humility.[6]

How did Ivan's personal qualities shape events of his time? The question is hard to answer. During the reform epoch Ivan's authority was restricted by his advisors, but with the oprichnina Ivan at last got rid of his initial counsellors and shook free of boyar tutelage. It seemed as though he had finally achieved the unlimited power he had striven to acquire, but this is obviously an exaggeration. The oprichnina was uniquely Ivan's creation, but he did not conceive and develop it alone, for during its most significant periods Ivan was constantly surrounded by hard, practical men like Basmanov, Viazemskii, and Skuratov. At first sight they appear as no more than the obedient executors of Ivan's decrees, but their authority in the oprichnina was substantial.

Ivan often told his son and heir "he should restrain people . . . be on his guard against them, and know how to attach them to his person," but Ivan himself had no idea how to manage men or even persuade intimate associates to follow his policies for any length of time. Ivan possessed one surprising characteristic: no matter how suspicious and cruel he might be, as Kliuchevskii has rightly observed, he was strangely credulous, and placed excessive, unlimited trust in men who had succeeded in convincing him of their loyalty. Unbalanced and highly suggestible, Ivan always was influenced by favorites and unable to decide important affairs of state or even choose his wives without their counsel. Silvester was the first to teach Ivan the lessons of life. Adashev intrigued him with his plans for major reform. Basmanov, one of the best commanders of the sixteenth century, suggested the oprichnina, a system of rule based on unrestrained force. Skuratov prodded him to deeds of violence. However, no matter how much Ivan fell under their influence, he would ultimately destroy his favorites without mercy, for once they lost power his attachment to them ceased. Adashev was disgraced and his pro-gentry reform program consigned to oblivion. When the oprichnina failed to achieve its goals Ivan had Basmanov's son behead his father. Skuratov alone managed to avoid his predecessors' fate, but no one can say what his destiny might have been if a Swedish cannonball had not ended his life at the peak of his glory.

When he abdicated the tsar experienced a severe emotional crisis that brought on serious illness. In following years the tsar enjoyed robust health, but he earnestly sought to attract competent physicians from abroad, and after the sack of Novgorod the zemshchina was filled with rumors that God had afflicted Ivan with an incurable disease. Witnesses swore the tsar was subject to fits, during which he was like a madman and foamed at the mouth. A nervous disorder may have caused his sudden flashes of rage and incredible suspiciousness, but the effect of Ivan's illness on events of his time should not be exaggerated. His cruelty was not exclusively pathological. The dark gloomy atmosphere of the middle ages, when men were prone to crude superstition, was impregnated with a cult of violence and contempt for the life and worth of the individual. Ivan was merely one of many medieval ruler-tyrants.

Ivan's harsh rule powerfully impressed contemporaries. The people bestowed the epithet of *groznyi* (awesome) on their mighty sovereign, which described the temperament of the first tsar of Muscovy with remarkable accuracy. Some 4,000 people perished in the oprichnina terror when the country's population was less than eight or ten million. As the terror intensified, fear and suspicion became more and more a fact of political life. Ivan himself was a victim. Towards the end of his life the tsar, an inveterate dissembler, no longer could conceal his emotions from outside scrutiny. The Austrian ambassador observed that those who saw him noticed the difference between his regal carriage and the expression in his eyes, which constantly darted about, watching everything closely. The papal envoy noted that although Ivan was very conceited because his courtiers incessantly praised and flattered him, he still remained suspicious. The same is true of his writing. D.S. Likhachev has pointed out that in the twilight of his life Ivan composed a canon to the Angel of Death which was filled with fear of death, paranoia, and loneliness. Fear drove Ivan to the Sloboda, where he lived for many years like a recluse, closely guarded and never going out unless attended by hundreds of soldiers armed to the teeth. In terror of conspiracies and assassination attempts he ceased to trust even his close family and friends, and his new confederates diligently nurtured his suspicions.

The tsar behaved like a man possessed by fear when oprichnina violence was at its height. Engels once noted that an epoch of terror is not the same thing as the dominion of those who can inspire it: "Quite the reverse; it is dominion by those who are themselves terrified. Terror is usually mindless cruelty undertaken to assuage the fears of those who are themselves frightened."[7] The brutal terror deeply impressed all elements of society. Fulsome obsequiousness and glorification of the ruler flourished as never before; Kurbskii remarked that flatterers and boon companions incessantly praised the tsar's wisdom and infallibility. Fear and flattery led Ivan's keen mind astray, so that he lost perspective, would brook no opposition, and stubbornly made mistake after mistake, until he ended up surrounded by dubious men, conscienceless scoundrels and careerists. The oprichnina made the autocrat seem omnipotent, but at the time of the terror he became a tool of opportunists like Maliuta Skuratov.

Men of his own time were impressed by Ivan's whimsical, aberrant behavior. At times his jokes were harmless. He joyfully celebrated his kinswoman's marriage to Duke Magnus. Guests danced while the psalm of St. Afanasii was chanted, and the ruler, now age 45, danced beside young monks and beat time over their heads with a rod. Ivan relaxed at such revels and joked at the expense of the monks and the great boyars. The chronicle narrates that he once summoned his boyars and "consigned (them) the royal cup without stint and (ordered) the cupbearer to give them to drink without cease. They began to frolic and talk all kinds of nonsense; some recited poetry; others sang songs, . . . and they uttered all sorts of indecent words. And . . . the tsar . . . asked men to listen to what they said and secretly take it down. Next morning he had copies brought to him and marvelled that the intelligent modest men of the royal council would say such things, and he showed the words to his counsellors, and they too marvelled at such a wonder."[8] Scribes had taken down the babblings of the drunken boyars, but the matter went no further. Not all the tsar's jests had such a happy outcome; his subjects dreaded his humor more than fire. Fusilier Captain Nikita Golokhvastov, celebrated for his daring, tried to become a monk to avoid Ivan's wrath, but this ploy failed to save him; the tsar had him brought before him and said he was glad to help a bold monk reach heaven sooner. Golokhvastov was seated on a powder keg, which was ignited.

As a youth Ivan was attracted to religion and as an adult became a fanatic. Many of his cruel incomprehensible actions were motivated by religious fanaticism. After the sack of Kazan Ivan ordered Moham-medans who had been brought to Novgorod executed for refusing to accept Christianity, and when he took Polotsk he had all the Jews drowned and personally murdered their children, who he considered were illegitimate and unpleasing to God. After perpetrating strange acts of cruelty Ivan was easily moved to penitence. He wrote to the Kirillov-Beloozero monastery: "Who can teach, who can punish, who can enlighten me, stinking dog that I am? I have ever been prone to drunkenness, lechery, fornication, vileness, murder, theft, rapine, hatred, and every evil."[9] The monks, who had been forced to endure much from Ivan during his lifetime, proclaimed him a pious tsar when he died, because churchmen were delighted with his devotion to re-ligion and his rhetorical self-accusation. None of the tsar's contem-poraries doubted his penitences were genuine; it never occurred to them. This affords an opportunity to look more closely at Ivan's be-havior and literary style, which strikingly display the combined traits of holy fool and jester, again as Likhachev has noted. In his writings Ivan could shift with ease from humility to a pride and anger which deprecated and denigrated his correspondent. The tsar would even engage in a verbal duel with a victim after the executioner had sharpened his axe.

Greed and coveting other persons' property were among the faults of which the tsar adjudged himself guilty. Ivan inherited ample re-sources from his ancestors and was not scrupulous in his choice of means to augment them. Shortly before the Tatar invasion he ordered his treasure transported from Moscow to Novgorod, a move which required 450 wagons. To judge from the number of vehicles, his treasure must have amounted to many thousand pounds of gold and silver ingots and coins. Ivan possessed one of the finest collections of precious stones in Europe. He knew how to appraise gems, which he acquired from all over the world, and like an inveterate collector he was fond of displaying them. Those who visited the royal treasury were impressed with the size and brilliance of the jewels, as well as with Ivan's mystical, obscure notions about them. The tsar believed rubies cleansed his tainted blood, sapphires contained secret power to protect him, and it meant death if a turquoise lost color when held in the hand. Diamonds, the most valuable eastern stones, kept a man from rage and voluptuousness; the tsar himself admitted he had never cared for them. Ivan considered jewels a gift from God which revealed the secret of nature for man's benefit and contemplation.

Since trustworthy data are lacking it is difficult to know what Ivan actually looked like. A very early portrait, which was painted by an unknown Moscow artist and taken to Copenhagen, is the best of the few that have survived. The appearance of the man is memorable: a high forehead, a receding hairline, a long aquiline nose, and an ample beard. But the portrait's value is lessened because it was painted in a conventional manner, like an icon. Another representation of Ivan is found on a fresco on the wall of the Novospasskii monastery in Moscow, but it is more conventional than the Copenhagen portrait; the ruler's handsome appearance is devoid of individuality. The defamatory pictures of the tsar found in German brochures which show a cruel, cunning Asiatic in a peak cap are worthless. Later portraits of Ivan in seventeenth-century works follow a pattern; he has an aquiline nose, and his eyebrows come together menacingly.

Visual representations of the tsar may be supplemented by literary descriptions, of which the most famous is by Prince I.S. Shakhovskoi, who wrote in the early seventeenth century: "Tsar Ivan was clumsily built. He had grey eyes and a jutting nose. Although of considerable height, he stooped, but his body was firm, his shoulders high, his chest broad, and his muscles thick."[10] Some details of this description are suspect. For example, Shakhovskoi said the tsar had grey eyes, but this does not agree with Ivan's celebrated reference to grey-eyed men. He asked Kurbskii: "Whenever you find a righteous man, will he not have grey eyes?" Shakhovskoi's description contains further incongruities, which are probably to be explained by the fact that the author had used the work of others to compose it. His assertion that Ivan was ungainly seems unduly harsh. Even the tsar's enemies, who criticized him unsparingly for acting like a tyrant, never said he was ugly. Less prejudiced authors, like Italian and English merchants, declared that Ivan had an attractive appearance and was indeed handsome. Ivan was evidently of a prepossessing exterior, or at least it did not reflect his innate cruelty. The first composite portrait of the tsar, painted by M.M. Gerasimov,[11] does not fully square with the sources in this regard. The Austrian ambassador, who was impressed with the tsar's regal carriage, gave a detailed description.

He said the tsar at age 45 was vigorous and stout. He was tall, and had a long thick reddish beard streaked with black. His head was shaven, and he had large darting eyes.

Chapter Twenty-Six

THE ROUT OF THE CRIMEAN HORDE

The plan to establish a vassal kingdom in Livonia collapsed after the unsuccessful siege of Reval. The author of the scheme, the oprichnina boyar Taube, betrayed the tsar and led a revolt in Dorpat, which the commanders suppressed in two hours, and Taube fled to Lithuania. Ivan demanded the king surrender him, and when he was refused ordered many Livonian prisoners executed. These events had no sustained impact on Russian foreign policy. Threat of hostilities with the Crimea aroused Moscow to seek peace with the Rzeczpospolita. Ivan sent a proposal to Cracow with the Lithuanian ambassador for an alliance against the Turks and Tatars, but the death of King Sigismund prevented its realization.

Collapse of the military alliance between Russia and Sweden and resumption of fighting in Swedish Livonia also stimulated Ivan's peace initiative, but considering John III a personal enemy, Ivan sent him an arrogant, insulting letter in which he demanded the Swedish king acknowledge himself a vassal of the Russian crown and cede Reval immediately. Diplomatic pressure was supplemented by military activity on the Swedish frontier. Alleging the war with Sweden required it, the tsar left the capital with his retinue and fusiliers in 1572 and went to Novgorod, although a Tatar attack was imminent. The Russian command was planning to send an army from Moscow to Novgorod to drive the Swedes out of Livonia as soon as the Tatars were defeated, but the struggle on the southern border was protracted. The army suffered severe losses fighting the Tatars and had to defer the incursion into Livonia. Ivan sent the Swedish king another offensive letter: "I had hoped you and your Swedes would now admit your folly, but I was mistaken. Your knavery is palpable; it flourishes in various forms, like a reptile."[1] The tsar warned King John he would soon invade his realm, and he kept his word. Late in 1572 he entered

Swedish Livonia with a large army and captured the fortress of Paida. Maliuta Skuratov perished when the fortress was stormed.

Events followed their normal course on the southern frontier. After Moscow was burned in 1571 Ivan told the khan he was ready to cede Astrakhan in return for peace, but the Crimean war-party prevailed and rejected Moscow's overtures. Famine and plague had ravaged Russia. The tsar's army had suffered serious defeats at Reval and below Moscow, and the Tatars considered the capital to be easy prey. Fire had destroyed the old fortifications and the new ones, which had been hastily erected, were not an effective substitute. The military reverses had shaken Russia's control of the Volga region and around the Caspian sea. The Nogai Horde finally had severed its vassal relationship with Moscow and adhered to the anti-Russian coalition. The subject peoples of the Volga area were aroused to throw off Russian domination. Many Adigesian princes in the north Caucasus had allied with the Crimea, and behind the Crimea stood the Ottoman empire, the most powerful military state in Europe. Given such resources, the khan hoped he could wrest the middle and lower Volga regions from Russia, capture Moscow, and restore Russia's ancient subjection to the Tatars. Shortly before the invasion Devlet-Girei had even distributed the regions and cities of Muscovy to his nobles. The sultan sent a special force to the Crimea to take part in the campaign.

Expecting a new attack around May, 1572, the Russians mustered about 12,000 gentry, 2035 fusiliers, and 3800 cossacks on the southern frontier. With units from the northern towns the army was reckoned at slightly higher than 20,000 men. The Tatars had an advantage in numbers; 40,000 to 50,000 knights from the Crimea, together with the Great and Little Nogai Hordes, took part in the attack, and they had Turkish artillery at their disposal. The Russian command stationed its basic forces south of Kolomna to interdict the routes from Riazan to Moscow, but considering it possible the Tatars might again advance from the Ugra region in the southwest, placed a commander, Prince D.I. Khvorostinin, with the vanguard in Kaluga on the far right flank where, contrary to tradition, he was given more soldiers than the regiments on the right and left flanks and a mobile river squadron to guard the fords across the Oka.

The Tatars invaded on July 23, 1572. Their mobile cavalry raced towards Tula and tried to cross the Oka above Serpukhov on the third day, but the Russian rearguard beat them back from the fords. By this time the khan and the entire Horde were approaching the main fords on the Oka at Serpukhov, while the Russian commanders awaited the enemy in heavily fortified positions north of the Oka. After clashing with the strong Russian defense the khan renewed his attack on the area about the Senkin ford above Serpukhov. During the night of July 28 Nogai cavalry dispersed the 200 gentry guarding it and seized the crossing points. Intensifying their nocturnal penetration, the Nogais ranged far to the north. At dawn Khvorostinin and the vanguard hastened to the place where the Tatars were crossing, but on encountering their main force declined to give battle. Next the army on the right flank tried to head off the Tatars on the upper reaches of the Nara river but were decisively repulsed. Khan Devlet-Girei emerged to the rear of the Russian army and began making his way without opposition along the Serpukhov road towards Moscow. The khan's sons, attended by a large body of picked cavalry, commanded the Tatar rearguards, and the Russian vanguard followed them, waiting for a favorable opportunity. When it came Commander Khvorostinin attacked. The battle took place near the village of Molodi, about thirty miles from Moscow. The Tatars were defeated and fled, and Khvorostinin pursued their rearguard to the khan's camp. Devlet-Girei had to send 12,000 Crimean and Nogai knights to assist his sons and retrieve the position. Fighting spread, and the commander-in-chief, Vorotynskii, while waiting for the Tatars, ordered a mobile fortress moved to the vicinity of Molodi. The main army hid within it and prepared for battle.

Since the enemy had three times as many troops Khvorostinin was compelled to withdraw, but while doing so executed a clever maneuver. His retreating regiment enticed the Tatars to approach the walls of the mobile fortress, where salvos from the Russian cannon, fired point-blank, decimated the Tatar cavalry and forced it to retire. The defeat at Molodi made Devlet-Girei suspend his march on Moscow. The Tatars waited a day at Pakhra expecting a Russian attack, but when it failed to occur they returned to Molodi. The Russian commanders had achieved a genuine success by diverting the khan from Moscow and forcing him to fight in a place of their own choosing. A hill lay at the center of the Russian defense position, on the summit of which stood the mobile fortress, surrounded by hastily dug trenches, with the main army concealed behind its walls. Outside, the remaining units covered the rear and flanks, and at the foot of the hill 3,000 fusiliers, ready to cover the commanders with their muskets, stood on the further side of Rozhai brook. Covering the distance from Pakhra to Rozhai quickly, the Tatars hurled themselves en masse against the Russian positions. The fusiliers were wiped out in the battle, but the soldiers in the movable fortress repulsed the cavalry attacks with heavy fire from their cannon and muskets. Alarmed at the setback, the Tatar commander-in-chief, Divei-Murza, wishing to reconnoiter, approached the Russian position closely, where daring lesser boyars captured him. The fighting raged until evening, July 30. Tatar losses were high; Tereberdei-Murza, commander of the Nogai cavalry, and three Crimean princes died. Having failed in his objective, the khan halted the attack and spent two days restoring order in his army. The Russians won the engagement, but their victory threatened to become a disaster, for the depleted units hiding in the mobile fortress soon exhausted their supplies and men and horses began to feel the pinch of hunger.

After two days of rest Devlet-Girei renewed his effort to storm the mobile fortress on August 2, concentrating all his cavalry and infantry units against it. The attack was led by the khan's sons, who had been told nothing must stop them from freeing Divei-Murza. Ignoring losses the Tatars kept trying to overturn the unstable walls of the fortress: "they stretched their hands out to the fortress wall; many Tatars were killed, and countless numbers had their hands cut off." Late in the day, when the Tatar onslaught weakened, the Russians executed a bold maneuver that decided the outcome. Commander M.I. Vorotynskii and his forces secretly left the fortress, made their way along the bottom of a declivity behind it, and came out to the rear of the Tatars. Prince D.I. Khvorostinin, who was left to defend the fortress, had artillery and a small group of German mercenaries at his disposal. At an agreed signal he ordered the cannon to fire, came out of the fortress, and fell upon the enemy at the moment Vorotynskii's units attacked them from behind. Unable to withstand the attack, the Tatars fled, and many were slain or taken prisoner. A son and grandson of Khan Devlet-Girei were killed and the commanders captured a large number of Crimean and Nogai princes. The Russians continued their pursuit of the enemy into the following day and routed the rearguard, comprising some 5,000 knights, which the khan had left on the Oka.

Time-honored tradition usually has assigned credit for the victory over the Tatars to Prince Vorotynskii, the commander-in-chief, but this is not really true. Vorotynskii had not been designated chief commander as a result of his superior military talents or service, but because of his patent of nobility. The real hero of the Battle of Molodi was the young oprichnina commander, Prince D.I. Khvorostinin, who formally held the rank of deputy commander of the main army. Giles Fletcher mentioned his outstanding service in the wars with the Tatars. Two years earlier he had defeated them roundly near Riazan, but the range of his military skills was not fully revealed until the Battle of Molodi in 1572, when he routed the Tatar rearguard on July 28, and took command of the mobile fortress during the decisive battle on August 2.

Molodi was one of the most important battles in the sixteenth century. Routing the Tatar Horde in the field enabled Russia to deliver a crushing blow to the military power of the Crimea. The destruction of the Turkish army near Astrakhan in 1569 and the defeat of the Crimean Horde near Moscow in 1572 limited Turkish and Tatar expansionism in eastern Europe, and the splendid victory won by the unified oprichnina-zemshchina armies affected domestic affairs and hastened the abolition of the oprichnina.

Chapter Twenty-Seven

THE ABOLITION OF THE OPRICHNINA

As soon as Moscow burned down in 1571 the government began gradual preparations to phase out the oprichnina. The danger of a Tatar invasion had hastened the fusion of the oprichnina and zemshchina armies; members of both were mingled indiscriminately and frequently served under senior zemshchina commanders. The Battle of Molodi was won by the combined army, which the military records bureau had formed without bothering to divide the gentry levy into two separate units. The authorities next moved to eliminate the extensive administrative overlapping that had grown up between the two institutions. Early in 1572 the tsar restored the office of governor in Novgorod and appointed Boyar I.F. Mstislavskii to the post. The oprichnina boyar P.D. Pronskii, who had been in charge of Novgorod, was transferred to the zemshchina section of the city and made subordinate to Mstislavskii. The separate administrations of Novgorod came to an end, although division of the region into two halves was maintained.

After reactivating the office of governor in Novgorod the authorities united the country's financial administration. The oprichnina

Keeper of the Seal was transferred to the zemshchina treasury bureau to assist the zemshchina treasurer, and the united treasuries supervised storage of the royal treasures, which had been transported to Novgorod, in church basements in the Yaroslav court. Interestingly enough, these changes in the military, administrative and financial structure occurred shortly before the Tatar invasion of 1572, when the tsar thought it highly likely he might lose the war. At the time Ivan celebrated his marriage to Anna Koltovskaia and made a disposition for his new wife in his draft will. Working on its text Ivan inserted a short but significant remark concerning the oprichnina: "It will be up to our sons, Ivan and Fedor, to do whatever they deem fit with the oprichnina we have established; the pattern is to hand."[1] In one sentence the tsar expressed indifference to the fate of the oprichnina, leaving his successors to decide whether to continue or abolish it. Many signs foretold its imminent end. Unlike the past, no further districts were incorporated into the oprichnina at the beginning of the year; construction of fortresses stopped, and the English ambassador was notified the secret negotiations to provide the royal family refuge in England were suspended. Ivan had long hesitated to proclaim dissolution of the guard, but the news of the defeat of the Tatars near Moscow apparently put an end to his doubts. He celebrated the victory for two weeks. In Novgorod bells rang constantly, and solemn prayers were said in all the churches. However, diversion and amusement did not interfere with executions. Amid the tales of rejoicing the Novgorod chronicler inserted a laconic statement: "That year the orthodox tsar hurled many of his lesser boyars into the Volkhov, weighted down with stones."[2] Trusted gentry members of the oprichnina accompanied the tsar to Novgorod in 1572, but they too fell victim to his wrath. The new leaders were trying to frighten the guardsmen, since it had been decided to dissolve the guard and abrogate its members' privileges.

Abolition of the oprichnina led to a review of service landholding in the territory it had controlled, which mainly affected its upper levels, gentry that had acquired rank and estates during the oprichnina, as well as those transferred into oprichnina territory from elsewhere. They were obliged to give up their lands, which had been confiscated earlier from zemshchina gentry. Many local serving-men who entered the oprichnina when their districts were incorporated into it probably kept their lands, but were deprived of the right to increase them. This abolished the main privilege of holding more land than their zemshchina counterparts, which members of the oprichnina had

enjoyed. Petty and middle oprichnina proprietors held their supplementary grants exclusively on service-tenure, so that this new land
review accomplished a second redistribution of the service-tenure
fund.

The tsar's last rescript on the oprichnina, which forbade even its
name to be mentioned, constitutes a fitting commentary on the institution. Those defying it were threatened with severe punishment:
"Anyone guilty of chattering about the oprichnina will be stripped
to the waist and beaten with a knout in the square." It would seem
this measure, which meant the end of the oprichnina, constituted
Ivan's and his new leaders' assessment of it, but another explanation
appears more likely. Fearing criticism, the authorities sought to stop
discussion of the hated oprichnina by forcing everyone to keep silent.

Chapter Twenty-Eight

THE PURPOSE OF THE OPRICHNINA

When it began the oprichnina showed a marked animus against the
princes. The disgraces, executions and confiscations that overwhelmed
the Suzdal nobility during its first months weakened the aristocracy's
political authority and strengthened the autocratic monarchy. Speak-
ing objectively, these measures helped overcome the survivals of
feudal fragmentation, which ultimately derived their tenacity from
the enormous estates owned by the princes and boyars. However,
the oprichnina was not consistent during the seven years it existed;
it did not pursue, either subjectively or objectively, a single goal,
principle, or plan. The time of massive terror in 1567-1570 followed
the brief period of compromise in 1566. At the center of its political
history lay the monstrous affair involving the supporters of the tsar's
cousin, Prince Vladimir Andreevich, which culminated in the sack of
Novgorod. It was not so much Novgorod's notorious separatism that
caused the terror as the efforts of the government, which had lost the
support of the ruling groups in the dominant class, to retain power
at any cost. The atmosphere of massive terror, universal fear, and
denunciation permitted the repressive forces inherent in the oprichnina to have a disproportionate effect on the political structure of

Ivan Vasilevich, Tsar and Grand Prince of All Russia

the leadership, and at last its creators lost control of the hellish terror machine. Members of the oprichnina became its ultimate victims.

Traditional estimates of the extent of the terror need to be re-examined. It is a gross exaggeration to say that thousands and thousands of people died. The synodical, based on genuine oprichnina records, shows that at the height of the terror some 3,000 to 4,000 individuals perished, including no less than 600 to 700 members of the gentry, apart from their families. The terror weakened the boyar aristocracy, but it also seriously damaged the gentry, the church, and the upper chancery bureaucracy, the very entities that provided the monarchy with its strongest support. To terrorize these social elements and groups was politically asinine.

V.I. Lenin characterized the political structure of seventeenth-century Russia as autocracy tempered by a boyar council and boyar aristocracy.[1] Sixteenth-century Russia may be similarly described, save that then the feudal aristocracy possessed more land and enjoyed greater political power. Autocracy was official doctrine and an appreciable political reality, but the head of state in the sixteenth century did not possess unlimited power. He ruled jointly with his council of mighty feudatories, as the boyar council and princes of the church were known. The establishment of the oprichnina constituted a form of revolution at the top to realize the concept of unlimited autocracy. The tsar could initiate measure in the oprichnina which otherwise would have been impossible without sanction from the council and higher clergy, and Ivan eventually shook off the tutelage of the boyar aristocracy.

The oprichnina circumscribed the council's competence, particularly in domestic matters. During the reform years the council regularly chose the regents who administered Moscow, and the whole country in the tsar's absence. In Adashev's time the titled nobility dominated the regency council, but after the introduction of the oprichnina the tsar substituted non-titled boyars for the princes, whom he expelled from the Moscow commission. By the end of the oprichnina period no boyars sat on it, and the capital was administered exclusively by chancery people. When the regency council was dissolved the boyar council lost one of its most important privileges. Council members traditionally had presided over important chanceries. The Master of Horse, head of the stable chancery, was considered the senior boyar in council, but after the execution of Cheliadnin-Fedorov the office was in effect abolished and administration of the chancery passed into the hands of gentry known as equerries.

During the oprichnina years the tsar scarcely ever convoked the full council and stopped regularly augmenting its membership. Deprived of almost all its influential leaders, the boyar council sharply contracted in numbers and its authority became slight.

Long before the oprichnina was established the eminent gentry publicist Ivan Peresvetov had urgently counselled the tsar to form a guard resembling the Janissaries in order to terrify insubordinate nobles. Fifteen years later many of Peresvetov's ideas had become reality. His prophecies were so prescient that certain scholars have been moved to assign his writings to the period following the oprichnina and regard them as a literary formulation of the oprichnina tragedy, but Peresvetov merely had been ahead of his time. His ideas apparently had no direct influence on the oprichnina, for Ivan and his intimates had no sympathy with gentry radicalism or the rationalism in Peresvetov's thought. Oprichnina policy had points of contact with the notions of gentry publicists but its practice was remote from their idealism. Ordinary soldiers, not just nobles and idle rich men, experienced the terror. The privileges given to members of the oprichnina hideously distorted Peresvetov's desire that a ruler should be generous to his soldiers and the gentry should enjoy equality. The gentry dreamed of a strong monarch whose rule would inspire awe and epitomize justice, yet this was transformed into the cruel despotism and abuse of the oprichnina. The monarchy had to rely on the gentry in its struggle with the fractious nobles, but it accomplished its purpose by forming an elite corps of serving-men from a few chosen districts, distinct from the rest, rather than by organizing the petty and middle gentry as a whole. The oprichnina proved that the middle and petty gentry did not yet possess sufficient moral and political potential, or adequate maturity and authority, to thrust aside and take the place of the boyar aristocracy as rulers of the country. The emergence of lowborn gentry praetorians merely led to brutal excesses, shameless pillage, and abuses of every kind.

The oprichnina threw up its own group of privy councillors. Expansion of the chancery system under the auspices of the boyar council created a number of conciliar secretaries, whose political power unquestionably grew during the oprichnina. Their senior representatives, who sat on the council, and privy councillors of gentry origin began to counterbalance the influence of the boyar nobles, and with the formation of these two new groups the council, which had been the exclusive preserve of the aristocracy, gradually assumed a more representative character. It was, however, the land assemblies that made the greatest contribution to developing genuine representation of the estates. The boyar council and the ecclesiastical assembly composed of princes of the church remained fixed components of any sixteenth-century assembly; the authorities invited gentry to participate only in a few exceptional circumstances. The most representative assembly of Ivan's era was the one held in 1566, when the oprichnina toyed briefly with compromise, which contained Moscow merchants as well as gentry and the chancery bureaucracy.

The oprichnina staunchly defended merchant capital. Ivan once observed to the English merchant Jenkinson: "We know we must hearken to what is said about the interests of merchants, for they form a bulwark of our state treasury." He assigned large tracts of land from the oprichnina to the merchant family of Stroganov, and granted substantial privileges to the English merchant company. The tsar was interested in foreign trade and did everything in his power to keep the sea route to Narva open.[2] The oprichnina offered the first concessions ever made in Russia to foreign industrial capital, but only as long as it derived profit from it. On occasion the authorities did not scruple to rob traders.

The oprichnina raids had demoralized society but they could not alter its basic patterns, which were set in the reform era. The growth of the chancery system fostered centralization; the role of the service gentry in the bureaucracy increased in importance, and the assemblies with more heterogeneous representation were harbingers of the monarchy of the future, which would come to rely on representatives from the estates. The confiscations carried out during the early existence of the oprichnina weakened the boyar aristocracy and strengthened the monarchy. The terror left deep traces on Russian life, and the grim spectre of the oprichnina long haunted the leaders of the ruling group. However, the oprichnina did not alter the general political contours of the monarchy, nor end the domination of the council as the highest body of state nor attack the system of precedence, which protected the privileges of the nobility. The oprichnina seriously harmed Russia. The cruel, confused terror cost many people their lives and the raids destroyed productive forces. The outrages perpetrated by members of the oprichnina were unprecedented and unjustifiable.

Chapter Twenty-Nine

A TATAR KHAN ON THE MUSCOVITE THRONE

Three years passed. Recollections of the oprichnina were less immediate, and people had begun to forget the tsar's idiosyncratic creation
when an ominous cloud appeared on the horizon portending another
oprichnina. Ivan abdicated a second time in 1575 and set a Tatar in
his service, Khan Simeon Bekbulatovich, on the throne. The Tatar
now dwelt in the royal chambers and the mighty sovereign had moved
to the Arbat, went about Moscow like an ordinary boyar, took residence in the Kremlin at a distance from the new grand prince on the
throne, and humbly obeyed his orders.

A long series of circumstances, the most dramatic of which occurred behind the scenes, preceded Ivan's abdication. The sources are
silent; only the synodical tells a portion of the story. It contains the
entry: "Remember, O Lord, Prince Boris Tulupov, Prince Vladimir,
Prince Andrei, Princes Nikita Tulupov, Mikhailo Pleshcheev, Vasilii
Umnoi, Aleksei, Fedor Starovo, Orina . . . and Yakov Mansurov." The
compiler deliberately put these names on one page, because after
serving in the oprichnina all these men had transferred to what was
called Ivan's court, which had taken the place of the guard after the
oprichnina was dissolved. The new court accepted only highly trusted
men, who never numbered more than a few hundred, among whom
these men occupied responsible positions. A year before Simeon's
enthronement the tsar celebrated his marriage to Anna Vasilchikova,
to which only a few very prominent people were invited. Interestingly
enough, all those celebrating the wedding were soon numbered among
the disgraced; no one suspected that their route from wedding feast
to scaffold would be so short. Before the wedding Ivan visited the
torture chambers and asked boyars' slaves roasting over fires: "Which
of our boyars are betraying us?" He himself suggested some names:
"Vasilii Umnoi, Prince Boris Tulupov, Mstislavskii? . . ." The first
persons he mentioned were his intimate counsellors who were standing beside him. He spoke in jest, but the boyars froze at hearing his
words.

The men listed in the synodical were not simply important officials at Ivan's court. Their biographies reveal that they were the leaders

of the first government formed after the oprichnina was abolished, which included Prince Boris Tulupov, who had achieved a dazzling career. Originally a humble armorer transporting the royal muskets, within a year or two he had become a member of the tsar's intimate council, disposing of high state affairs. The synodical also lists Vasilii Umnoi, Skuratov's successor, who continued Maliuta's hunt for treason among the boyars so zealously that he was immediately awarded boyar rank at Ivan's court. His numerous relatives in the Kolychev family followed him there.

Little or nothing is known about conflicts among the leaders of Ivan's court before Simeon arrived, but one point is clear: they permitted power to pass to extremists who wished to restore the style of rule practised in the oprichnina. The first symptoms of this conflict among Ivan's court leaders can be discerned in the fierce squabbles over precedence between members of the Kolychev and Godunov and Saburov families. Boyar F.I. Umnoi lost a suit against Boyar B. Yu. Saburov and had to give way to him, and his cousin, Boyar B.I. Umnoi, barely survived a challenge from the royal chamberlain, D.I. Godunov.

After Tulupov's execution his estate in Staritsa was assigned to Boris Godunov in recompense for an insult he had suffered. The nature of the insult Tulupov offered Godunov will never be known, but the latter was requited in full; Tulupov was impaled on a stake. It is well to remember that the property of disgraced persons usually was divided between the treasury and the informer. Boris tried to divest himself of the estate he had acquired unjustly, and when Ivan died he assigned Tulupov's property to a monastery with instructions to pray in perpetuity for the Umnoi brothers Vasilii and Fedor, Tulupov, and the latter's mother Anna.[1] Fedor Umnoi ended his life as a monk, and witnesses reported that Anna was tortured to death the day her son died. Since Boris had been instrumental in disgracing all of them, he had them remembered on August 2, obviously the day they were executed, as described in the synodical.

The tsar sent the leaders of the first post-oprichnina government to the scaffold on August 2, 1575. The executions provide a clue to unravelling the second treasonable affair involving Novgorod. Once set in motion, the terror machine could not be stopped. Many members of Ivan's court were arrested, including his personal physician, Elijah Bomel. The people remembered Elijah, considered a wicked seer, with revulsion.[2] He rendered the tsar services of a sinister nature, preparing poison for courtiers fallen from grace, some of whom, for example, Grigorii Griaznoi, he poisoned with his own hand. Bomel was the first royal astrologer. He would inform the tsar that the position of the stars was unfavorable, foretell frightful disasters, and then show him how to escape his fate. Ivan trusted him completely. At last the astrologer became involved in a web of his own intrigues and decided to flee Russia. Adopting his servant's name en route, Bomel set out for the frontier, first sewing his gold into the lining of his coat, but the suspicious-looking foreigner was arrested in Pskov and returned in chains to Moscow. Ivan was dumbfounded that his favorite had betrayed him and ordered him roasted on a large spit. Under torture Bomel implicated Leonid, archbishop of Novgorod, and many prominent individuals. Contrary to legend, it was not spite but weakness that caused the seer and wizard to urge the tsar to slay his boyars; he could not endure torture.

The Englishman Horsey, who saw the doctor carried half-dead from the torture chambers to prison, has related curious tales about his last days. The tsar ordered his son Ivan and his associates, who were suspected of concerting with the physician, to examine him. Bomel had hoped these courtiers would help him avoid his fate, but when he realized his friends had forsaken him he started talking and told the tsar more than he wished to know. He compromised the prominent courtier, P.N. Yurev, a cousin of the heir, whose name is found in the synodical. Archbishop Leonid died in disgrace on October 20, 1575, and Zakharin-Yurev was beheaded four days later.[3] These events form a pattern.

The new round of executions in Moscow was occasioned by the situation in Novgorod, of which the chief figure was Leonid. The archbishop was among the clerics who had advocated friendly relations with the oprichnina and Ivan's court. Enjoying the tsar's confidence he became archbishop after the sack of Novgorod, where he subordinated the church to the oprichnina administration, headed by Aleksei Staroi, probably the Staroi (again, no coincidence) executed shortly before Leonid's trial. Contemporaries stated that two other high churchmen shared the fate of the Novgorod archbishop. Their names are coupled with Leonid's in a short synodical of disgraced public functionaries: "Archbishop Leonid, Archimandrite Evfimii, Archimandrite Iosif of Simonov."[4] The chronicles also mention that Evfimii, who presided over the Chudov monastery in the Novgorod Kremlin, perished with Leonid. All these men were closely connected with one another. During the oprichnina years Levkii, a notorious supporter of the tsar whom Kurbskii bitterly assailed, was in charge of the Chudov monastery. He was followed by Leonid, who in turn named Evfimii his successor. They were tainted by their cooperation with the oprichnina, as was the archimandrite of the Simonov monastery, which had achieved the unusual distinction of being enrolled in the oprichnina.

The compliant churchmen had put up with the tsar's numerous marriages and other violations of church law, but their tolerance ceased as soon as Ivan announced that no more land could be willed to great monasteries. He made clear that he was disappointed with his former favorites. Two years before the executions he wrote that the Chudov and Simonov monasteries were inhabited by monks in name only, for everyone knew they were men of this world in every respect. The archimandrites set a poor example for the brethren; the tsar was informed that the Simonov archimandrite "did not want to retain his office; washed, received the Eucharist improperly, and spoke without understanding."[5] Monks had no need to worry about cases of mere impiety, but other charges were levelled against them. The tsar grew angry with his clerics because they constantly pursued the boyars with the ingenious justification that religious establishments would become impoverished without boyar legacies. Ivan wrote that "in olden times holy men did not pursue boyars," but now monks associated and had friendly relations with the fractious boyars. Very likely Leonid and the archimandrites paid for their friendship with the boyars of Ivan's court who were executed.

Leonid's death spawned numerous legends. Some told that the tsar stripped the robe from the archbishop, sewed him in a bearskin, and incited dogs to worry him. In another version Leonid was strangled in the square in front of the Cathedral of the Dormition. The best-informed author, Horsey, asserted that after a court sentenced Leonid to death the tsar took pity on him and commuted the sentence to perpetual confinement. The archbishop was locked in a cellar, kept on bread and water, and soon died. Horsey noted that Leonid was charged with practising witchcraft and maintaining a coven in Novgorod, whose members were burned after his trial. Is this credible, or did Horsey invent it? A brief entry in the synodical list proves it: "Remember, O Lord, fifteen women, the witches of the coven." They were Leonid's witches, of whom Horsey wrote.

The court condemned Leonid as a heretic and state criminal for supposedly having had treasonous contacts with the Polish and Swedish kings. These charges were so inept that only a completely cowed people could possibly believe them. Fearing criticism from church leaders, the tsar resorted to blackmail. The catalog of the royal archive refers to an investigation concerning "Moscow Metropolitan Antonii, and concerning Krutitsa Bishop Tarasii in the years 7083 and 7084."[6] The date of the investigation is significant: the year 7083 ended August 31, and 7084 began September 1, 1575. This means the tsar was pressuring the metropolitan when Leonid's trial was being energetically prepared.

Certain historians have considered Ivan's abdication and the elevation of Khan Simeon to be one of the former's whims or caprices, devoid of political significance and whose purpose was unclear, but the above facts demonstrate that a serious internal crisis precipitated Ivan's abdication. The second Novgorod affair implicated many highly-placed boyars and princes of the church. Fear of total betrayal haunted the tsar like a nightmare. He longed to proceed against the conspirators but no longer possessed reliable military forces. Ivan's court had failed to live up to his expectations; its chief leaders were charged with high treason and ended their lives on the block.

The basic problem with which Ivan and his associates were wrestling lay elsewhere. Abolition of the oprichnina had abrogated the unlimited powers inherent in the original proclamation establishing it. No one could prevent Ivan from executing intimates in his court, and he secured the condemnation of a few church hierarchs unpopular in the zemshchina because of their identification with the oprichnina, but he dared not attack his mighty vassals without the approval of the boyar council and church leaders. The threatening oprichnina no longer existed, and it had failed to crush the boyar aristocracy. As had been the case before, when planning action Ivan had to reckon with the attitude of the nobility. It was risky to ignore the boyar council, especially when it was known that the tsar's guard, his court, was not entirely reliable. Ivan and his associates long agonized over the problem of how to reactivate the oprichnina without the consent of council and also preserve an appearance of legality, until the tsar's fondness for jesting and mystifying suggested what he ought to do. A new figure, Grand Prince Simeon, appeared upon the scene. Tragedy had unexpectedly become farce.

A few details are known about Sain Bulat Bekbulatovich. He played a role suitable only for a weak and mediocre man. Ivan could do whatever he liked with his tame khan. He had first made him tsar of Kasimov, then removed him from that Islamic appanage duchy, baptized and renamed him Simeon, and married him to the widowed daughter of Prince Mstislavskii. A service Tatar khan, formerly a Muslim, could enjoy no authority among the boyars or with the church, but Simeon's royal blood impressed Ivan; he appreciated his submissiveness even more, and made him president of the zemshchina council. However, even this office could not endow the tame khan with sufficient authority to decide affairs in the name of the boyar council on his own. To overcome the impasse Ivan abdicated in favor of Simeon and proclaimed the president of the boyar council grand prince of all Russia. Next, without difficulty he had Simeon declare a state of emergency. By entering on what he termed his appanage Little Ivan of Moscow (as the tsar now called himself) no longer had to make submissions to the council. He issued his orders in the form of petitions addressed to the grand prince.

Soon after Archbishop Leonid's death Ivan submitted his first petition to Simeon, asking him "to show your generosity by making men available to scrutinize boyars, gentry, lesser boyars, and court servitors. You should free and dismiss some and you should free and accept others." The petition clearly put the grand prince in a position inferior to the appanage prince. Little Ivan of Moscow could take any subject of Grand Prince Simeon into his appanage, but Simeon was forbidden to accept serving-men from the tsar's appanage. The newly-organized appanage army was identical with the old oprichnina guard. Gentry enrolled in the appanage lost their service-tenure estates in the zemshchina and were given land in the appanage principality as recompense. The new appanage prince said nothing about an exchange of holdings between the grand duchy and the appanage and kept everything under his control. Little Ivan of Moscow deliberately used expressions in his petition to convince his subjects he had no intention of again dividing the state into an oprichnina and a zemshchina, but was merely conducting a regular reorganization of his court and reviewing personnel.

When the first oprichnina was established the tsar left Moscow before announcing his decision to abdicate, but when the second one was organized Ivan refused to leave the capital and deposited the crown and other regalia in his appanage treasury. Explaining his unusual action to the English ambassador, among other things Ivan said: "Behold. Seven crowns remain at our disposition, with the sceptre and the rest of the royal regalia." The regalia the dethroned grand prince showed the Englishman can be determined: rescripts from the appanage were issued by Lord Prince Ivan Vasilevich of Moscow, Pskov and Rostov. Little Ivan added the titles of the two appanage principalities of Dmitrov and Staritsa, as well as those of Rzhev and Zubtsov, to the three ancient princely titles.

The prince of Moscow needed approximately a month to structure his appanage and form a new oprichnina guard in it. The appanage included the Pskov region, sacked during the oprichnina years, and Rostov and its district. Neither had been part of the original oprichnina; hence, it is reasonable to conclude that the prince of Moscow had no wish to take into his appanage petty service gentry residing in former oprichnina districts, who had once comprised the oprichnina guard. The appanage was governed by its own council, headed by the Nagoi and Godunov families, and Bogdan Belskii. The tsar's old chamberlain, Dmitrii Godunov, had adopted the career of political investigator, and his chancery now handled conspiracies against the tsar's person. His services were appreciated, and he was awarded boyar rank in spite of his humble birth. His nephew Boris entered the appanage council with the rank of steward, and his brother-in-law, Belskii, became armorer. Afanasii Nagoi had rendered the tsar valuable service when he was envoy to the Crimea by uncovering imaginary boyar plots to benefit the Crimean khan, which assured him advancement. He persuaded Ivan to bring his brother Fedots into the appanage council, make him an associate boyar, and later to marry his niece, Mariia Nagaia. The triumvirate that now had formed, consisting of representatives of the Nagoi and Godunov families, and Belskii, preserved its influence at Ivan's court to the end of the tsar's life.

Public executions, which took place a month after Ivan abdicated, made a painful impression on contemporaries. The chronicles describe them in detail, but even a brief perusal reveals that the chronicle entries differ. The synodical must again be consulted to establish the facts. It lists the following individuals: "Prince Petr Kurakin, Iona Buturlin and his son and daughter, Dmitrii Buturlin, Nikita Borisov, Vasilii Borisov, Druzhina Volodimerov, Prince Daniel Drutskii, Iosif Ilin, a protopope, three assistant secretaries, and five peasants."

Who were these victims of the second oprichnina? Boyar Prince Petr Kurakin had been lucky to escape the first oprichnina, when his brother Ivan was immured in a monastery. He had been exiled to Kazan, where he spent ten years, only to be brought back to Moscow to perish on the scaffold. Boyar Ivan Buturlin and Associate Boyars Dmitrii Buturlin and Nikita Borisov had a different experience. They had become part of the oprichnina council when that institution was in decline, and after it was abolished they abandoned their dark oprichnina habits and transferred to the zemshchina council. The other disgraced persons listed in the synodical had enjoyed comparable careers. Prince Daniel Drutskii and the eminent secretaries Druzhina Volodimerov and Osip Ilin had risen in the oprichnina and then went to preside over chanceries in the zemshchina. Ivan, protopope of the Cathedral of the Archangel in the Kremlin, met the same fate as these former members of the oprichnina; they "sat him in the water," or, to speak plainly, drowned him in a river. The sources establish that the tsar executed these former members of the oprichnina in late November, 1575. This date forms the final link of a long chain: Ivan slew the leaders of his court in August; hunted treason in Novgorod in September and October; abdicated late in October; a month later created his new oprichnina, now known as his appanage; and, finally, ordered the execution of prominent zemshchina boyars.

Contemporaries hinted that strife in the royal family caused the new round of sentences of disgrace. The Moscow chronicler tells the following story in a contrived and complicated way: the tsar "had begun to think about his son and heir, Ivan Ivanovich, and about his desire to rule." The heir already was suspected of intending to overthrow his father and seize the throne, so Ivan abdicated and assigned the grand duchy to Simeon in order to block his son, but boyars close to the heir supposedly said: "Sovereign, it is not fitting for you to overlook your own progeny and set a foreigner upon the throne."[7] In a rage the tsar ordered these opponents executed. It is difficult to assess the credibility of the chronicle account. Perhaps the Bomel affair implicated boyars among the heir's intimates, and the tsar decided to get rid of them. Apparently he considered Ivan Buturlin the chief conspirator, since he had his son and daughter beheaded with him while sparing the families of other disgraced persons.

After the first serious quarrel with his son Ivan declared in the presence of boyars, clergy and foreign envoys that he would disinherit him and make the Danish Duke Magnus his heir. Five years later he made good his threat, but awarded the crown to Simeon, not to Magnus. The royal family was rent with faction, as relatives feuded. The headstrong father's actions seemed to say to his adult son: "I am executing your cousins and intimates and I shall give the throne to a foreigner, not to you." Historical songs preserve a confused tradition to the effect that only the intervention of his beloved uncle, Nikita Yurev, saved young Ivan from death, but whether this is true or not cannot be determined. The tsar did not forget other zemshchina leaders; boyars' severed heads rolled in their courtyards, but although Ivan bullied and cudgelled the heir he never intended to bring him to trial, and actually took him into his appanage and proclaimed him co-ruler. Decrees from the appanage were issued jointly in the name of the two princes of Moscow, Ivan Vasilevich and Ivan Ivanovich.

Three days after the public executions in the Kremlin Ivan summoned the English ambassador to inform him Simeon had become grand prince, and added: "This came about because of the criminal deceitful behavior of our subjects, who murmur against us and oppose us for demanding an oath of fealty, and hatch conspiracies against our person." The sense of his declaration was clear: Ivan of Moscow had executed the boyars for refusing to take an oath of allegiance to him. Fearing the envoy might not take his abdication seriously, Ivan declared: "I have bestowed the office on a foreigner; neither he, his realm, nor his throne are akin to me."[8] In his discussion with the envoy Ivan had unwittingly revealed the truth. Simeon had been called upon to play the principal role in the charade because he had no real claim to the Russian throne. Conjuring up the hateful spectre of the Tatars by deliberately allowing a khan to exercise the powers of the grand prince, to whom the prince of Moscow humbly submitted petitions, Ivan prudently had sought a successor who would arouse fear in his subjects and thereby further bar him from seeking the throne. The ceremony at which power was transferred to Simeon was ambiguous. The chronicle noted that the khan ruled only at Ivan's pleasure, and foreigners observed this also. Horsey wrote that the tsar had elevated Simeon and crowned him without approval by the boyar council, and omission of the ceremony at which council members took an oath to the new ruler deprived the act of legal sanction. Simeon's position was rendered even more anomalous by the fact that although he sat on the royal throne he was not tsar, but merely grand prince.

After Simeon had been on the throne for three months Ivan told the English ambassador he could reassume office whenever he wished and act as God ordained, because Simeon had not been crowned officially nor elected by the people, and merely ruled on his own recognizance. But even after this statement the tsar was slow to end the charade, and the Tatar khan stayed on the Muscovite throne approximately a year. Assuming he might need the compliant Simeon in the future, Ivan retired him honorably instead of destroying him. When he left Moscow Simeon became grand prince of Tver.

The tsar had in effect reestablished the oprichnina under the guise of an appanage, but this time his persecutions affected no more than a few persons, and the previous sacks and devastation did not occur.

The appanage was a kind of postscript to the oprichnina, when the tsar destroyed the group of boyars that had dominated the oprichnina in its last phase. Simeon's rule had no real impact on Russia's domestic situation.

Chapter Thirty

IVAN'S FAMILY LIFE

Royal marriages served political not private ends and were influenced by dynastic considerations. Muscovite diplomacy had counted heavily on arranging a good marriage for Ivan before he attained his majority; the boyars had hoped to contract a marriage with a Polish princess, but negotiations with the Polish royal house were unproductive and the council was compelled to forgo the advantages such a dynastic marriage promised. In the chronicle version forcible arguments were suggested to the sixteen-year-old grand prince, which he rehearsed in a speech to the council: "You have planned to contrive a marriage for me in other realms (which was literally true) with some king or some tsar, but I . . . reject this notion. I do not wish to marry in other realms because I lost my father and mother when I was young. For me to bring a wife from another country means that our habits will somewhat differ, and there will be vanity between us, and so I . . . am minded and wish to marry someone within my own realm."[1] Ivan's musings about incompatibility of character were secondary in comparison with religious considerations. In the eyes of the orthodox Muscovites neighboring ruling houses professed heretical beliefs; it was such a difficulty that had prevented Vasilii III from marrying until he was 25. Finally young Ivan decided to emulate his father's example. The council issued a proclamation ordering the prettiest girls in the land to present themselves at court. Boyars and associate boyars spread out over the country to look at them, preceded by couriers bearing a stern injunction that all gentry with daughters twelve years or older must take them to the governors at once for scrutiny; anyone who concealed his daughter faced disgrace and execution. Poor road conditions threatened to drag the scrutiny out for months, and the boyars, without waiting for girls from the provinces to assemble, took advantage of the situation to bring their daughters and nieces to court. One of the girls presented to the tsar at this review was Anastasiia, daughter of Associate Boyar Roman Yurevich Zakharin. Her father was undistinguished, but her uncle had been one of the regents during Ivan's minority, and the grand prince had known Anastasiia's family from childhood. The tsar's relatives, the Glinskii family, not considering the Zakharin family dangerous rivals, did not oppose the choice of Anastasiia.

Ivan's first marriage lasted thirteen years; six children were born of it, but only two survived. The two first, Anna and Mariia, died when they were less than a year old. The third was Dmitrii, whom at six months his parents took on a pilgrimage to the Kirillov monastery. On the way back the child died in an unexpected manner. When travelling the heir was attended by an elaborate entourage; his nurse was supposed to be invariably accompanied by two noble boyars. Returning from Kirillov the royal barge put into shore and the procession was marching down the gangplank when it overturned, precipitating everyone into the river. The child fell from his nurse's arms, and although rescued immediately, he was already dead. Thus perished Dmitrii, Ivan's eldest son and original heir. Anastasiia's second son, Ivan, was born on March 28, 1554, and two years later she had a daughter, Evdokiia. The son survived, but the daughter died at three. The royal family's third son was born May 31, 1557, but this child, Fedor, was sickly and feeble-minded, for by this time Anastasiia's health was failing and she was constantly ill. The frequent bouts with childbirth had exhausted the queen, who died before she was thirty, and was buried in the Voznesenskii monastery in the Kremlin. Many attended her obsequies, and the chronicler said: "There was much lament for her, as she was gentle and kindly disposed to all." Little is known of Anastasiia. Reared in seclusion among boyar ladies, it was unlikely she bore any resemblance to Sofia or Regent Elena Glinskaia. She seldom became involved in her husband's affairs. Those ill-disposed towards her were fond of comparing her with the impious Empress Eudocia, who had persecuted St. John Chrysostom, an allusion to Anastasiia's hostility to Silvester. She was alarmed at the unbounded influence Ivan's advisor had over him, but could do nothing about it, for her own was not as great.

Relations between husband and wife could not be termed unclouded, especially towards the end of Anastasiia's life. Many years later when Kurbskii reproached Ivan for his immorality the latter replied openly and frankly: "Perhaps you will say I did not endure my lot and did not display continence, but we are all human."[2] The tsar's remark about reprehensible conduct found reflection in the chronicle: "When Queen Anastasiia died the tsar became wild and very lustful." Nevertheless, Ivan was attached to his first wife and remembered her with affection and regret all his life. At her obsequies he sobbed, and "from great groaning and from sadness of heart" could barely stand up. A week after Anastasiia's death Makarii and the bishops made an unusual proposal to the tsar, asking him to lay aside his grief and "marry soon for the good of Christians, and not place constraint upon himself." Political calculation lay behind the concern for Ivan's morals. Many at court were dissatisfied with the predominance of the Zakharin family and hoped that relatives of a new queen would expel the late Anastasiia's kin.

Ivan made an impetuous second marriage. Meeting with no success in Poland and Sweden, his diplomats found the tsar a young bride in Kabardia, Princess Kuchenei, daughter of a Kabardian prince, Temir Guki. Ivan scrutinized the girl at court, and the official chronicle declares he fell in love with her. Kuchenei was converted to Orthodoxy and took the name of Mariia. The marriage celebration in the Kremlin lasted three days, and during this whole time inhabitants of the capital and foreigners were forbidden on pain of punishment to leave their homes. The authorities were afraid the commons might mar the festivities, for everyone remembered what had happened after Ivan's first wedding.

At first Mariia, who knew no Russian, did not understand what her husband said to her, but later she learned the language and even advised the tsar how to set up a guard such as the princes of her mountain homeland had, and on some other matters. This marriage produced a son, Vasilii, who died in infancy. Vague rumors that Mariia was poisoned are only legend. Before her death Ivan and she went to Vologda, where she was taken ill. Reports about the conspiracy in Novgorod forced the tsar to rush back to Moscow, telling Aleksei Basmanov to convey his sick wife later. The road was hard and long. On orders Mariia was brought to the Sloboda, where she soon died.

After the sack of Novgorod the tsar announced he would remarry immediately, requested another bride-show, and 1500 daughters of the gentry were assembled at court from all over the country. Ivan, now 40, was faced with a difficult choice. Health and beauty were the essential criteria, but a good half of the girls possessed these qualities in abundance. The tsar finally listened to his loyal confidant,

Maliuta Skuratov, who chose Marfa Sobakina. After the betrothal she began to decline, and should properly have been eliminated from the competition, but putting his trust in God the tsar proceeded with the wedding, although the bride was at death's door and died before the marriage could be consummated, as the higher clergy certified. It was stated officially that evil persons had poisoned her, but it is not difficult to guess the source of the rumor. The marriage had taken place, and the lowborn Maliuta was now related to the royal family. Various rumors circulated about Marfa's death. It was said that her mother had arranged for a courtier to transmit to her some herbs and potions. When Marfa's grave was opened a surprising biological phenomenon was disclosed: the pale royal bride lay in her grave unaffected by decay after more than 360 years.

The bride-shows had been held several times. During the last one the number of girls was narrowed from 24 to 12, until Maliuta Skuratov's protegeé finally won, but when she died the choice fell on Anna Koltovskaia, whom the tsar married a few months later. She was of even more humble origin than the Sobakin family, and the queen's relatives could not be given conciliar rank. The Koltovskii family never became accustomed to the court, and Anna's fresh beauty was not enough to keep her on the throne at such a difficult time. The marriage lasted less than a year. The tsar sent Anna to a nunnery and deprived her relatives of their estates.

When the new favorite, Vasilii Umnoi-Kolychev, took Skuratov's place the tsar married Anna Vasilchikova. The ceremony was attended by only a few people, but nearly twenty representatives of the Kolychev family were among the guests. Can this be explained by the tsar's caprice, or because the favorite had arranged for the tsar to marry his relative? Afterwards the destinies of the Kolychev and Vasilchikov families became closely intertwined. A few months later ominous clouds gathered over Umnoi's head. Anticipating disaster he sent money to the Troitsa monastery to have prayers said for his soul, and Queen Anna's brothers hastened to follow his example, surely no chance occurrence. Tradition has it that the tsar sent Vasilchikova to a nunnery three days after Umnoi's execution.

Emotion played no part in the tsar's marriages, even when foreign-policy considerations were absent. Ivan's family life was exposed to domestic vicissitudes, and his subjects were unable to distinguish among the queens who followed the various favorites to court. It seems that only one of the tsar's marriages caused surprise. The *Chronograph of the Marriages of Tsar Ivan Vasilevich* reveals that he "married a widow, Vasilisa Melenteva, whose husband was slain by members of the oprichnina; she was unusually comely and pretty, more so than the girls who normally passed before the tsar's eyes."[3]

Students of the Chronograph on occasion have expressed the view that the entry pertaining to Queen Vasilisa was the work of Sulakid- zev, a notorious forger of old Russian materials, but though attractive the theory fails to correspond with the facts. Vasilisa was an actual historical personage, who was mentioned, apart from the Chronograph reference, in a chronicle belonging to N.M. Karamzin, which reported that people said: "Tsar Ivan Vasilevich prayed with the widow Vasi- lisa Melenteva, that is, with his wife." A notation from the cadastral book of the Viazma district assists in dissipating any lingering doubts about Vasilisa: "The sovereign, Tsar and Grand Prince, Ivan Vasile- vich of all Russia, in summer 7087 bestowed an hereditary estate upon Fedor Melentev and Mariia Melenteva, Ivanov's children."[4]

This entry underscores something which was rare in the sixteenth century. The children of an obscure Melentii Ivanov, who was not a member of the Muscovite nobility, received a hereditary estate com- prising some 4,000 acres of land, extensive forests, and a meadow. Few noble boyars had been so lavishly rewarded for major state ser- vice, but the orphans of the undistinguished Melentii had performed one service: before they were granted their land their mother had become Ivan's sixth wife. His marriage to a secretary's widow, proba- bly not even of gentry origin, was not occasioned by political con- siderations. Vasilisa, who was older than the other queens, died soon afterwards, but Ivan's brief sixth marriage coincided with the period during which he achieved his greatest success.

The court favorite A.F. Nagoi arranged for Ivan to marry his niece three years before the tsar died. This seventh marriage contravened church law, and many regarded it as illegal. The tsar too apparently did not take it seriously and was prepared to jettison his last wife to win the hand of an English princess. At the height of the Livonian war Moscow tried to forge a military alliance with England in order to use that country's fleet in the Baltic, but without success, for Elizabeth's council refused to ratify the treaty, which had been struck in Vologda. This aroused the tsar to criticize the English queen harsh- ly: "We understood you were sovereign in your realm and ruled it alone, but others share your authority; they are not responsible people, but petty traders, while you continue to vaunt your maidenly state like a vulgar girl."[5] His scorn of the "old virgin" did not prevent Ivan from scheming to marry her, but his plans came to naught.

At the end of the war the Russian court entered into fresh negotiations in London with a view to arranging a marriage between the
tsar and Mary Hastings, a relative of the queen. Fedor Pisemskii,
Ivan's representative in England, officially stated that the tsar intended to get rid of Mariia Nagaia because "he, the sovereign, has
taken a boyar's daughter from his domain unto himself, but this is
not immutable; if the queen's niece is comely and worthy of so great
an honor, our sovereign . . . will put away his wife and come to terms
with the queen's niece."

Ivan calculated a marriage to an English princess would enhance
the prestige of the royal dynasty, which had been shaken by military
reverses. In addition to dynastic considerations such a move would
free Russia from international isolation, and the marriage would lead
to a military alliance between the two countries. Ivan expended extraordinary energy in pursuit of this eighth marriage, and the negotiations took on greater urgency when Ivan further sought to arrange
a refuge in England.

The tsar instructed Pisemskii to make careful inquiries about Mary's
dowry and be sure to ascertain "whose daughter she is; of what
appanage prince . . . and whether she has a brother or sister."[6] He
wanted to know the extent of the Hastings family's property and
whether his potential wife might inherit an independent principality.
He obviously hoped he would obtain both Mary Hastings' hand and
her appanage principality, which could be the ultimate refuge for
himself and his feeble-minded son. However, Ivan's marriage plans
fell through; Elizabeth refused, on the grounds that the thirty-year-
old bride was in poor health. The English ambassador said: "The
queen's niece is inferior to her other relatives; she is ill, and not at
all pretty."[7] Her face was marked by smallpox. This setback did not
discourage Ivan, who expressed his firm intention to send a new embassy to London to arrange a marriage with another of the queen's
relatives. Ambassador Bowes claimed the tsar had confided his most
cherished wish to him: if Queen Elizabeth failed to include a bride
with the next embassy, "one whom he wanted, he intended to collect all his treasure, go to England, and there marry one of the queen's
relatives." Bowes may be charged with considerable exaggeration,
but there is no doubt Ivan was attracted to England. If he had succeeded in arranging a marriage with the English court, Queen Mariia
would have had to take the veil, and the fate of Ivan's young son
Dmitrii would have been unenviable.

Chapter Thirty-One

TRIUMPH IN LIVONIA

The destruction of the Turkish army at Astrakhan and the rout of the Crimean Horde south of Moscow decisively altered the military balance in eastern Europe. In 1575 Russia's southern frontiers were free from Tatar raids for the first time in many years. Khan Devlet-Girei died two years later and the Crimea experienced a protracted civil war. Peace also descended upon the western frontiers. An interregnum had occurred in the Rzeczpospolita, which weakened Poland-Lithuania and diverted attention from Livonia. Muscovite diplomacy attempted to influence the electoral struggle in Poland. Some Orthodox gentry there were in favor of electing Ivan to the Polish throne, but he evidently was not seriously interested. He said to Polish envoys: "To rule is no novelty for me, and my son is young; he cannot cope with affairs of state." Wrestling with domestic problems, Ivan was afraid to assume further responsibilities in Poland. During his reign King Sigismund II was in a difficult position; finances were in disarray and the turbulent gentry refused to obey him. Ivan was well informed about developments. The boyars had written at his direction: "Our great sovereigns freely exercise their royal autocratic prerogatives, unlike your wretched kingdom ... where you are an elected, not a hereditary sovereign; the magnates have granted you power only because they tolerate you."[1] Ivan despised an elected king. He could not foresee the blows which the West would soon rain upon him.

While the Rzeczpospolita was preoccupied with domestic problems Russia strove to win back fortresses in Livonia from the Swedes. In two campaigns during 1575-1576 the Russians acquired control of the two maritime fortresses of Pernau and Hapsal, and conquered almost all the littoral between Reval and Riga, but an attempt to take Reval, the main fortified post in Swedish Livonia, undertaken early in 1577, met with failure, and the Russian army withdrew after a siege of six weeks.

The interregnum in the Rzeczpospolita was now over. Moscow supported the Austrian candidate for the throne, and the two countries secretly had discussed plans to sever the union between Poland

and Lithuania: when the Austrian candidate was elected Poland would become part of Austria and Lithuania and Livonia would go to Russia. Backed by the Muscovite faction the Austrian archduke was proclaimed king of the Rzeczpospolita, but proved unable to establish himself in Poland. Austria's opponents elected Stefan Batory, prince of Transylvania; a struggle broke out between the two kings, and the energetic and far-seeing Batory prevailed.

Protracted feudal anarchy had weakened the Rzeczpospolita. Seeking to take advantage of the situation, while still at war with Sweden the Russians invaded Polish Livonia under Ivan's personal command, but in spite of his best efforts the tsar could muster no more than some 16,000 gentry and fusiliers for the campaign. With such a small force the Russians hesitated to besiege Riga, the key defence post in southern Livonia, but although the invasion from the outset was limited, in seven weeks the tsar's armies captured the fortresses of Dünaberg, Kokenhausen, Wenden, and a score of castles. The Muscovites' triumphant march produced a strong impression on the gentry of Livonia. Most of the fortresses surrendered without resistance, and Alexsandr Polubenskii, commander of the Lithuanian armies on the Daugava was taken prisoner. This success brought Ivan nearer his cherished goal. He now controlled almost all Livonia from the Narova river to the northern Daugava, except for Riga, Reval, and the Duchy of Courland, which had formed on the other side of the Daugava. His military achievement encouraged Ivan to take his pen in hand. He informed his enemies that all of Livonia was now subject to his will, and soon afterwards sent letters to Batory, the Lithuanian commanders, the renegade Kurbskii, and others. Ivan's derisive letter to Kurbskii clearly revealed the feelings that animated him during this last successful campaign: "Although my transgressions are more numerous than the sands of the sea, I hope for the grace of God, Who in the magnitude of His mercy can efface all of them. In our old age we have gone beyond the far-off towns where you sought refuge." He further lectured Kurbskii: "And there to your haven God brought us, but still we write to you not from pride, but to correct you, to make you think about saving your soul."[2]

The military operations undertaken in 1577 against Sweden and Livonia had conflicting ends in view. After attacking Reval the tsar's army managed to drive the Swedish forces out of Livonia, but the plans for the part of Livonia under Lithuanian control were much less clear-cut. The Russian command made no effort to capture the fortress of Riga, the key to southern Livonia, and was content merely to confine the Lithuanian garrisons northeast of the Daugava. Knowing that Batory's hold on the Polish throne was tenuous, Ivan hoped he could enforce peace terms without major warfare, and to further this aim arranged for some Polish prisoners to be sent home. Before they left, the leading nobles among them were invited to a party at court, where they received lavish gifts of fur coats and goblets. Ivan had them convey a message to Batory: "The king should send envoys, and the king should defer to the sovereign's will in all things; as to this, he bids you tell the king the sovereign's hand is lofty."[3] Ivan had manifestly underestimated his opponent's resolution and energy.

The goals Ivan formulated for the Livonian campaign were optimistic, but his achievements were fleeting. As long as Riga remained under enemy control the Russian position in southern Livonia was insecure, and no sooner had the tsar returned to Moscow than two of the strongest fortresses he had taken, Dünaberg and Wenden, fell. The tsar's attempt to end the protracted war by undertaking extensive offensive operations against the Swedes and Livonians simultaneously had unfortunate results; Russia's enemies succeeded in coordinating their military activity for the first time since the Livonian war had begun. Twice in 1578 Ivan sent troops to retake Wenden, even though his commanders begged him to rescind the order, arguing that their forces were too small. The tsar's representatives with the army were told to lead the troops to the fortress and "take appropriate action apart from the commanders, whereas the commanders should cooperate with them." This badly-planned attack was a disaster. Unified Polish-Lithuanian and Swedish contingents suddenly fell upon the Russian camp near Wenden and routed the Russian commanders. The victories in Livonia were in danger of becoming defeats.

Chapter Thirty-Two

THE POLICY OF IVAN'S COURT

Ivan's court was not abolished, but merely reorganized when Simeon stepped down. Almost all its appanage territories, including Pskov and Rostov, remained within its administration, as well as the north coast and the Dvina lands, to which were added the outlying regions of Kozelsk, Vologda, and Kargopol, formerly parts of the oprichnina. Inclusion of these northern regions was dictated by the need to increase the court's revenue and enable it to maintain such chanceries as the Dvina unit, the court's great treasury, the court's military records unit, and others, which were distinct from the zemshchina chanceries and situated in the section of Moscow under the court's jurisdiction. The military records for 1577-1579 distinguish clearly between court and zemshchina units. Contemporaries considered Ivan's court a reincarnation of the oprichnina, but the two institutions were not the same. Possibly the basic difference was that Ivan's new court was not associated with particular territories as closely as the oprichnina and his appanage had been, or, in other words, his court was regarded as the tsar's private army rather than a special region which the tsar controlled as an appanage prince. Privy Councillors A.F. Nagoi and B. Ya. Belskii and members of the Godunov family, who had presided over Little Ivan of Moscow's appanage, were in charge or it.

As defeats in the field multiplied the government of Ivan's court took great pains to conceal military expenditures and maintain the court's forces. An assembly convoked in Moscow in January, 1580 approved a decree forbidding the church to acquire new lands and enacting that monasteries must disgorge all hereditary estates princes had bequeathed to them, no matter when obtained: "Those who have purchased princes' patrimonies hold them for the sovereign, and only God and the sovereign know their worth."[1] The treasury had long coveted land held in hereditary tenure by the Suzdal and other nobles which had survived from the original appanage period. During the oprichnina years the princes had lost a great deal of land, and this had greatly benefited the monasteries, which acquired the lands of the disgraced. Refusing to allow such lands to revert to their original

owners, the administration of Ivan's court forbade them to buy back
their ancestral lands from the church, but although this seemed a
concession to the church, it was more apparent than real, for it point-
edly omitted the princes' patrimonial estates the treasury wanted,
which was the most valuable category. The measures taken by the
court's administration against the monasteries were bound ultimately
to increase the service-tenure fund of land available to impoverished
gentry.

Military reverses compelled the authorities to resort to extraordinary measures to finance the war. Supplementary exactions were laid
upon the entire country, particularly upon the "black-plough" or
crown lands in the northern regions and along the north coast. Towns
and merchants had to pay large sums; on several occasions the English merchant company alone was assessed 2,000 rubles. Ivan's court
did not hesitate to cancel the immunities enjoyed by great landowners, the *tarkhanshchiki,* a Tatar word denoting those who paid no
or reduced taxes on their lands. Monasteries and churchmen were required to assign their fees to the treasury. These financial exactions
affected the entire population, and the increased tax burden was disastrous for the economy, which was experiencing crisis. The economic crisis of the second half of the sixteenth century is usually attributed to increasing feudal exploitation, the oprichnina, and the war,
but its basic source was the steady and ruinous diminution of the
amount of arable land, peasant impoverishment, and the decrease of
the rural and urban population. It is reasonable to assume that the
decline gradually accelerated over two decades, until the economy
collapsed in the early 1580s, but scholars advocating this view have
overlooked one important factor.

The famine lasting for the three years 1601-1603 is known to have
destroyed Russia's economy in the early seventeenth century. A similar decline had occurred during the time of disaster in the 1570s and
1580s caused by the three-year famine and plague of 1569-1571. The
harm done by oprichnina violence cannot be compared with mam-
moth natural misfortunes, but here it chanced that both reached
their height simultaneously. Under ordinary circumstances the country would have needed no more than a decade or two to recover, but
the war forced the state to increase taxes, the fundamental reason
why the economy continued to decline, assailing the rural and urban
population alike. Towns in the center and the northwest were particularly hard hit. Moscow lost a third of its people, and rural areas
were depopulated; for hundreds of miles travellers saw nothing but

abandoned villages, for the peasants had fled to the borderlands.
Those who remained decreased their harvests in hope of avoiding the
state's ruinous exactions. The taxation unit known as *obzha*[2] in olden
times had included no more than one to three peasant households,
but during these disastrous years it comprehended four or eight, or
even more. The peasants on their dwarf holdings considered that the
exceptional imposts levied during the last years of the war were in-
tolerable.

Population decline and the contraction of peasant holdings caused
the bulk of the land to fall out of cultivation. At the time of Ivan's
death five-sixths of the land around Moscow was unworked, and the
peasants tilled barely one-thirteenth of the land around Novgorod,
which had been ravaged by the enemy. As one historian has expressed
it graphically, the villages and hamlets in the Novgorod region resembled large cemeteries where a handful of the living wandered to and
fro. The disaster disturbed the traditional relationships between peasant and landlord.

The custom of permitting peasants to depart on St. George's day
was complicated by the quitrent system, but if a peasant discharged
that obligation and paid up his rent he was free to leave his landlord
and move elsewhere. As long as peasants remained tied to the patrimonial estates the dominant group never questioned the legality of
St. George's day. Circumstances altered, however, towards the end of
the sixteenth century, when the gentry everywhere ceased observing
St. George's day and force alone determined peasant movement. The
gentry, themselves under a form of indenture, used coercion to keep
peasants on their lands and bring them from neighbors' lands. St.
George's day lost its meaning at a time when no new laws had been
framed to take its place. The service-tenure chancery characterized
the situation as one in which "peasant movement is fraught with
great disturbances and denunciations; the weak are constrained by
the strong."[3]

In these parlous times the gentry grew seriously impoverished and
petty proprietors of service-tenure estates lost most of their peasants.
Cadastral surveys are filled with references to ruined proprietors,
some of whom became beggars wandering from house to house, while
others died without providing for their children. Exhausted by the
war, the gentry lost its former pugnacity and its members were willing
to fight only for a few acres of land. Poland heard reports that Muscovite serving-people had appealed urgently to the tsar to end the
war because neglect of their land prevented them from rendering

service. Many gentry deserted and were relentlessly hunted by the authorities, beaten with the knout, put in chains, forced to post large bonds, and saw their children and servants arrested. By the end of the war such measures were applied even to prominent members of the gentry, who formed the army's officer corps, but even so mobilization was becoming constantly more difficult. Commanders on occasion had to defer attacks because lesser boyars had failed to mobilize, and sometimes even after they were successfully mustered the gentry fled the battlefield and dispersed to their estates. The agricultural disarray and enforced movement of the peasants meant that the service-tenure system was in danger of collapse because landlords had to be absent over long periods.

The government of Ivan's court could not rely solely on force to deal with service people, and it adopted measures to aid impoverished gentry such as levying extraordinary imposts on those who enjoyed immunities and limiting monastery landowning. Contemporaries believed the monastery decree helped allay dissatisfaction in the zemshchina, but although this may be true Ivan's court did not consistently favor the gentry. The first moves to enserf the peasantry had nothing to do with Ivan's court or the oprichnina. Like its predecessors, his court kept control of criminal investigation and surveillance, but repression did not automatically follow. After the appanage was dissolved, executions ceased and the penalties meted out to disgraced zemshchina boyars were comparatively mild.

Chapter Thirty-Three

THE END OF THE WAR

The Lithuanian army had borne the brunt of many years of war with Russia; Poland did not enter the fray until the final stages. It should be remembered that the Rzeczpospolita, which comprehended Poland, Lithuania, the Ukraine, Belorussia, and Courland, was the most powerful state in eastern Europe, and when Stefan Batory came to power it was able to mobilize strong forces to attack its eastern neighbor. The new king rapidly overcame his initial international isolation, and his military reforms restored Poland's armed might.

Batory made thorough preparations for war with Russia, hiring mercenaries in Hungary and Germany, and securing abundant supplies.

Moscow knew the Rzeczpospolita was preparing for war, but evidently failed to appreciate the full extent of the danger. Envoys returning from Poland assured the tsar that although Batory was supported by a few hotheads among the Lithuanian gentry the Poles
would refuse to participate in any campaign. A little later a courier,
Timofeev, communicated that the king intended to attack Polotsk,
but the tsar refused to believe it and the Polotsk garrison was not
reinforced in time. In hopes of forestalling an invasion the Russian
commanders decided to attack the area they called German Livonia,
and their plan was partially implemented. Arriving with his forces in
Pskov, Ivan assigned Commander Khilkov, a gentry unit, and some
Tatar cavalry to Courland. Khilkov defeated the Germans there, but
his achievement was limited; the Russian army was split when the
enemy invaded.

Batory had made careful preparations and mounted his first attack to the east by striking at Polotsk. After a siege lasting four weeks,
accompanied by numerous assaults, the Poles managed to set fire to
the wooden walls of the fortress, Polotsk fell August 31, 1579 and a
week and a half later Batory routed approaching Russian advance
guards. When the Poles were storming Polotsk the tsar and his main
force were in Pskov. V.V. Novodvorskii, the distinguished authority
on the Livonian war, has asserted that Ivan was personally responsible
for the defeat because he lost his head and refrained from resisting
the enemy even though he had an army consisting of 300,000 men at
his disposal. Novodvorskii has erred in his calculations, since he did
not have access to Russian sources, the archival lists of the military
records bureau, which show that with great effort Ivan was able to
muster only 10,352 gentry, and 3,119 fusiliers and cossacks in Pskov.
His whole army, including town levies and Tatars, amounted to
23,641 men, or, with the slaves in attendance, approximately 30,000
or 35,000 men. Russia could employ but a portion of her forces in
the west, for the southern frontiers, which were under constant threat
from the Tatars, had to be guarded, and substantial garrisons maintained in the subjugated areas of Livonia, the lower Volga area, and
the Caucasus. The military capacities of the gentry levy had been
weakened by the war, which had lasted for twenty years, and the
catastrophic devastation of the country.

The army Batory had raised to attack Russia has been calculated
at 41,814 men, itself a formidable force, and Russia had also to fight

Sweden. The Swedish king had 17,000 men in the field, and 8,000 to 10,000 Swedish soldiers attacked Russian fortresses in Livonia, supported by a first-class fleet. The Polish invasion forced the tsar to send Commander Khvorostinin and the main army to Nevel, which was closest to Polotsk, where Commander I.P. Shuiskii and the right guard followed. They though the king's army would grow exhausted from a protracted siege and then might be attacked, but their calculations proved incorrect. The tsar and his forces had to remain in Pskov because Swedish armies were building up in the rear. In July the Swedish fleet bombarded and set fire to the suburbs of Narva and Ivangorod, and a large Swedish force landing at Reval advanced in September to besiege Narva. The Russians were caught between two fires. The enemy armies were larger and attacking on all fronts. Ivan was alarmed by the developments at Narva because he considered Russia's first Baltic port infinitely more important than Polotsk. He sent Commander Khilkov to Narva as soon as the latter returned from his foray into Courland, but when Polotsk fell Russia's military position became more difficult and the anticipated campaign against the Swedes did not take place. However, the Swedish army withdrew after sustaining heavy losses during a siege of Narva that lasted two weeks.

In early spring, 1580 the Tatars resumed their attacks on Russia's southern frontier. The country had to fight without allies and the number of Russia's enemies had increased. Attempts to reach agreement with the Rzeczpospolita were unsuccessful. Batory ignored Ivan's peace overtures, as he had no wish to discuss peace. To launch his new campaign he collected the largest force ever used in an eastern war. The Russians were not certain of the enemy's plans and expected an attack in any one of three directions, against Livonia, Pskov, or Smolensk, but Batory, refusing to make the moves that promised him greatest strategic gain, attacked the minor fortress of Velikie Luki.

In Russia the summer mobilization in 1580 was accomplished with great difficulty. In spite of threats the gentry did not arrive to join their regiments, and the authorities had to expend much effort to find those failing to appear and send them to their posts. The military records bureau devised three defense strategies in the west. A detailed plan to mobilize and concentrate the army if Pskov were attacked has survived. It provided that Pskov should be garrisoned with some 2500 gentry, 2500-2700 fusiliers, and 500 mounted cossacks, while a field army of 1394 gentry and some 3,000 Tatars was to operate outside the walls. This meant that Russia had available some 7,000

Conquests during Ivan IV.   Losses during the Troubles.
Losses during Ivan IV   Conquests during Alexis.

Muscovy in the 16th and 17th Centuries

men, or 12,000-15,000, including Tatars and armed slaves, directly to oppose an invading army. The remaining troops were massed to defend the southern redoubts from the Tatars and protect the numerous fortresses.

The Russian command had no plan to counter Batory's attack on Velikie Luki, because for fifteen years it had not been considered a front-line fortress. The town's wooden walls were in disrepair and the small garrison did not receive reinforcements in time. The king's army invested Velikie Luki on August 27, 1580. Enjoying an enormous advantage in numbers the Poles expected to take it quickly, but they encountered stubborn resistance. During the first days of the siege the defenders made a daring sortie, overran part of Zamojski's regiment, and captured the king's standard. An attempt to storm the fortress failed and the attackers sustained losses, but the tsar's commanders had to surrender on September 5 after the enemy set fire to the wooden walls and the whole town went up in flames. The king's mercenaries massacred prisoners. Two weeks after Velikie Luki fell the Poles defeated Commander Khilkov near Toropets. While the king was besieging Velikie Luki a Lithuanian army attacked Smolensk and was repulsed by the commanders, but this limited success could not alter the general pattern of military activity.

The Rzeczpospolita had devoted large forces and substantial resources to the second Russian campaign—48,399 men were under arms—but the results were meagre, mainly because Batory had not received effective support from Sweden. After the defeat at Narva the council of state had advised King John III to make peace with Moscow, but Batory's success encouraged the war party. After careful preparation the Swedes invaded Karelia and seized the fortress of Korela in November, 1580.

The military defeats compelled Russian diplomacy to take a step unprecedented in the country's history by turning to the Catholic world with a request to mediate peace. Moscow's offer, which hinted at possible Russian participation in an anti-Turkish league, sparked interest in Vienna and the Vatican. The pope sent a legate, Antonio Possevino, to Cracow and Moscow to mediate, and his efforts made peace easier to achieve. Soberly assessing Russia's military posture, the tsar was prepared to make substantial concessions to end the war. His personal emissaries informed Batory that Russia would cede Poland all of Livonia, including the towns of Dorpat, Fellin, and Pernau, and all other castles except Narva and its environs. Ivan was ready to sacrifice the interests of Russian landlords in Livonia and

give up all the territory he had conquered in order to keep the port
of Narva. The tsar's initiative increased chances for a peaceful settlement, but Batory considered the concessions inadequate and demanded Narva and payment of a huge indemnity of 400,000 gold
pieces.

The issue of Narva was the stumbling-block during the Russo-
Polish negotiations. Russia's enemies were determined to destroy the
port. Chancellor Zamojski told the Diet in Warsaw the king would
not allow the Russians to hold the important ports in Livonia and
called on Poland to hit the enemy hard and push him back from the
sea in order to prevent him from obtaining foreign military equipment and artisans. Ivan sent Batory a personal message affirming Russia's historical right to Livonia and sneering at the demand for an
indemnity. Ivan assiduously emphasized the difference between himself, a sovereign born to the throne, and Batory, an elected king: "We,
humble Ivan Vasilevich, lord of mighty realms through God's will,
not by unruly men's desire." Behind the tsar's affected humility
lurked unbounded pride. Allowing his anger free reign, at the end of
the letter Ivan threatened his adversary with war in the foreseeable
future: "And if you refuse to behave properly and return our envoys
to us, not an envoy nor a courier will move between us for forty or
fifty years."[1] Apparently recovering his former energy and confidence, the ruler of Russia ordered commander Khvorostinin to cross
the Dneiper and strike at Orsha and Mogilev. The Russian attack
achieved its purpose, for Batory hesitated to order his main army into action until he learned the Russians had withdrawn from Lithuania.

Pskov was the target of Batory's third eastern campaign, as the
king knew the capture of this fortress would decide the fate of Livonia. Divining his intention the Russian command reinforced Pskov
with men from adjacent castles in Livonia. This weakened the Livonian defense line but was justified by military necessity. The battle
to decide Russia's fate was fought at the walls of Pskov, which was
one of the country's strongest fortresses, girt with three massive
stone walls 300 feet long, 26 to 29 feet high, and some 16 feet thick.
The enemy found the city ready to defend itself. The commanders
had amassed much heavy artillery and obtained ample supplies and
provisions. The tsar entrusted the defense of Pskov to Boyar I.P.
Shuiskii, a member of his court and one of his best commanders.

The size of the garrison in Pskov cannot be determined exactly.
The Poles estimated 7,500 to 9,000 fusiliers and gentry, or 12,000 in
all, counting the population under arms. Captured members of the

garrison said Pskov contained 1,000 mounted lesser boyars, 2,500 fusiliers, some local and some from Narva, and 500 Don cossacks led by Mishka Cherkashenin. The number of fusiliers and cossacks is credible, for the military records bureau, anticipating a siege, had put just such forces into Pskov in May, 1580. The local commanders also disposed of 2,500-2,700 gentry, and thus the military complement of the Pskov garrison in 1580 exceeded 5,500, or 7,000 including armed slaves. A force of approximately the same size protected Pskov the following year. The city had some 20,000 inhabitants, and almost the entire adult population took part in its defense. Batory's army was estimated to number as many as 47,000 men during the third campaign. Its core was the mercenaries, 15,000 cavalry and 12,000 infantry. Attacking from Polotsk and Opochka Polish advance guards reached the outskirts of Pskov in August, 1581, and Lithuanian detachments simultaneously attacked Rzhev. When the Lithuanians attacked Ivan and his family were at Staritsa. Enemy outriders set fire to villages near his residence and from its windows the glow of flames could be seen. The Lithuanian commanders discussed plans to capture the tsar, but Ivan showed no fear in face of the danger. Sending his wife and young son away he remained to prepare Staritsa for defense, although he had no more than 700 gentry and fusiliers, but the Lithuanians avoided battle with Russian units concentrated at Rzhev and moved to join the main force at Pskov.

Early in September Batory's army began an intensive siege of Pskov. After digging trenches the besiegers forced their way to the moat at the southern edge of the city and trained batteries on the Svinuzskii tower. On September 7 the fortress was subjected to heavy bombardment from morning until late at night and large holes appeared in the south wall. Next day the king's infantry tried to storm the city. Columns moved through the holes, climbed the walls, and seized two towers, but their efforts to penetrate the city were shattered by the invincible bravery of the defenders, who fought stubbornly and fiercely for more than six hours. The Russians blew up the Svinuzskii tower when enemy forces were inside, and compelled the foe to withdraw.

After failing to storm the city the king's army began a protracted siege. Sappers bored tunnels to set powder charges beneath the walls, but the people of Pskov, adopting their tactics, destroyed them. Batteries pounded the city in late October with molten balls in an attempt to set it on fire, and on November 2 the king's infantry made a last unsuccessful attempt to storm the city, which was repulsed by the defenders. Frosts came early in October and the situation of the besiegers took a turn for the worse, since the Polish army was not equipped for a winter campaign. In November the soldiers left the trenches and withdrew to a camp, and front-line batteries and all siege artillery also were brought there. The siege had failed, and henceforward the enemy could do no more than blockade Pskov. Heavy losses, cold, and lack of supplies demoralized the soldiers, many of whom dispersed among the villages to forage for food. While the army was rapidly disintegrating Batory left it and returned to Poland. His departure caused alarm, but this diminished when reports started circulating that peace with Russia was imminent.

The defenders also had to endure great hardship, but although their supplies were exhausted and famine was rife their courage was undaunted. The garrison made constant sorties to harass the enemy and, aware that Batory's army was in a difficult position, Shuiskii tried to destroy it. On January 4, 1582 he led the garrison out of the city in an attempt to capture the king's camp but was unable to do so, and after an unsuccessful encounter the Russians retreated into the fortress. However, Batory had suffered his worst setback in the war with Russia. Pskov was the rock which shattered the enemy invasion. Piotrowski, who participated in the campaign, was amazed at the steadfastness of the city's defenders: "Their determination and capacity to defend themselves are stouter than their walls." [2] Possevino, who was in the vicinity of Pskov several times during the siege, shared this opinion: "The Russians resolutely defend their towns; women fight alongside the soldiers; no one spares either his strength or life, and the besieged endure hunger stoically."[3] Batory's official historian, Heidenstein, in paying tribute to the firmness with which the Russians defended their country, wrote that they displayed "unbelievable fortitude defending and protecting their fortresses in time of war,"[4] and opposition hardened as the enemy invasion went deeper. In the first eastern campaign the king's 40,000-man army had produced an impressive result in the capture of Polotsk, but during the second campaign almost 40,000 men had wasted their energies to reduce the insignificant fortress of Velikie Luki, and 47,000 men proved unable to take Pskov in the third campaign. The Rzeczpospolita was exhausted and after three years of war was as anxious for peace as Russia. Ivan understood that the position of Batory's army was critical, but he issued orders to avoid open conflict, and refrained from offensive action to lift the siege of Pskov. The Russian command had to keep its reserves in Novgorod because the Swedes had launched a new invasion and Russia again was forced to fight on two fronts.

The Swedes experienced little difficulty capturing the Russian fortresses in Livonia and around Narva since scarcely any Russian troops remained in them, and Pontus de la Gardie, the Swedish commander-in-chief, reached Narva, which after a fierce bombardment he succeeded in taking on September 9, 1581. The commanders in Ivangorod tried to help Narva in its hour of need but the Swedes routed the small force they had dispatched on the bridge between the two towns. The ancient Russian rearguard fortresses of Ivangorod, Yam and Kopore were not equipped for defense and offered no real resistance to the enemy. The loss of Narva had far-reaching military and economic consequences. Russia was deprived of the port, acquired with so much difficulty, which had assured uninterrupted commercial relations with western Europe.

Loss of these strong outposts on the northwestern frontiers posed an immediate threat to Novgorod and Pskov. The Swedes now possessed good fortified bases from which to strike at the heart of Russia, and a direct road lay open to Pskov, under siege by the Poles. However, Swedish success in Livonia intensified the differences between Poland and Sweden. When Batory asked King John to surrender Narva and other fortresses he had won from the Russians, cooperation between the two countries proved impossible.

Ivan felt that the loss of his Baltic port rendered it pointless to continue to fight with the Rzeczpospolita for Livonia. Admitting he could not wage war on two fronts at once, the tsar was prepared to cede his conquests in Livonia to Poland in order to concentrate his resources on war with Sweden and to recover Narva at any price. The boyar council's resolution on peace with Poland contained a clause concerning the war with Sweden: "We must come to terms with Lithuania and King Stefan, but we must take a stand against Sweden and not make peace with her." The tsar employed the good offices of Possevino, the papal legate, to resume peace negotiations with Batory, which took place in a ruined village not far from Yam Zapolskii, on the road from Novgorod to Velikie Luki, where intense quarrels broke out concerning the future of Narva. The Polish envoys demanded all Livonia, but the Russian envoys rejected their claim and the Narva issue was omitted from the text of the treaty.

The envoys engaged in a furious dispute over titles, which clearly revealed the fundamental aims of Russian diplomacy. Although he believed he was infinitely superior to a mere elected king, Ivan was willing to omit the title of tsar from the peace treaty. He was moved to make the concession by the following haughty calculation: "When one is a sovereign from old, it matters not what you call him; he is known as lord in all lands, and that he is a sovereign." At the same Ivan had no intention of allowing Batory to assume the title of lord of Livonia, for he was planning immediately to renew the contest for Narva. The Yam Zapolskii negotiations ended on January 15, 1582, when a truce for ten years was signed. Russia gave up to Poland all its conquests in Livonia, including the fortress of Dorpat and the port of Pernau, and Batory returned the fortresses of Velikie Luki, Kholm, Nevel, Velizh, and the suburbs of Pskov, but kept Polotsk.

Even before the truce was signed the Russian command was preparing an assault on the Swedes and in February, 1582 Commanders M.P. Katyrev and D.I. Khvorostinin moved against the Russian fortresses they held. Khvorostinin's advance guard encountered enemy troops near the village of Lialitsa on the road to Yam. The main force rushed to his assistance, but, according to the military registers, "the other commanders made no haste to do battle." Although unable to deploy all their forces the Russians defeated the Swedes, but a general assault on Narva failed to materialize. In the spring the Russian command recalled regiments from Novgorod and sent them to the Crimean frontier. Moscow was also under heavy pressure from the Rzeczpospolita, which delivered an ultimatum not to send armies to Narva on pain of abrogating the treaty.

Relying on Russia's domestic problems, as did Batory, John III and the ruling group in Sweden planned to attack and dismember the country. De la Gardie was instructed to take advantage of popular discontent in Novgorod in order to occupy that city, and Pskov too. A large army, including mercenary units from Germany, France and Italy, was concentrated in Finland. The immediate goal of the invasion was the Russian fortresses of Oreshek and Ladoga, and the Swedes attempted to occupy both banks of the Neva to cut Russia off from the Baltic. On September 8 the Swedish army attacked Oreshek and after a long bombardment made a general assault a month later, but the ancient Russian fortress, situated on an island in the middle of the Neva, successfully repulsed the enemy attack, and a week later reinforcements arrived by boat. The enemy suffered heavy casualties during a second attack and de la Gardie withdrew from Oreshek in November.

Sweden could not wage war with Russia alone, but the understanding about Narva dictated by Batory and ominous developments on the southern and eastern frontiers prevented Moscow from using its military superiority. An incursion by the Great Nogai Horde provoked the peoples of the Volga region to undertake a major uprising against Russian domination which lasted more than three years and was only suppressed with great difficulty after Ivan died, and a new war with Kazan forced the Russian government to initiate peace talks with Sweden, whose diplomats strove to have the Russians cede the entire coast of the Gulf of Finland but failed in their endeavor. These negotiations, conducted on the river Pliussa, ended in August, 1583, when a brief truce for three years was signed. The Swedes kept the Russian towns they had captured, Korela, Ivangorod, Yam and Kopore and its environs, while Russia retained a small area on the coast of the Gulf of Finland, including the mouth of the Neva. Thus ended the Livonian war, which had lasted for twenty-five years and came to involve the major Baltic powers. Russia's first effort to establish a presence on the Baltic had failed, and defeat in the Livonian war had placed the country in a difficult position.

Chapter Thirty-Four

FINAL CRISIS

These defeats caused Ivan to lose all trust in his boyars and commanders. The military records bureau officially declared that commanders' treachery had caused Polotsk's fall, just as the tsar had written in his letters to Batory. Fearing the boyars would betray him, Ivan selected zemshchina commanders among trusted persons at his court to serve as personal emissaries, but the results were disappointing; some were captured and others perished. Confronted with such misfortune the tsar vacillated and hesitated but at last reopened the secret negotiations to secure him refuge in England. Rumors reached the zemshchina and intensified the split among prominent figures, which became so widely known that Russian diplomats abroad were called upon to explain the situation. The tsar's ambassador officially told the English queen that some Muscovites were unstable, but those identified as such "had recognized their guilt, petitioned the sovereign, begged the sovereign for mercy, and the sovereign had shown them his mercy." The envoy's words referred to events that had occurred a year earlier, when Prince I.F. Mstislavskii, the president of the boyar council, and two of his sons were prosecuted and publicly repented that "in the tsar's eyes they were guilty of many transgressions." Members of Mstislavskii's family appealed to the tsar and the accused were forgiven.

At age 48 Ivan fell seriously ill, and senior boyars and clergy hastily were summoned to the Sloboda. Despairing of recovery, Ivan proclaimed: "I have chosen my elder son, Prince Ivan, to rule Muscovy after me." The tsar's illness aroused speculation among the boyars about the heir. Contemporary observers noted young Ivan's popularity, and his name was linked with hopes of change for the better. When he recovered, Ivan's trust in his son, who was now 27, was eroded and he had become afraid of him. Horsey wrote: "The tsar feared for his power, believing the people entertained too high an opinion of his son."[1] Ivan was frequently ill at the end of his life and signs of senility multiplied, while his son was reaching maturity and, as Secretary Ivan Timofeev observed, the tsar "spitefully breathed out fires of rage against his enemies, like a rhinocerus." The army and people thought young Ivan would soon insist his father give him an army to rout the Poles at Pskov. The heir was supposed to have told the ruler angrily that he preferred glory to glitter and although he possessed less wealth than his father he could still devastate the latter's realm with fire and sword and take away most of his kingdom. Pskov long entertained legends of how the father "impaled his brave son on a stake to teach him not to talk about delivering the city of Pskov."[2]

A year and a half before young Ivan died a relative of the notorious favorite, Bogdan Belskii, fled and told the Poles that the Muscovite tsar detested his older son and frequently beat him. The incessant quarrels in the royal family arose from various sources. The despotic father constantly interfered in his son's personal life. Ivan immured Evdokiia Saburova and Petrova-Solovaia, his son's first two wives (whom he had personally chosen) in a nunnery, but perhaps young Ivan picked Elena Sheremeteva, his third wife, himself, as his father was hostile to the Sheremetev clan. The tsar had one of Elena's uncles executed; another, whom he called a demon's son, was packed off to a monastery, and Ivan publicly charged Elena's father with maintaining treasonable relations with the Crimean khan. Her only surviving uncle was captured by the Poles, and Russian couriers reported he swore loyalty to the Polish king and advised him to strike at Velikie Luki. Again boyar treason had made its way into the palace.

The final quarrel between father and son broke out at the Sloboda, where the family was spending the autumn, as it usually did. The customs of the time did not consider a woman properly dressed unless she wore no less than three chemises, but one day Ivan came upon his daughter-in-law sitting on a bench in a warm room attired in one chemise. Elena was pregnant, but the tsar had no mercy and struck her, and the blows and her fright caused a miscarriage. Trying to protect his wife young Ivan grasped his father's hands, whereupon the tsar struck him too. This scene was described by the Jesuit, Antonio Possevino, who arrived in Moscow soon after the heir was buried and was at pains to learn the details of the tragedy. An Italian interpreter, who had been at the Sloboda at the time of the quarrel, told him young Ivan had died from a severe wound on the temple inflicted by the tsar's staff. He had been listening to court gossip, but there are questions as to its reliability.

Sir Jerome Horsey, who had many friends at court, described the heir's death somewhat differently. In a rage Ivan boxed his son's ear hard enough to induce a fever, from which he died two days later. Horsey specifically stated that young Ivan died of fever, not from a murderous blow on the temple. Heidenstein, the well-informed contemporary Polish chronicler, supports Horsey. He heard that young Ivan went into a decline, caused by either a blow from the staff or serious mental illness and contracted fever, from which he died. The Russian chronicler gives much the same version: "His father's wrath made him ill, and death came from his illness."

Which version of the heir's death should be accepted? An authentic letter the tsar sent to some boyars who quitted the Sloboda November 9, 1581 after meeting with him helps provide the answer: "The day you left us was the day my son Ivan was taken ill. He is now deathly ill . . . and as long as God spares my son Ivan we cannot leave this place."[3] This means the fatal quarrel took place on the day of the boyars' departure, but four days elapsed before the tsar wrote the letter filled with anxiety over his son's extreme illness. The blows, combined with a severe nervous disorder, brought young Ivan to his grave. He contracted fever and died after an illness lasting eleven days. His father nearly went out of his mind. Ivan had destroyed both his son and his long-awaited heir. His brutality had consigned his dynasty to oblivion.

Chapter Thirty-Five

IVAN'S DEATH

Days of mourning were proclaimed throughout the country when the heir died. The tsar went to Troitsa to do penance. Secretly he asked the archimandrite to send the cellarer and, falling on his knees before him, "weeping and sobbing bowed to the ground six times." The tsar asked that his son be accorded the exceptional privilege of a weekly remembrance, and other monasteries and churches received large sums of money to remember young Ivan's soul.

In his state of deep spiritual crisis Ivan behaved in a most unusual manner: he decided posthumously to pardon all the disgraced boyars he had ordered executed. It is hard to say whether he was alarmed by premonitions of his own imminent death, or anxious to save his soul, burdened as it was with grave sins, or motivated by the sober calculation that he should become reconciled with the boyars and clergy in order to improve the position of Fedor, the new heir. In any event, Ivan ordered secretaries to compile detailed lists of all those slain during the oprichnina, which were sent with substantial contributions to major monasteries. This was a pure windfall for the clergy, for rough calculation shows that the monks received thousands and thousands of rubles in less than three years. The posthumous rehabilitation of the disgraced, whose names it had been forbidden to mention for many years, had political as well as moral overtones. Essentially the tsar was admitting that his long struggle against boyar dissent had been useless, and the council considered his action a guarantee that prosecutions and disgraces would not reoccur. The new policy was confirmed by a decree that threatened those making false denunciations with stern punishment and authorized the execution of anyone who groundlessly charged boyars with conspiring against the tsar. Boyars' slaves were also liable for accusing their masters falsely, and petty slanderers were beaten and sent to serve as cossacks on the southern frontier.

The death of young Ivan made the feeble-minded Fedor heir to the throne, but since it was general knowledge that he was incapable of ruling, Secretary Ivan Timofeev declared "even the lame and the halt" mistrusted him, and the boyars hesitated to believe Fedor could govern the country after the defeats and devastation it had suffered. The tsar displayed his customary skill in order to save the dynasty. After young Ivan had solemnly been interred he delivered a speech to the council in which he began by saying that his sins were responsible for his older son's demise, and since, he continued, there was reason to doubt that power should pass to his younger son he would request the boyars to consider which great nobleman should ascend the throne.

During his long stormy career Ivan had abdicated twice, but the threat of a third abdication in favor of his feeble-minded son was designed to guarantee that his chosen heir would succeed him. The boyars, knowing what would happen to another candidate and anyone rash enough to support him, earnestly entreated the tsar to abandon his plans to retire to a monastery until the country's affairs were restored to order and loyally declared they wished no other tsar than his son. Ivan still did not trust the boyars and made ready to remove his family to England if fresh defeats or risings should occur, but fearful of publicity he concealed his intention from his intimates, entrusting negotiations in London to an obscure English interpreter.

Feeling his end was near Ivan dictated a new will to a trusted secretary, Savva Frolov, one of the handful privy to the secret English negotiations. Like his father, Ivan established a regency council for his son, but refused to recreate the one that previously had existed and decreased the number of the regents. Fedor was placed under the tutelage of four men: Ivan's uncle, Boyar N.R. Yurev, council President Prince I.F. Mstislavskii, the illustrious victor at Pskov, Boyar Prince I.P. Shuiskii, and the armorer, B.Ya. Belskii. The tsar had united boyars recently disgraced with the base-born nephew of Maliuta Skuratov, whose name alone was enough to inspire fright among his subjects. Legend holds that Ivan's favorite, Boris Godunov, was one of the regents, but this is inaccurate. Fedor had no children from his marriage to Irina Godunova, and, in hopes of preserving the dynasty the tsar had contemplated making his son obtain a divorce, but after young Ivan's death he hesitated to take drastic measures with his son. Ivan did not include Boris Godunov among the regents because, if Fedor were divorced, the former might interfere with the tsar's plans.

In his speech Ivan had asked the council to consider which nobleman was worthy to occupy the throne. The boyars dared not fulfil the tsar's injunction, and Ivan soon indicated the man he suspected of harboring such a design by briefly disgracing Boyar Vasilii Shuiskii, an ambitious, intelligent and crafty prince of the blood, as foreigners called members of the Shuiskii clan, who later did become tsar.

The death of his elder son had so shattered Ivan mentally and physically that he survived the former by no more than two years. His health deteriorated markedly in late February, 1584, when he instructed the monks of the Kirillov monastery to pray for his deliverance from mortal illness, and witnesses said his body became greatly swollen. Confused rumors circulated to the effect that the tsar's intimates, Belskii and Godunov, had poisoned him, but they are groundless, for these favorites owed their rise to Ivan and were terrified he might die and everything would inevitably be different. Belskii supposedly dispatched a courier to remote villages on the north coast to find seers able to divine the future and old women foretold him the exact day and hour Ivan would die. Many such legends were fabricated after the tsar's death.

The day he died, March 19, 1584, the tsar ordered his will brought and read to him. During the day he bathed at length, then had a chessboard set up, and after a game died suddenly. The tsar's death occasioned great turmoil. In fear of disturbance, the regents tried to conceal the truth from the people, but after issuing a proclamation that Ivan might still recover, they requested the Kremlin gate be closed and the palace guard placed on alert.

Ivan's reign of fifty years had come to a close.

Chapter Thirty-Six

CONCLUSION

When the Livonian war came to an end reports circulated abroad that revolts were expected in Moscow, the tsar had been taken prisoner by his boyars, and the gentry were fractious. These unfounded rumors were premature, because Russia did not experience such developments until after Ivan died. Writers who lived through the Time of Troubles were fond of recalling the peace and tranquility of Fedor's reign because the misery that followed it obscured many ominous developments that rocked the state to its very foundations during his rule.

Popular disturbances were widespread in the 1580s and involved taxpaying townsmen, indentured serfs, rich merchants, and disaffected gentry. The nobility took advantage of the risings to exile Belskii, the tsar's principal executor, but the regency council collapsed in less than a month and the new boyar rulers abolished Ivan's court and freed those still held in prison from the oprichnina years They now had a chance to pry hereditary estates, maintenance, and salaries from the treasury and admit other boyar nobles into the council, whose members suddenly became numerous, whereas before they had been no more than ten. Witnesses asserted that the boyars took a long time to convince themselves that Ivan was dead, but when they finally came to believe it they put on fancy clothes, annointed their grey hair with oil, and treated Fedor as though he did not exist.

The collapse of strong central authority led to the Time of Troubles, but its previous success made it difficult for the aristocracy to reassume power. Ivan's reforms had created a strong chancery bureaucracy, which brought base-born privy councillors and crown secretaries representing the zemshchina estates into the boyar council, and made the gentry politically important. Boris Godunov relied upon them to establish his own powerful centralized authority.

Even today Russia in the sixteenth century presents a fascinating panorama. It was then the newly united country took its first steps, which were accompanied by great triumphs and defeats. Russia achieved significant success in foreign policy. After throwing off the yoke of the Golden Horde, Moscow eradicated the Tatar khanates in the Volga region and severely defeated the Crimean Horde, which had become a tool of the Turks. Russia's victories confined Turkish conquests to the Balkans and the Black Sea region, although Turkish expansionism continued to cast a shadow over the whole of Eastern Europe. Russia also penetrated to the Urals and Siberia, and engaged in commercial relations with western Europe, first through the northern seas and later via the Baltic, although the first attempt to establish a foothold on the Baltic coast met with disaster.

During the sixteenth century Russia enjoyed great economic success, but also experienced major devastation. Old regions were depopulated, but fertile lands in the newly-acquired border regions were brought under cultivation. Production and trade increased, to be followed by decline at the end of the century, and the peasantry was enserfed. This turbulent time placed its distinctive stamp upon the character and fate of those who were part of it. Ivan the Terrible was very much a man of this time.

NOTES

CHAPTER 1

1.   Khan Mamai, to whom the Glinskii family owed its element of Tatar blood, was the effective ruler of the Golden Horde at a crucial juncture in its history, when combined Russian armies under Grand Prince Dmitrii Donskoi of Moscow defeated him at Kulikovo Pole in 1380, allaying the myth that the Tatars were invincible and demonstrating that Moscow would lead Russia to independence from the Golden Horde. Mamai himself was slain in the Crimea later that year (ed.).

2.   "Piskarevskii letopisets," *Materialy po istorii SSSR (XV-XVII vv.)*, 2 (1955) (hereafter PL), p. 86.

3.   *Pis'ma russkikh gosudarei*, Vol. 1 (1848), pp. 2-5.

4.   *Polnoe sobranie russkikh letopisei* (hereafter PSRL), 8 (1859), p. 285.

5.   PSRL, 13 (1904), p. 76.

6.   *Pskovskie letopisi* (hereafter PsL), 1 (1941), p. 106.

7.   Ivan I (1304-1341), nicknamed Kalita ("Moneybags"), grandson of Alexander Nevskii, became grand prince of Vladimir and Moscow in 1325. He followed a policy of avoiding conflict with the Golden Horde at any cost, which left the Muscovite principality comparatively free from Tatar punitive raids while Ivan began the "gathering of the Russian lands," the source of Moscow's subsequent power. Later grand princes, including Vasilii III and Ivan the Terrible, considered Kalita the founder of their dynasty (ed.).

8.   PSRL, 4 1 3 (1926), pp. 554-560.

9.   The Time of Troubles (smutnoe vremia), which began at the death of Tsar Fedor, Ivan the Terrible's son, in 1598, was characterized by massive internal disturbance throughout Russia, rapid rise and fall of four rulers, popular uprisings, and finally intervention by Poland and Sweden. The country closed ranks to expel the invaders, but Russia lay in ruins. The Time of Troubles ended with the accession of Mikhail Romanov to the throne in 1613 (ed.).

10.   Prince Yurii Ivanovich (1480-1536) had the town and district of Dmitrov for his appanage. As the second son of Grand Prince Ivan III he could harbor legitimate aspirations to the throne of Moscow (ed.).

CHAPTER 2

1.   PSRL, 4 1 3, p. 558.

2.   Sigismund von Herberstein (1486-1556), a diplomat in the service of the Holy Roman Empire, on two occasions undertook delicate missions to negotiate with the court of Vasilii III. His sojourns in Muscovy gave him opportunity to learn much about the country, which he embodied in his famous *Commentary on Muscovite Affairs*, accessible in R.H. Major, ed., *Notes Upon Russia: Being a Translation of the Earliest Account of That Country, Entitled Rerum Moscoviticarum Commentarii by the Baron Sigismund von Herberstein*, Hakluyt Society, 1st. series, Vols. X & XII, London, 1851-1852; Oswald P. Backus III, *Commentaries on Muscovite Affairs by Sigismund Freiherr von Herberstein, Nyberg and Guttenhag*, Lawrence (Kan.), 1956, and an abridged version, J.B.C. Grundy, ed., *Description of Moscow and Muscovy*, 1557, New York, 1969 (ed.).

3.   PSRL, 13, p. 95.

CHAPTER 3

1.   D.S. Likhachev and Ya.S. Lur'e, eds., *Poslaniia Ivana Groznogo* (Moscow and Leningrad, 1950) (hereafter POI), p. 33.

2.   Ibid., p. 34.

3.   The point of this ponderous joke seems to be an allusion to Shuiskii's financial position. The prince would have behaved better if he had had a new fur coat made instead of obtaining costly utensils, because only men who have money are in a position to do this (ed.).

4.   "Sochineniia kniazia A.M. Kurbskogo," *Russkaia istoricheskaia biblioteka,* 31 (1914) (hereafter RIB), p. 113. (The correspondence between the tsar and the prince is available in *The Correspondence Between Prince A.M. Kurbsky and Tsar Ivan IV of Russia, 1564-1579,* edited, with a translation and notes by J.L.I. Fennell, Cambridge, 1955 (ed.)).

5.   The *Domostroi,* from which Professor Skrynnikov quotes, is a compilation of precepts and aphorisms designed to regulate Russian urban family life in the sixteenth century. It may have grown up in the previous century as a manual to guide the deportment of the nobility and wealthy burghers of Novgorod, and it well reflects the patriarchal attitude in society at the time. Silvester revised it for young Ivan's consumption and benefit, preserving the popular language in which it was written. It remains a moot question to what extent existing realities accorded with the ideal the *Domostroi* sought to depict (ed.).

6.   PSRL, 13, p. 145, 444.

7.   RIB, p. 166.

CHAPTER 4

1.   Vladimir Vsevolodovich Monomakh (1053-1125) was summoned by the people of Kiev to be their grand prince in 1113, when disturbances, which he successfully mediated, were rife in the city. Vladimir's writings that have survived reveal that he was a monarch imbued with the principles of the Orthodox Christianity of his time, which he sought to exemplify in his life, and a redoubtable warrior and hunter. His memory was so popular that a legend arose to the effect that when Vladimir defeated the Byzantine emperor, Constantine VIII, in a battle, the latter sued for peace and, as a token of his sincerity, sent the Cap of Monomakh to Kiev, which was used to crown Muscovite grand princes down to Ivan's time. Vladimir was born in 1053 and Constantine died in 1054, and the Cap, as Professor Skrynnikov points out, reflected an eastern style; hence, it was symbolic of Russian subservience to the Tatars rather than Russian triumph over the Byzantine Empire (ed.).

2.   POI, p. 35.

CHAPTER 5

1.   St. George's day, an important holiday in the Russian Orthodox church, was celebrated on November 26, which coincided with the end of the annual agricultural cycle, the time when peasants who had discharged their obligations to their landlords traditionally were free to move elsewhere a week

before and after St. George's day. By the middle of the fifteenth century, certain local statutes began providing that St. George's day was the only time in the year peasants might move, a limitation that was extended throughout the country by the Law Code of 1497 and affirmed in the Code of 1550. A further major infringement of this ancient custom is thought to have occurred in 1581, when the Forbidden Years were introduced, during which peasants were not allowed to move at all. This was a milestone along the road to the full enserfment of the peasantry (ed.).

2.   Professor Skrynnikov alludes to the fact that for centuries Novgorod had followed its own path of development. Always an urban complex based on trade rather than agriculture, Novgorod had evolved a distinctive form of government (also found in Pskov), some features of which were: contracting with princes of its choice to defend the city in return for substantial commercial privileges, the presence of a powerful class of rich merchants, and, above all, vesting of political control in the city assembly (veche). No measure could become law until the assembly had passed it, which meant that Novgorod was governed by a form of direct-action democracy, although the ability of various pressure groups, such as the great merchant-traders, to distort this process should be recognized. These unique practices came to an end in 1479, when Ivan III completed Novgorod's subjection to Moscow, but, as Professor Skrynnikov frequently points out, memories of them long lingered among the city populace (ed.).

3.   POI, p. 35.

CHAPTER 6

1.   At the instigation of Metropolitan Makarii church leaders and the boyar council met with the tsar in February, 1551 to discuss reform. Ivan put a series of questions to the council in which he raised a number of issues of general social significance, including the touchy matter of church landowning, upon which certain limitations were placed, perhaps because at the time the Non-possessors had Silvester's ear. The council derived its name from the 100 decisions taken at its sessions, which called for sweeping changes to improve the ecclesiastical establishment, but most of them were never implemented (ed.).

2.   *Domostroi* (Odessa, 1887), pp. 12-13.

3.   POI, p. 309.

4.   Loc. cit.

5.   RIB, p. 169.

CHAPTER 7

1.   POI, p. 47.

2.   Cf. A.A. Zimin, *I.S. Peresvetov i ego sovremenniki* (Moscow, 1958), p. 332.

3.   Cf. D.P. Golokhvastov and Leonid, *Blagoveshchenskii ierei Sil'vestr i ego pisaniia* (Moscow, 1874), p. 91.

4.   The Nogai Horde emerged in the late fourteenth century after the decline of the Golden Horde. Its members occupied considerable territory,

largely southeast of the Volga, with their center in Saraichik at the mouth of the Yaik river. The state these nomad pastoralists formed was composed of enclaves (ulus) ruled by noble leaders (murzy) who originally had been tribal chieftans. When the Horde fragmented in the second half of the sixteenth century the tribes ruled by Prince Izmail, who voluntarily submitted to Moscow in 1555-1557, became known as the Great Nogai Horde (ed.).

5.   The Tatars also formed enclaves in western Siberia after the collapse of the Golden Horde, with a social and economic structure like that of the Nogais. In 1555 Khan Ediger became a Muscovite vassal, agreeing to pay an annual tribute, but Khan Kuchum, who had seized the throne, refused to continue payment and opposed Moscow until he was defeated by the Cossack adventurer Ermak in 1581. The Siberian khanates came under Moscow's permanent control by 1598 (ed.).

6.   The north Caucasus region, known as Kabardia, contained the town of Piatigorsk as its chief settlement. Its inhabitants, the Adegisian and Cherkassian tribes, had long resisted Tatar attempts to dominate them and were grateful when Russian success eventually helped relieve the pressure upon them. Unity eluded all the tribes of Kabardia, but those adjacent to Piatigorsk came to terms with Moscow and appealed for Russian assistance against the Crimea in 1552. Russians and the Piatigorsk Cherkassians, as the local tribes were now called, cooperated in raids on the Crimean Tatars several times in the 1550s, and Moscow built a fort at the mouth of the Terek river in 1567. A sign of the growing relationship between the two groups was Ivan's marriage to a Kabardian princess, Kuchenei, in 1561, who is known in Russian sources as Mariia Temriukovna (ed.).

CHAPTER 8

1.   PSRL, 13, p. 237.
2.   Ibid., p. 525.
3.   Ibid., p. 524.
4.   Ibid., p. 237.
5.   Ibid., p. 525.

CHAPTER 9

1.   PSRL, 13, p. 268.
2.   Ibid., pp. 268-269.
3.   PL, p. 56.
4.   Holy fools were wayfaring mendicants, not directly associated with the church, of whom there were many in Russia. Some undoubtedly were of unsound mind, and their behavior was often strange and bizarre. They enjoyed considerable influence because it was believed that God spoke through them to the people, as demonstrated by the example of Nikola of Pskov, of whom Professor Skrynnikov later writes. The notorious Rasputin is perhaps the most celebrated example of this genre (ed.).
5.   Professor Edward L. Keenan, Jr. of Harvard University, in *The Kurbskii-Groznyi Apocrypha* (Cambridge, Mass., 1971), has aroused considerable controversy by claiming that the exchange of epistles between Tsar Ivan and

Prince Kurbskii, vital as a source for this period of Russian history, was a seventeenth-century forgery. Professor Skrynnikov, in *Perepiska Groznogo i Kurbskogo. Paradoksy Edvarda Kinina* (Leningrad, 1973), undertook to refute him (ed.).

　　6.　　RIB, pp. 619-620.
　　7.　　POI, pp. 37-38.

CHAPTER 10

　　1.　　Germans began settling the northeastern Baltic area and establishing a commercial presence in strategic towns like Riga during the first half of the thirteenth century. Next, a band of military zealots left over from the Crusades, the Knights of the Sword, came there to advance the cause of Christianity and soon established themselves as the dominant force in the region, enslaving the native populations. After 1237 they became affiliated with the powerful Teutonic Order to the southwest, but kept their separate identity, ruled by a grand master (chosen for life), assisted by a small group of grandees. The knights, known collectively as the Livonian Order, employed the subject people to work the land and lived in castles throughout the area, but by the fifteenth century their crusading zeal had waned; they grew secularized, were at odds with the burghers in the towns, and the Reformation, which spread rapidly among them, caused serious religious division. These circumstances had created a power vacuum in Livonia, of which Ivan the Terrible and his associates hoped they might take advantage (ed.).

　　2.　　Scandinavians (known as Varangians) appearing in north Russia in the ninth century soon proceeded in annual trading flotillas south along the Dnieper river and the Black Sea coast to Constantinople, the great emporium of medieval Europe and Asia Minor. Their movement was already known in Kievan times as the "Route from the Varangians to the Greeks" (ed.).

CHAPTER 11

　　1.　　Cf. RIB, pp. 260-261.
　　2.　　POI, pp. 37-38.

CHAPTER 12

　　1.　　Reval is today known as the city of Tallinn, capital of the Estonian SSR (ed.).
　　2.　　PSRL, 13, p. 369.

CHAPTER 13

　　1.　　Ivan's second wife, Mariia Temriukovna. Her brother, called Prince Mikhail Cherkasskii, accompanied her to Moscow and rose to a high position before he fell from favor and was executed in 1571 (ed.).
　　2.　　PSRL, 13, p. 331.
　　3.　　RIB, p. 221.

4.   POI, p. 537.
5.   Ibid., p. 38.
6.   RIB, pp. 114-115.
7.   S.O. Shmidt, ed., *Opisi tsarskogo arkhiva XVI veka i arkhiva posol'-skogo prikaza 1614 g.* (Moscow, 1960) (hereafter OAP), p. 36.
8.   7071 is 1563. The chronological starting point for Russian materials of the sixteenth century was the year of the creation of the world (anno mundi) thought to have been 5508 years before the birth of Christ (ed.).
9.   Yurii Vasilevich (1532-1563), Ivan the Terrible's brother, was born deaf and dumb. Given Uglich as his appanage, he lived there quietly until his death, taking no part in affairs. He was married to a member of the Palitskii family in 1548, but had no children. Yurii never figured in the dynastic questions that beset Ivan's reign after the tsar's illness in 1553 (ed.).
10.   PSRL, 13, p. 525.
11.   RIB, pp. 276-277.
12.   This passage shows that actual lawsuits could be filed in order to determine rank under precedence. Since the tsar decided important cases, his verdict might indicate a shift in the relationship among those in power. In this instance Basmanov's successful suit foretold his rise to prominence and presaged the decline of the Zakharin family (ed.).
13.   In exile Kurbskii composed his *History,* a sombre indictment of Ivan's reign and policies. It is available in *Prince A.M. Kurbsky's History of Ivan IV,* edited, with a translation and notes, by J.L.I. Fennell (Cambridge, 1965) (ed.).
14.   RIB, p. 279.
15.   The reference is to the sensational but unsubstantiated charge Kurbskii made in one of his letters that Ivan maintained a homosexual relationship with Fedor Basmanov, a son of his new favorite (ed.).
16.   POI, p. 536.

CHAPTER 14

1.   RIB, p. 381.
2.   *Tsentral'nyi gosudarstvennyi arkhiv drevnikh aktov* [The main archival repository for materials on early Russian history, located in Moscow] (hereafter TsGADA), Fond 79, *knigi posol'skogo dvora,* No. 12, p. 278 ob. Ivan's envoys were guilty of exaggeration, but the situation was somewhat comparable. (Svidrigailo (c. 1370-1452) struggled to separate the Grand Duchy of Lithuania from the Kingdom of Poland and supplant his older brother, Jagiello, as grand prince. He managed to win and hold office for two years, 1430-1432 and, after being expelled, tried again without success on a number of occasions. His activities were a source of constant disruption in Poland-Lithuania (ed.)).
3.   POI, p. 535.
4.   See "Pis'mo Sigizmunda II Avgusta ot 13 ianvaria 1563 g.," *Arkhiv Kurnik. Korn* (Poznan), No. 1536. B.N. Floria located this source in Polish archives and kindly brought it to my attention.
5.   F. Nyestadt, "Livonskaia letopis'," *Sbornik materialov i statei po istorii Pribaltüiskogo kraia,* 4 (1883), p. 36 (Professor Skrynnikov is citing Franz Nyenstädt, *Livländische Chronik,* in the Russian version (ed.)).

6.   *Gosudarstvennyi arkhiv Latviiskoi SSR* (Riga), Fond A-2, op. K8, d. 35, pp. 5-6.
7.   RIB, p. 395.
8.   The archives of the Grand Duchy of Lithuania are known as the *Lithuanian Metric*. Once maintained in Trokhi and then Vilna, and now housed in TsGADA, the Metric, comprising some 600 books, is an invaluable source for the history of the Grand Duchy of Lithuania from the fifteenth to the eighteenth centuries (ed.).
9.   POI, pp. 14-15; 19; 61.
10.   *Gosudarstvennyi arkhiv Latviiskoi SSR* (Riga), Fond A-2, op. K8, d. 43, p. 10.

CHAPTER 15

1.   PSRL, 13, p. 392.
2.   S.V. Bakhrushin and L.V. Cherepnin, eds., *Dukhovnye i dogovornye gramoty velikikh i udel'nykh kniazei* (Moscow-Leningrad, 1950) (hereafter DDG), 426-427. (This work is available in selected form: Robert C. Howes, ed. and trans., *The Testaments of the Grand Princes of Muscovy* (Ithaca, N.Y., 1967) (ed.).).
3.   RIB, p. 3; DDG, p. 426.
4.   PSRL, 13, p. 392.
5.   Few members of the Livonian nobility came over to the Russian side, save Johann Taube and Elert Kruse, whom Ivan enrolled in the oprichnina and rewarded lavishly. They rose to high positions and were entrusted with confidential missions, but later defected. They have left an important first-hand account of this turbulent time, but their narrative must be utilized with caution because they tended to emphasize Ivan's brutality and Russian cruelty in their desire to rehabilitate themselves after their flight. In his later citations Professor Skrynnikov uses the Russian translation of their work: M.G. Roginskii, "Poslanie Ioganna Taube i Elerta Kruse," *Russkii istoricheskii zhurnal,* 8 (1922), pp. 8-59. This work is not available in English (ed.).

CHAPTER 16

1.   POI, p. 193.
2.   *Razriadnaia kniga 1375-1605 gg.* (hereafter RAZ), *Gosudarstvennaia publichnaia biblioteka im. M.E. Saltykova-Shchedrina* (hereafter GPB), *otdel rukopisei, sobranie Ermitazhnoe,* d. 390, p. 327 ob.
3.   R.G. Skrynnikov, "Oprichnaia zemel'naia reforma 1565 g.," *Istoricheskie zapiski,* 70 (1961), 223-250.
4.   TsGADA, Fond pomestnogo prikaza 1207, Book 643, pp. 238 ob.-282, 333-369, 424-500 ob.
5.   G. Fletcher, *O gosudarstvom russkom* (SPb., 1906), p. 41. (Giles Fletcher (1546-1611), who had enjoyed a distinguished career as a scholar and politician in England, spent portions of the years 1588-1589 in Russia to renegotiate the status of the Muscovy Company, England's trading entity, with the government of Tsar Fedor. Like his predecessor Herberstein, he employed much of his time gathering materials, which he used after his return to compose

a perceptive analysis of the Russian scene, available in three modern English editions: Lloyd E. Berry, ed., *The English Works of Giles Fletcher, the Elder* (Madison, 1963); Albert J. Shmidt, ed., *Of the Rus Commonwealth* (Ithaca, 1966), and the facsimile edition of Richard Pipes and John V.A. Fine, Jr., eds., *Of the Russe Commonwealth, 1591* (Cambridge, Mass., 1966). It also has been reproduced with a good introduction and careful notes in Lloyd E. Berry and Robert O. Crummey, eds., *Rude and Barbarous Kingdom. Russia in the Accounts of Sixteenth-Century English Voyagers* (Madison, 1968), pp. 87-246 (ed.)).

6.   Georg vom Hoff, *Erschreckliche, greuliche und unerhoerte Tyranney Iwan Wasilowitz* (1582), p. 7. (Here Professor Skrynnikov is citing a variant of the Taube and Kruse narrative (ed.)).

7.   *Istoricheskii arkhiv,* 3 (1940), p. 245.

8.   DDG, p. 442.

9.   RIB, p. 285.

CHAPTER 17

1.   PL, p. 76.

2.   *Sobranie gosudarstvennykh gramot i dogovorov,* Part 1, No. 193 (Moscow, 1813) (hereafter SGGD), p. 557.

3.   PL, p. 76.

4.   *Sbornik Imperatorskogo russkogo istoricheskogo obshchestva* (hereafter SIRIO), 71 (1898), p. 465.

5.   Albert Schlichting was a German taken prisoner by the Russians during the Livonian campaign of 1564, but little is known of him beyond the information he gives about himself in his writings. Professor Skrynnikov draws subsequent citations from the Russian translation of Schlichting made by A.I. Malein: *Novoe izvestie o Rossii vremeni Ivana Groznogo. "Skazanie" Al'berta Shliktinga* (Leningrad, 1934). Both of Schlichting's reports are available: Hugh F. Graham, "'A Brief Account of the Character and Brutal Rule of Vasil'evich, Tyrant of Muscovy' (Albert Schlichting on Ivan Groznyi)," *Canadian-American Slavic Studies,* 9/2 (1975), pp. 204-272 (ed.).

CHAPTER 18

1.   SIRIO, 71, pp. 464-465.

2.   POI, pp. 163-164.

3.   Ibid., p. 444.

4.   PSRL, 13, p. 526.

5.   Yu. Tolstoi, *Pervye 40 let snoshenii mezhdu Rossieiu i Anglieiu* (SPb., 1875), p. 40.

6.   PsL., Vol. II, p. 262.

7.   Heinrich von Staden, another German renegade, also fled abroad, where he set down a first-hand account of his experiences in the oprichnina in which he sought to vilify the tsar in an attempt to advance his own fortunes by arousing western states to attack Muscovy. Professor Skrynnikov takes his subsequent citations from Staden from the Russian translation made by I.I. Polosin: *G. Staden. O Moskve Ivana Groznogo. Zapiski nemtsa-oprichnika* (Leningrad,

1925). Staden's narrative is available in *Heinrich von Staden. The Land and Government of Muscovy*, trans. by Thomas Esper (Stanford, Calif., 1967) (ed.).

CHAPTER 19

1.   "Sinodik opal'nykh tsaria Ivana Groznogo," in R.G. Skrynnikov, *Oprichnyi terror* (Leningrad, 1969) (hereafter Sinodik), p. 267.
2.   *Novgorodskie letopisi* (SPb., 1879) (hereafter NL), p. 98. Cf. *Zhitiie Filippa mitropolita.* GPB., *Solovetskoe sobranie,* No. 1073/963, p. 67.
3.   Hoff, op. cit., p. 12.
4.   Sinodik, p. 269.
5.   RIB, p. 350.
6.   Schlichting, p. 22.
7.   Filipp later was confined in a monastery in Tver, where he was murdered by Maliuta Skuratov in December, 1569 (ed.).

CHAPTER 20

1.   D.Ya. Samokvasov, *Arkhivnyi material. Novootkrytye dokumenty pomestno-votchinnykh uchrezhdenii Moskovskogo gosudarstva XV-XVII vv.* Vol. I, Part 2, (Moscow, 1905), pp. 12, 34, 91. (Quitrent was an obligation peasants had to render their masters. It originally meant farming their lords' land, but gradual specification of function led the latter in the fifteenth century to accept other forms of payment, which were first collected in kind and later in cash. In Ivan's time both modes of payment were current (ed.)).
2.   *Ustiuzhskii letopisnyi svod* (Moscow-Leningrad, 1950), p. 109.

CHAPTER 21

1.   SIRIO, 71, p. 591.
2.   Taube and Kruse, p. 46.
3.   SIRIO, 71, p. 777.
4.   NL, pp. 395-405. Cf. *Eigentliche Warhafftige Beschreibung etlicher Handlung* . . . (a pamphlet whose complete title is given as Item F20a in Andreas Kappeler, *Ivan Groznyj im Spiegel der ausländischen Druckschriften seiner Zeit* (Bern and Frankfurt a/M, 1972), p. 255 (ed.)).
5.   PsL, Vol. 1, p. 116.
6.   A.I. Turgenev, ed., *Historia Russiae Monumenta,* Vol. 1 (SPb., 1841) (reissued, Vancouver, B.C., 1973), p. 214. Describing treason in Novgorod, a recently discovered source for the history of the oprichnina refers to the courier. It is a German report on the sack of Novgorod based on testimony from a witness: *Warhafftige Newe Zeitung vom grausamen Feindt der Christenheit dem Moskowiter . . . .*, p. 3 (The title of this pamphlet is also given in full as F19 in Kappeler, loc. cit. (ed.)).
7.   SIRIO, 71, p. 777.
8.   DDG, p. 480.

CHAPTER 22
1. Fletcher, p. 96.
2. RAZ, p. 270.

CHAPTER 23
1. DDG, p. 483.
2. Ibid., p. 480.
3. Schlichting, p. 62.
4. Ibid., p. 46.
5. *Istoricheskie pesni XIII-XVI vekov* (Moscow-Leningrad, 1960), p. 358.
6. E.F. Shmurlo, *Rossiia i Italiia,* Vol. II, No. 2, (SPb., 1903), p. 230.
7. DDG, p. 480.

CHAPTER 24
1. NL, p. 121.
2. Ibid., p. 107.
3. A.N. Nasonov, "Letopisnye pamiatniki khranilishch Moskvy," *Problemy istochnikovedeniia,* 4 (1955), p. 255.
4. NL, p. 105.

CHAPTER 25
1. Staden, pp. 95-96.
2. Loc. cit.
3. RIB, p. 155.
4. POI, p. 567.
5. RAZ, pp. 455 ob. -456 ob.
6. O.A. Derzhavina, ed., *Vremennik Ivana Timofeeva* (Moscow-Leningrad, 1951), pp. 17, 150.
7. Professor Skrynnikov uses the standard Russian edition of the works of Marx and Engels for this reference: "Pis'mo F. Engel'sa k Marksu 4 sentiabria 1870 g.," in K. Marks i F. Engel's, *Sochineniia,* Vol. 33, p. 45.
8. PL, p. 85.
9. POI, pp. 162-163.
10. RIB, p. 619.
11. M.M. Gerasimov (1907-1970), a distinguished anthropologist and ethnographer, conducted a number of significant archaeological excavations at various sites throughout the Soviet Union, but was best known for the techniques he pioneered whereby to make a sculptural reconstruction of an historical personage from analysis of remains, particularly the skull (ed.).

CHAPTER 26
1. SIRIO, 129, p. 222.

CHAPTER 27

1.　　DDG, p. 444.
2.　　NL, p. 120.

CHAPTER 28

1.　　V.I. Lenin, *Polnoe sobranie sochineniia,* 17, p. 346.
2.　　Tolstoi, *Pervye 40 let . . . ,* p. 135.

CHAPTER 29

1.　　TsGADA, Fond 181, No. 141, p. 91.
2.　　PsL, Vol. II, p. 262. (Bomel (early 16th century-1579), originally from Westphalia, went to England, distinguished himself in the study of medicine at Cambridge, and soon attracted an aristocratic following, which brought him to prominence. He took advantage of his position to practise astrology, which acquired him further notoriety and aroused the ire of the church. Archbishop Parker had him imprisoned, but he was released on condition that he leave England at once. Ivan's request for an "English" physician thus had proved providential; Bomel departed for Moscow in early summer of 1570. It is difficult to avoid the conclusion that Queen Elizabeth and her advisors had taken advantage of Ivan in order to escape from an embarrassing situation (ed.)).
3.　　NL, p. 148.
4.　　Sinodik, p. 288.
5.　　DDG, p. 483.
6.　　OAP; TsGADA, Fond 138, op. 3, No. 2, p. 426.
7.　　V.I. Buganov and V.I. Koretskii, "Neizvestnyi moskovskii letopisets XVII v.," *Zapiski otdela rukopisei GBL,* 32 (1971), p. 145.
8.　　Tolstoi, *Pervye 40 let . . . ,* p. 181.

CHAPTER 30

1.　　PSRL, 13, p. 450.
2.　　POI, p. 210.
3.　　GPB., *otdel rukopisei,* sb. O. XVII. 17, p. 157. (The reference is to A.I. Sulakidzev (1771-c. 1830), an official in the Finance Ministry at St. Petersburg who became an eminent bibliophile. He collected more than 2,000 documents pertaining to Russian history from the fifteenth century onward, some both rare and valuable, which he then proceeded to mark and annotate. At last, using archival and literary materials, he constructed what he asserted were several early chronicles, and thus his name has become synonymous with forging what seem to be authentic historical sources (ed.)).
4.　　TsGADA, Fond 1209, Book 619, pp. 89-89ob.
5.　　POI, p. 142.
6.　　SIRIO, 38, p. 6. (Mary Hastings was a daughter of Henry, second earl of Huntingdon, and, although not the queen's niece, was a member of one of England's most powerful families. Elizabeth considered the match merely a

counter in the negotiations to secure continuation of the privileges the Muscovy Company enjoyed in Russia and thus was willing to let Pisemskii see Lady Mary and have Sir Jerome Bowes, recently named ambassador, take her portrait to Moscow. But, knowing before he left that Lady Mary had begun to express misgivings about the marriage, Bowes sought to deprecate her charms and qualities to the tsar, and the project collapsed in a series of acrid exchanges between the two men that ended only a month before Ivan's death (ed.)).

7.   Ibid., p. 105.

CHAPTER 31

1.   POI, p. 259.
2.   Ibid., p. 211.
3.   RAZ, p. 445.

CHAPTER 32

1.   SGGD, Part 1, No. 200.
2.   *Obzha* was a taxation unit based on the amount of land a peasant held. The increase in the number of peasant families meant the same amount of tax had to be paid on a lesser amount of land with a correspondingly smaller yield (ed.).
3.   *Istoricheskii arkhiv,* 4 (1949), p. 82.

CHAPTER 33

1.   POI, p. 213; p. 232.
2.   O.N. Milevskii, trans., *Dnevnik pokhoda S. Batoriia na Rossiiu* (Pskov, 1881), p. 107.
3.   Antonio Possevino, *Moskoviia,* trans. L.N. Godovikova. *Istoricheskie sochineniia A. Possevino o Rossii XVI veka,* Dissertation, Moscow State University, Supplement, p. 91. (Professor Skrynnikov cites from this Russian version. Possevino is available in Hugh F. Graham, ed. and trans., *The Moscovia of Antonio Possevino, S.J.* (Pittsburgh, 1977) (ed.)).
4.   Reinhold Heidenstein, *Zapiski o Moskovskoi voine* (SPb., 1889), p. 125.

CHAPTER 34

1.   Dzh. Gorsei, *Putesheshestviia: Chteniia v Imperatorskom obshchestva istorii i drevnostei rossiiskikh pri Moskovskom universitete,* 2 (1907), p. 35 (Little is known of the career of Sir Jerome Horsey prior to his association with the Muscovy Company, but he spent almost twenty years (1573-1591) in its service, almost continuously in Russia, where he not only learned to speak the language well, but came to know many prominent people and eventually was used by both England and Russia to carry out a number of diplomatic missions of interest to both sides. He was not noted for his high standard of commercial ethics, and his attempts to enrich himself eventually caused him

trouble and led to his expulsion. Horsey wrote an account of his travels which is invaluable for historians of the period, but from a man as well connected and as experienced as Horsey was, more and better detail might have been expected than is found in his narratives, which must be used with extreme caution. His *Travels,* with a useful introduction and notes, are available in Berry and Crummey, *Rude and Barbarous Kingdom . . . . ,* pp. 249-369 (ed.)).

2.   PsL, Vol. II, p. 263.

3.   N.P. Likhachev, "Delo o priezde v Moskvu Antoniia Possevina," *Letopis' zaniatii Arkheograficheskoi komissii,* 9 (1903), p. 58.

AUTHOR'S BIBLIOGRAPHY

S.V. Bakhrushin,"Ivan Groznyi," in his *Nauchnye trudy,* Vol. 2, Moscow, 1954.

S.B. Veselovskii, *Issledovaniia po istorii oprichniny,* Moscow, 1963.

R.Iu. Vipper, *Ivan Groznyi,* 3rd edition, Moscow-Leningrad, 1944.

A.A. Zimin, *I.S. Peresvetov i ego sovremenniki,* Moscow, 1958.

Id., *Reformy Ivana Groznogo,* Moscow, 1960.

Id., *Oprichnina Ivana Groznogo,* Moscow, 1964.

N.M. Karamzin, *Istoriia gosudarstva rossiiskogo,* Vol. 9, Book 3, SPb., 1831.

V.O. Kliuchevskii, "Kurs lektsii po russkoi istorii," in his *Sochineniia,* Vol. 2, Moscow, 1959.

V.B. Kobrin, "Sostav oprichnogo dvora Ivana Groznogo," *Arkheograficheskii ezhegodnik za 1959 god,* Moscow, 1960.

V.I. Koretskii, *Zakreposhchenie krest'ian i klassovaia bor'ba v Rossii vo vtoroi polovine XVI v.,* Moscow, 1970.

V.D. Koroliuk, *Livonskaia voina,* Moscow, 1954.

A.K. Leont'ev, *Obrazovanie prikaznoi sistemy upravleniia v Moskovskom gosudarstve,* Moscow, 1961.

D.S. Likhachev, *Chelovek v literature Drevnei Rusi,* Moscow, 1970.

V.V. Novodvorskii, *Bor'ba za Livoniiu mezhdu Moskvoi i Rech'iu Pospolitoi (1570-1582 gg.),* SPb., 1904.

N.E. Nosov, *Stanovlenie soslovno-predstavitel'nykh uchrezhdenii v Rossii. Izyskaniia o zemskoi reforme Ivana Groznogo,* Leningrad, 1969.

S.F. Platonov, *Ivan Groznyi,* Prague, 1923.

Id., *Ocherki po istorii smuty v Moskovskom gosudarstve XVI-XVII vv.,* Moscow, 1937.

P.A. Sadikov, *Ocherki po istorii oprichniny,* Moscow-Leningrad, 1950.

A.M. Sakharov, *Obrazovanie i razvitie edinogo Rossiiskogo gosudarstva v XIV-XVII vv.,* Moscow, 1969.

R.G. Skrynnikov, *Nachalo oprichniny,* Leningrad, 1966.

Id., *Oprichnyi terror,* Leningrad, 1969.

Id., *Perepiska Groznogo i Kurbskogo,* Leningrad, 1973.

I.I. Smirnov, *Ivan Groznyi,* Leningrad, 1944.

Id., *Ocherki politicheskoi istorii Russkogo gosudarstva 30-50kh godov XVI v.,* Moscow-Leningrad, 1958.

S.M. Solov'ev, *Istoriia Rossii s drevneishikh vremen,* Vol. 3, Moscow, 1960.

M.N. Tikhomirov, *Rossiia v XVI stoletii,* Moscow, 1962.

G.V. Forsten, *Baltiiskii vopros v XVI i XVII stoletiiakh,* Vol. 1, SPb., 1893.

S.O. Shmidt, *Stanovlenie rossiiskogo samoderzhestva,* Moscow, 1973.

INDEX

Adashev, Aleksei Fedorovich, Associate boyar, 24-27, 30, 32, 36, 41-46, 48-50, 53-56, 58, 60, 66, 69, 72, 79, 81, 82, 94, 114, 147, 159
Adashev, Daniel, associate boyar, 69, 112
Adashev, Fedor, 37
Afanasii, metropolitan, 71, 97, 114
Alenkin-Zheria, A.F., prince, 92
Aleksandrovskaia Sloboda, 77, 84-86, 102, 108, 114, 119, 121, 122, 125, 134, 140, 148, 173, 193, 195
Anastasiia Romanovna Zakharina, wife of Ivan IV, 9, 38, 55, 58, 60, 92, 172, 173
Andrei Ivanovich, prince of Staritsa, 6-9, 58, 65, 130
Anfim, son of Silvester, 31
Anna, daughter of Ivan IV, 172
Antonii, metropolitan, 166
Armus, 76
Artemii, elder, 29, 40
Arts, count, 74, 75
Assemblies; reconciliation, 25; stoglav, 26, 28, 29, 44
Astrakhan, 32, 35, 132, 133, 152, 156, 177
Austria (and Vienna), 178, 187
Azov, 132
Babylon, 72, 73
Balakhna, 87
Bartenev, Novgorod secretary, 141
Bashkin, Fedor, 40
Bashkin, Matvei, 39, 40
Bashkirs, 33, 35
Basmanov, Aleksei Danilovich, boyar, 50, 69, 71, 81-83, 86, 87, 116, 138, 139, 143, 144, 146, 147, 173,
Basmanov, Fedor, 71, 80, 87, 138, 139
Basmanov, Petr, 81, 138, 139
Batory, Stefan, king of Poland, 178, 179, 183, 184, 187-193
Battles; Molodi, 153-155; Sudbishche, 69; Ula, 57

Bekbulatovich, Simeon, 162, 163 166, 167, 169-171, 180
Belev, 62
Beloozero, 10, 40, 63, 138, 139
Belorussia, 183
Belskii, Bogdan Ya., boyar, 168, 180, 194, 197-199
Belskii, Dmitrii Fedorovich, prince, 3, 4
Belskii, I.D., prince, 9, 10
Belskii, I.F., prince, 62, 96, 102
Bezhetskii Verkh, 113
Beznosov, Andrei, secretary, 126, 127
Bomel, Elijah, physician, 163, 164, 169
Boris and Gleb, saints, 121
Borisov, B.N., 115
Borisov, Ivan, 40
Borisov, N.V., associate boyar, 91, 168
Borisov, Vasilii, 168
Bowes, Sir Jerome, English ambassador, 176
Bundov, K.S., boyar, 98, 99
Buturlin, Afanasii, boyar, 14
Buturlin, Dmitrii, associate boyar, 168
Buturlin, Ivan, boyar, 168, 169
Buturlin, V.A., boyar, 127
Cap of Monomakh, 15, 16
Cathedrals; Dormition, 15, 20, 84, 101, 112, 116, 165; Annunciation, 24, 30, 40, 71; St. Sophia, 123, 124; Trinity of Pskov, 125; Archangel, 169
Chronicles; Synodal, 66; Moscow (Royal Book), 66, 67; Lithuanian Metric, 76; Franz Neustadt, 74; Pskov, 2, 4; Voskresenskii, 2
Caucasus, 35, 132, 152, 184
Cheboksarai, 93
Cheliadnin, Ivan Ivanovich, Master of Horse, 5, 13, 16
Cheliadnin-Fedorov, I.P., Master of Horse, 16, 17, 67, 75, 96, 97, 99 102-104, 106-108, 113-116, 121, 127, 159
Cheliadnina, Agrafena Vasilevna, 5

Cherkashenin, Mishka, 189
Cherkasskii, Mikhail, prince, 87, 139
Cherkasy, 62
Crimea (and Crimean Tatars), 14,
    15, 34, 50, 53, 56, 62, 69, 80,
    83, 103, 132, 133, 145, 151-
    153, 155, 156, 177, 185,
    194, 199
Christian III, king of Denmark, 39
Chrysostom, St. John, 172
Chuvash, 33, 91
Circassia (and Adigesia), 132
Coinage and counterfeiting, 8
Constantine VIII, emperor of
    Byzantium, 16
Constantinople, capital of
    Byzantine empire, 14, 16, 24, 55
Copenhagen, 150
Courland, duchy of, 178,
    183-185
Cracow, 151, 187
Daniel, metropolitan, 10
Danilov, Fedor, boyar, 115
Danilov, V.D., prince, 96, 127, 128
Denmark, 49, 56, 57, 131
Devlet-Girei, khan of the Crimea,
    83, 152-154, 177
Divei-Murza, 154
Dmitrii, grandson of Ivan III, 1
Dmitrii, son of Ivan IV by
    Anastasiia, 36, 37, 67, 79, 172
Dmitrii, son of Ivan IV by Mariia
    Nagaia, 176
Domostroi, 12, 31
Dorogobuzhkii, Ivan, prince,
    16, 17
Dorpat (formerly Yurev), 50,
    53-55, 72-76, 151, 187, 192
Drutskii, Daniel, prince, 168, 169
Dubrovskii, Kazarin, secretary,
    112
Dünaberg, 178, 179
Elders, transvolga, 29
Elizabeth I, queen of England,
    175, 176
Empire, Byzantine, 15, 26
Empire, Ottoman (Turks, and
    Turkey), 26, 32, 103, 106,
    131-133, 151, 152, 177, 199
Empire, Roman (and Caesar
    Augustus), 14, 103

Engels, Friedrich, 148
England, 105, 119, 131, 175, 176,
    193, 197
Erik XIV, king of Sweden, 57, 74,
    120, 131
Ermes, 53
Ermolai Erazm, 44
Estonians (and Estonia), 49, 56
Eudocia, empress of Constantinople,
    172
Evdokiia, daughter of Ivan IV, 172
Evfimii, archimandrite, 164, 165
Evfrosiniia, princess, mother of
    Vladimir Andreevich, 37-39, 41,
    64, 66, 104, 115, 121
False Dmitrii I, 47
Fedor Ivanovich, son of Ivan IV,
    4, 92, 156, 172, 196-199
Fellin, 53, 54, 187
Filipp, saint and metropolitan
    (Kolychev, Fedor Stepanovich),
    97-99, 112-114, 116, 129, 134
Finland, 75, 192
Fletcher, Giles, English writer, 91,
    155
France, 192
Frankfurt-am-Main, 123
Frolov, Savva, secretary, 197
Funikov, Nikita, secretary, 60, 135
Funikov, Vasilii, prince, 69
Gerasimov, M.M., sculptor, 150
Gerio, Venetian abbot, 126
Germany, 184, 192
Glinskaia, Anna, princess, grand-
    mother of Ivan IV, 16, 17, 20
Glinskaia, Elena, grand princess,
    mother of Ivan IV, 1-3, 5-9, 16,
    38, 47, 81, 172
Glinskii, I.M., prince, 145
Glinskii, Yurii Vasilevich, boyar,
    17, 20
Glinskii, Mikhail Lvovich, prince, 16
Glinskii, Mikhail Vasilevich, prince,
    3-8, 16, 17, 20, 21, 61, 62
Glinskii, Vasilii Mikhailovich,
    prince, 62
Godunov, Boris, boyar, 47, 145, 163,
    168, 197-199
Godunov, D.I., chamberlain, 163, 168
Godunova, Irina, 197
Golden Horde, 14-16, 32, 199

Golokhvastov, Nikita, captain, 149
Gorodets, 139
Golovin, P.P., associate boyar, 88
Gorbatyi, A.B., prince, 34, 41, 58, 86, 88, 144
Gorenskii, Petr, prince, 58, 81
Gorodishche, 123, 124, 127
Griaznoi, Grigori, 164
Griaznoi, Vasilii, 87, 122, 139, 145
Gulf of Finland, 50, 193
Hapsal, 177
Hastings, Lady Mary, 176
Heidenstein, R., chronicler, 190, 195
Helmet, 74, 76
Herberstein, Sigismund von, 6, 8, 16
Horsey, Sir Jerome, English merchant, 164, 165, 170, 194, 195
Hungary, 184
Ilin, Osip, secretary, 168, 169
Ioasaf, metropolitan, 11
Iosif, archimandrite, 164
Islands; Valaam, 40; Oesel, 56; Hare, 132
Italy, 192
Ivan I. Kalita, 3
Ivan III, grand prince, 1, 15, 71, 104, 120
Ivan IV Vasilevich (Ivan the Terrible; Little Ivan of Moscow), 1-4, 6, 8, 9-17, 19-23, 25, 26, 28-32, 34-47, 29, 46-49, 53, 55, 57, 58, 60, 63-67, 69, 70-73, 75-77, 79-88, 91, 94, 95, 97-119, 121, 122, 125, 126, 128-130, 132, 134, 135, 137, 138, 140-146, 148-152, 156, 159-164, 166-171, 173, 175-177, 180-182, 183, 188, 189, 191, 192, 195-199
Ivan Ivanovich, son of Ivan IV, 104, 136, 156, 164, 169, 170, 172, 194-197
Ivan, protopope, 169
Ivangorod, 50, 185, 191, 193
Ivanov, Savluk, 64
Izborsk, 119-121
Jagiello, king of Poland, 73
Jenkinson, Anthony, English ambassador, 103, 105, 161
John III, king of Sweden, 74, 131, 151, 187, 191, 192

Joseph of Volokolamsk, 29
Karbardia, 35
Kaluga, 152
Karamyshev, I.M., boyar, 98, 99
Karamzin, N.M., 175
Karelia, 187
Kargopol, 87, 180
Kashin, Ivan, prince, 70, 89
Kashin, Yurii, prince, 57, 89
Katyrev, M.P., commander, 192
Katyrev-Rostovskii, A.I., prince, 91, 92, 114-116
Kazan, 2, 19, 32-36, 40, 42, 43, 49, 58, 69, 83-97, 115-117, 132, 134, 149, 168, 193
Keenan, E.L., historian, 47
Kettler, Gotthardt, 53
Khilkov, D.I., boyar, 54, 93, 184, 185, 187
Khiron-Zakharin, I.P., boyar, 137
Khlyznev-Kolychev, Boris, prince, 64
Kholkholkov, I.Iu., prince, 92
Kholm, 192
Kholyn, 140
Khovanskii, A.P., prince, 144
Khvorostinin, D.I., prince, 152-154, 185, 188, 192
Kirill, metropolitan, 134
Kliuchevskii, V.O., historian, 10, 48, 146
Kokenhausen, 178
Kolomenskoe, 132
Kolomna, 19, 108, 152
Koltovskaia, Anna, 156, 174
Kolychev, Mikhail, I., 114, 115, 116
Kopore, 191, 193
Korela, 187, 193
Kostroma, 24, 32, 43, 54, 100
Kozelsk, 180
Kuchenei (Princess Maria Temriukovna), 173
Kurakin, Fedor, prince, 66
Kurakin, Petr, prince, 66, 91, 104, 168
Kurakin, Ivan, boyar, 66, 89, 104, 168
Kurbskii, Andrei Mikhailovich, prince, 11, 13, 31, 32, 34, 35, 46-48, 53, 60, 61, 70-77, 79-81, 84-86, 92, 103, 122, 144, 148, 150, 164, 172, 178
Kurliatev, Dmitrii Ivanovich, prince, 38, 41, 58, 63

Ladoga, lake, 64
Ladoga, town, 129, 141, 192
Lenin, V.I., 46, 159
Leonid, archbishop of Novgorod, 164-167
Letts, 49
Levskii, abbot of Chudov monastery, 85, 164
Lialitsa, 192
Likhachev, D.S., historian, 148, 149
Lithuania, 1, 7, 21, 25, 40, 53, 56, 57, 62-64, 68, 70, 71, 73-77, 80, 102, 103, 119, 128, 131, 138, 151, 178, 188
Livonia, 49, 50, 53, 54, 56, 57, 72, 74-76, 94, 105, 117, 120, 131, 151, 152, 177-179, 184, 187, 188, 190-192
Livonian order, 15, 49, 53
Livonian war, 43, 45, 49, 50, 53, 57, 69, 95, 131, 175, 193, 198
London, 105, 176, 197
Lublin, union of, 131
Lykov, Mikhail M., boyar, 114, 116
Magnus, duke of Oesel, king of Livonia, 56, 131, 137, 148, 169
Maintenance (*kormlenie*), 22, 43, 44
Makarii, metropolitan, 15, 23, 24, 29, 38, 68, 69, 71, 173
Maksim (Mishka), cannoneer, 127
Mamai, khan, 1
Mansurov, Yakov, 162
Mari (tribe), 33
Mariia, daughter of Ivan IV, 172
Meissenheim, Hans, 39
Melenteva, Vasilisa, 175
Melentii Ivanov, (Melentev, Fedor; Melenteva, Mariia), 175
Menshoi-Sitskii, D.Yu., prince, 92, 115
Menshoi-Ushatyi, S.Yu., prince, 92
Minsk, 57
Mishurin, Fedor, secretary, 9, 10
Mitnev, M.S., 114, 115
Mohammed, sultan, 26
Mogilev, 188
Moliava, cook, 122
Monasteries and nunneries;
    Bogoiavlenskii, 110, 116
    Chudov, 71, 85, 97, 165
    Goritskaia, 115, 121

Joseph of Volokolamsk, 40
Kirillov, 29, 39, 54, 64, 101, 102, 104, 119, 149, 172, 198
Nizhegorod-Pechorskii, 110
Novospasskii, 150
Pechora, 71, 72, 75, 125
Simonov, 32, 165
Troitsa, 36, 174, 196
Voskresenskaia, 64, 65
Voznesenskii, 172
Mordva (tribe), 33, 91
Morozov, Mikhail, prince, 58, 68, 69
Morozov, Vladimir, prince, 81
Mosalskii, V.V., prince, 146
Moscow the third Rome, 14, 23
Mozhaisk, 53, 77, 87, 88
Mstislavskii, Ivan Fedorovich, prince, 53, 58, 96, 102, 155, 162, 166, 194, 197
Muromtsev, Vasian, elder, 71
Nagaia, Mariia, 168, 176
Nagoi, Afanasii F., 168, 175, 180
Nagoi, Fedots, 168
Narva, 50, 69, 116, 161, 185, 187-189, 191, 192
Nemoi, D.I., boyar prince, 38, 66, 89
Nevel, 185, 192
Nikola, holy fool, 125
Nil of Sorsk, 29
Nizhnii Novgorod, 34, 89, 121, 122
Nogai Hordes; Great, 35, 132, 152; Little, 132, 152
Nosov, N.E., historian, 30, 44
Novgorod, 7, 8, 18-20, 30, 31, 50, 53, 65, 66, 107, 114, 117, 118, 120-122, 124-131, 134, 135, 137-143, 145, 147, 149, 151, 155-157, 163-165, 169, 173, 181, 191, 192
Novodvorskii, V.V., historian, 184
Novosil, 95
Obraztsov, F.R., 115
Ochin, I.I., 130
Ochin-Pleshcheev, Z.I., boyar, 139
Odoev, 95
Odoevskii, N.R., prince, 144
Olferev-Nashchekin, Roman, privy councillor, 145, 146
Opochka, 19, 189
Oprichnina, 71, 80, 82, 83, 85-100, 102-122, 125, 127-132, 134-136, 138, 139, 141-148, 155-157,

159-166, 168, 169, 171, 175, 180, 181, 183, 196, 199
Opukhtin, Nikita, boyar, 113
Oreshek, 192
Orsha, 188
Ovchina-Telepnev-Obolenskii, Fedor, prince, 81
Ovchina-Telepnev-Obolenskii, I.F., prince, 5-9, 16
Pafnutii, bishop, 114
Paida (Weissenstein), 54, 57, 152
Paisii, abbot of Solovki, 116
Pakhra, 153
Paleologue, Sofia, grand princess, 1, 27, 47, 172
Pereiaslavl, 54
Peresvetov, I.S., publicist, 25-27, 34, 48, 160
Pernau, 177, 187, 192
Petrov, Pavel, 122
Petrova-Solovaia, 194
Piatigorsk, 35
Pimen, archbishop of Novgorod, 85, 114, 122, 129, 134, 135, 138
Poland (Rzeczpospolita), 49, 53, 83, 94, 126, 131, 137, 151, 173, 177, 178, 182-185, 187, 188, 190-192
Polotsk, 56, 57, 64, 68, 70, 72, 75, 80, 83, 99, 102, 103, 149, 184, 185, 189, 190, 192, 193
Piotrowski, S., chronicler, 190
Pisemskii, Fedor, secretary, 176
Platonov, S.F., historian, 88
Pleshcheev, Mikhailo, 162
Polev, German, 97, 98
Polubenskii, Aleksandr, 178
Pontus de la Gardie, Swedish commander, 191, 192
Possevino, Antonio, papal legate, 187, 190, 191, 195
Precedence (mestnichestvo), 22, 27, 69
Presniakov, A.E., historian, 3
Pskov, 19, 20, 50, 66, 120, 124, 125, 128-130, 137, 138, 164, 167, 180, 185, 188-192, 194
Pronskii, P.D., boyar prince, 144, 155
Pronskii, S.D. Boyar prince, 144
Pronskii, V.F., prince, 98, 99
Radoshkovich, 107

Radziwill, Ju.N., commander-in-chief of Lithuania, 73-75
Randolph, Thomas, English ambassador, 119, 131
Reformation, 49
Repnin-Obolenski, Vasilii Ivanovich, prince, 57, 70
Reval, 50, 56, 131, 151, 152, 177, 178, 185
Riapolovskii, 92
Riazan, 43, 83, 132-134, 152, 155
Riga, 54, 74, 75, 94, 177-179
Rivers; Daugava, 57, 83, 178, 179; Dneipr, 188; Don, 132; Nara, 153, Narova, 50, 178; Neglinnaia, 100, 101; Neva, 50, 192, 193; Oka, 83, 132, 152-154; Pliussa, 193; Rozhai, 153; Sheksna, 121; Volga, 33-35, 132, 139; Ugra, 132; Volkhov, 122, 123, 142, 156; Volkhovets, 141
Rome (Pope, Vatican, Catholic Church), 24, 49, 106, 187
Rop, a German, 127
Rostov, 61, 93, 132, 167, 168, 180
Rostovskii, Nikita, prince, 40
Rostovskii, Semen Borisovich, boyar prince, 38, 40, 41, 62, 66, 67, 89
Rumiantsev, Kuzma, secretary, 126, 127
Rusinov, Leontii, boyar, 113
Rzhev, 21, 167, 189
St. George's Day, 18, 27, 182
Saburov, B.Yu., boyar, 163
Saburova, Evdokiia, 194
Saburova, Solomoniia, 1
Sadikov, P.A., historian, 98
Safa-Girei, khan, 33
Saltykov, F.I., boyar, 139
Saltykov, L.A., prince, 67, 139
Schlichting, Albert, German writer, 98, 106, 107, 127
Schlitte, Hans, 39
Seas; Baltic, 49, 50, 175, 192, 199; White, 50; Black, 132, 199; Caspian, 152
Serebrianyi, Petr, prince, 103
Serpukhov, 132, 152, 153
Shah-Ali, khan, 33, 34
Shakhovskoi, I.S., prince, 150
Shcheniatev, P.M., prince, 38, 66, 104

Shchetinin, Yu.I., armorer, 92
Shcherbatyi, D.M., associate boyar
  prince, 144
Sheremetev-Bolshoi, Ivan Nikitich,
  boyar, 56, 58, 69, 70, 137
Sheremetev, Nikita, boyar, 70
Sheremeteva, Elena, 194, 195
Shevyrev, Dmitrii, prince, 89
Shibanov, Vasilii (Vaska),
  76, 77, 81
Shishkin-Olgov, Ivan, commander,
  69
Shmidt, S.O., historian, 21, 23
Shuiskii, Andrei Mikhailovich,
  prince, 10, 13
Shuiskii, D.I., prince, 145
Shuiskii, I.A., prince, 144
Shuiskii, I.P., boyar, 185, 188,
  190, 197
Shuiskii, Ivan Vasilevich, prince,
  4, 10-12, 37
Shuiskii, Vasilii, future tsar, 198
Shuiskii, Vasilii Vasilevich, prince,
  4, 9, 10
Siberia, 35, 199
Sigismund II, king of Poland, 64,
  74, 151, 177
Silvester, priest, 30-32, 34, 38-41,
  46, 48, 53-55, 58, 60, 61, 63,
  67, 69, 71, 79, 147, 172
Sitskii, V.A., boyar prince, 144
Skuratov-Belskii, Maliuta, 102, 113,
  122, 134, 137, 139, 144-148,
  152, 163, 174, 197
Smirnov, I.I., historian, 3, 28, 42
Smolensk, 57, 63, 68, 185, 187
Sobakina, Marfa, 141, 145, 174
Sol Galitskaia, 87
Sol Vychegodskaia, 87
Staden, Heinrich von, German ad-
  venturer, 106, 107, 124, 143, 144
Staraia Rus, 87
Starodub, 61, 69, 92, 93
Staroi, Aleksei, 162, 164
Staroi, Fedor, 162
Stepanov, Vasilii, secretary, 122
Stockholm, 120
Strigin-Riapolovskii, A.I., prince, 93
Sulakidzev, A.I., 175
Suzdal, 61, 65, 87, 88, 93, 94, 96

Svidrigailo, grand prince of
  Lithuania, 73
Sviiazev, Anton, secretary, 122
Sviiazhsk, 34, 91, 116
Sweden, 49, 50, 56, 57, 120, 121,
  131, 151, 173, 178, 185, 187,
  191-193
Synodicals, 108-114, 122, 127, 128,
  138, 162, 163, 165, 168
Tarasii, bishop, 166
Taube, Johann, and Kruse, Elert, 85,
  91, 122, 144, 151
Teliatevskii, Andrei, prince, 58
Temkin, Yu.V., prince, 92
Temkin, V.I., prince, 92, 139, 143
Tereberdei-murza, 154
Teterin, Timokha, 60, 77, 119, 120
Time of Troubles, 4, 198
Timofeev, Ivan, secretary, 184,
  194, 196
Tiutin, Kh.Yu., treasurer, 115
Toporkov, Vassian, elder, 39, 48
Toropets, 187
Torzhok, 7, 125
Transylvania, 178
Trifonov, Maksim, secretary, 92
Troekurov-Lvov, F.I., prince, 92,
  115, 116
Trubetskoi, F.M., prince, 144
Tuchkov, Mikhail Vasilevich, prince,
  4, 8-10
Tula, 34, 134, 152
Tulupov, Andrei, prince, 162
Tulupov, Boris, prince, 162, 163
Tulupov, Nikita, prince, 162
Tulupov, Vladimir, prince, 162
Tulupova, Anna, 163
Turov, Petr, 69
Turuntai-Pronskii, I.I., boyar, 37
Tver, 113, 118, 125, 129, 170
Uchin, Zakharii, boyar, 87
Udmurty (tribe), 33
Uglich, 66
Ukraine, 183
Umnoi-Kolychev, B.I., boyar, 115,
  163
Umnoi-Kolychev, F.I., boyar, 58, 163
Umnoi-Kolychev, Vasilii, 162, 163,
  174
Ushatyi, D.V., prince, 115

Ustiug Velikii, 86, 118
Vasilii III Ivanovich, grand prince,
  1-10, 14, 16, 29, 39, 47, 58,
  62, 66, 71, 171
Vasilchikova, Anna, 162, 174
Vasilii, son of Ivan IV, 173
Vasilii Vladimirovich, son of Prince
  Vladimir Andreevich, 122
Velikie Luki, 56, 185, 187, 190-192,
  194
Velizh, 192
Veselovskii, S.B., historian, 88, 89,
  90, 91, 108-112
Viazemskii, Afanasii, prince, 56, 82,
  87, 105, 106, 138, 139, 146
Viazma, 87, 96, 115, 175
Vilna, 56
Vishnevetskii, Dmitrii, prince, 62
Viskovatyi, I.M., secretary, 24, 40
  60, 134-137
Vitebsk, 74
Vladimir (town), 10, 32
Vladimir Andreevich of Staritsa,
  prince, 37, 38, 40, 41, 64-66,
  73, 79, 104, 106-108, 111, 112,
  115, 120-122, 138, 145, 157
Vladimir Monomakh, 15, 16
Volodimerov, Druzhina, secretary,
  168, 169
Vologda, 32, 87, 101, 103, 118-120,
  131, 140, 173, 175, 180
Volokolamsk, 3
Volovich, E., vice-chancellor of
  Lithuania, 73
Volynets, Petr, 126, 127
Volynskii, Grigorii, boyar, 127
Vorobevo, 20
Vorontsov, Andrei, 40
Vorontsov, I.F., boyar, 139
Vorontsov, Mikhail Semenovich,
  prince, 4, 6, 7, 13

Vorotynskii, Aleksandr, prince, 62, 63
Vorotynskii, Mikhail, prince, 62, 63,
  95, 102, 112, 153, 154
Vorotynskii, V.I., prince, 37, 62
Yurev, Mikhail, 4, 7-9, 25
Vyrodkov, Ivan, 50
Warsaw, 188
Wenden, 178, 179
Wild Field, 18
Wolmar, 73, 76, 77
Yakovlev-Zakharin, I.P., boyar, 58,
  82
Yakovlev-Zakharin, N.S., boyar, 137
Yakovlev-Zakharin, S.V., boyar, 137,
  138
Yakovlev-Zakharin, V.P., boyar, 137
Yam, 191-193
Yam Zapolskii, 191, 192
Yurevich, Mikhail, boyar, 4, 7-9
Yurev-Zakharin, Daniel Romanovich,
  boyar, 37, 58, 82
Yaroslavl, 61, 92, 93
Yurev-Zakharin, N.R., boyar, 96,
  137, 169, 197
Yurev-Zakharin, P.N., 164
Yurev-Zakharin, Roman, associate
  boyar, 172
Yurev-Zakharin, V.M., boyar, 58, 137
Yurii Ivanovich, prince of Dmitrov, 5
Yurii Vasilevich, prince of Uglich;
  brother of Ivan IV, 1, 10, 13, 66
Zaitsev, Petr, prince, 82, 87, 139
Zamojski, Jan, chancellor of Poland,
  187, 188
Zemshchina, 86, 88, 95-100, 102-107,
  112, 113, 115, 116, 122, 127, 129,
  130-132, 134-136, 138, 143, 147,
  155, 156, 166, 167, 169, 180, 183,
  193, 199
Zimin, A.A., historian, 3, 28, 42
Zubtsov, 167

THE AUTHOR

Ruslan Grigorevich Skrynnikov was born in 1931 in Kutais. His parents, natives of a small Cossack village in the Kuban region of southern Russia and schoolmates there, attended professional schools, his father becoming an hydrological engineer and his mother a chemistry instructor. Lovers of music and literature, the parents named their three children after characters in Pushkin's tales—Liudmila, Ruslan and Ratmir. In the 1930s the family moved to North Russia to help build an electrical plant on the Svir river. The construction crew erected for themselves a large building in Leningrad where Professor Skrynnikov met his future wife and where he lives today.

Returning to Leningrad from the Urals after World War II, he was drawn to physics and mathematics but, to everyone's surprise, began to study history at Leningrad State University where he worked with the noted historians D.S. Likhachev and B.A. Romanov. With their help he found his greatest interest, success and satisfaction in applying new analytical methods to old sources in search of new information of significance for the history of his country. Professor Skrynnikov's most recent success has been the reconstruction of the records of Ermak's sixteenth-century expedition which opened Siberia to Russian influence. Meanwhile, he has continued his portrayal of Old Russian life through a series of scholarly-popular biographies of the leading personalities of that time.

A teacher for practically all of his life and now professor of history at Leningrad State University, where students flock to his lectures, Professor Skrynnikov continues to make many appearances before large public audiences fascinated by the heroes and villains of Old Russia. All these activities leave him little time for his violin, which he played for fifteen years in the university symphonic orchestra, although he still finds time for music with his family and for his film and stamp interests. With his son and daughter, aged twelve and nine, he and his family enjoy the theater and concerts, and frequent visits to historical sites throughout his country.

ACADEMIC INTERNATIONAL PRESS

THE RUSSIAN SERIES

1 S.F. Platonov *History of Russia* Out of print
2 *The Nicky-Sunny Letters, Correspondence of Nicholas and Alexandra, 1914-1917*
3 Ken Shen Weigh *Russo-Chinese Diplomacy, 1689-1924* Out of print
4 Gaston Cahen *Relations of Russia with China. . . 1689-1730* Out of print
5 M.N. Pokrovsky *Brief History of Russia* 2 Volumes
6 M.N. Pokrovsky *History of Russia from Earliest Times. . .* Out of print
7 Robert J. Kerner *Bohemia in the Eighteenth Century*
8 *Memoirs of Prince Adam Czartoryski and His Correspondence with Alexander I* 2v
9 S.F. Platonov *Moscow and the West*
10 S.F. Platonov *Boris Godunov*
11 Boris Nikolajewsky *Aseff the Spy*
12 Francis Dvornik *Les Legendes de Constantin et de Methode vues de Byzance*
13 Francis Dvornik *Les Slaves, Byzance et Rome au XIe Siecle*
14 A. Leroy-Beaulieu *Un Homme d'Etat Russe (Nicolas Miliutine). . .*
15 Nicholas Berdyaev *Leontiev* (In English)
16 V.O. Kliuchevskii *Istoriia soslovii v Rossii*
17 *Tehran Yalta Potsdam. The Soviet Protocols*
18 *The Chronicle of Novgorod*
19 Paul N. Miliukov *Outlines of Russian Culture* Vol. III (3 vols.)
20 P.A. Zaionchkovskii *The Abolition of Serfdom in Russia*
21 V.V. Vinogradov *Russkii iazyk. Grammaticheskoe uchenie o slove*
22 P.A. Zaionchkovsky *The Russian Autocracy under Alexander III*
23 A.E. Presniakov *Emperor Nicholas I of Russia. The Apogee of Autocracy*
24 V.I. Semevskii *Krestianskii vopros v Rossii v XVIII i pervoi polovine XIX veka*
25 S.S. Oldenburg *Last Tsar! Nicholas II, His Reign and His Russia* 4 volumes
26 Carl von Clausewitz *The Campaign of 1812 in Russia*
27 M.K. Liubavskii *Obrazovanie osnovnoi gosudarstvennoi territorii velikorusskoi narodnosti. Zaselenie i obedinenie tsentra*
28 S.F. Platonov *Ivan the Terrible* Out of print
29 Paul N. Miliukov *Iz istorii russkoi intelligentsii. Sbornik statei i etiudov*
30 A.E. Presniakov *The Tsardom of Muscovy*
31 M. Gorky, J. Stalin et al., *History of the Civil War in Russia* (Revolution) 2 vols.
33 P.A. Zaionchkovsky *The Russian Autocracy in Crisis, 1878-1882*
43 Nicholas Zernov *Three Russian Prophets: Khomiakov, Dostoevsky, Soloviev*
44 Paul N. Miliukov *The Russian Revolution* 3 vols.
45 Anton I. Denikin *The White Army*
55 M.V. Rodzianko *The Reign of Rasputin—An Empire's Collapse. Memoirs*
56 *The Memoirs of Alexander Iswolsky*

THE CENTRAL AND EAST EUROPEAN SERIES

1 Louis Eisenmann *Le Compromis Austro-Hongrois de 1867*
3 Francis Dvornik *The Making of Central and Eastern Europe* 2nd edition
4 Feodor F. Zigel *Lectures on Slavonic Law*
10 Doros Alastos *Venizelos—Patriot, Statesman, Revolutionary*
20 Paul Teleki *The Evolution of Hungary and its Place in European History*

FORUM ASIATICA

1 M.I. Sladkovsky *China and Japan—Past and Present*

THE ACADEMIC INTERNATIONAL REFERENCE SERIES

The Modern Encyclopedia of Russian and Soviet History 50 vols.
The Modern Encyclopedia of Russian and Soviet Literature 50 vols.
Soviet Armed Forces Review Annual
USSR Facts & Figures Annual
Military-Naval Encyclopedia of Russia and the Soviet Union 50 vols.
China Facts & Figures Annual

SPECIAL WORKS

S.M. Soloviev *History of Russia* 50 vols.